Rapid Application Development with OutSystems

Create applications with OutSystems up to seven times faster than with traditional technologies

Ricardo Pereira

BIRMINGHAM—MUMBAI

Rapid Application Development with OutSystems

Associate Group Product Manager: Pavan Ramchandani
Publishing Product Manager: Rohit Rajkumar
Senior Editor: Sofi Rogers
Content Development Editor: Feza Shaikh
Technical Editor: Simran Udasi
Copy Editor: Safis Editing
Project Coordinator: Manthan Patel
Proofreader: Safis Editing
Indexer: Sejal Dsilva
Production Designer: Shankar Kalbhor

First published: January 2022

Production reference: 3080222

Published by Packt Publishing Ltd.
Livery Place
35 Livery Street
Birmingham
B3 2PB, UK.

978-1-80020-875-9

www.packt.com

First of all, I would like to dedicate this book to my wife, Carmen, my son, Afonso, and my daughter, Maria, for being my source of energy and support, for being part of my life, and for all the love they give me.

I would also like to thank all my family, my parents, brother, grandparents, in-laws, brothers-in-law, cousins, and nephew, for believing in me and for all their love. Thanks to my brother from another mother, João Roque, for walking beside me in this adventure that is life.

I would like to give special thanks to Andreia Tulcidás and Ana Lopes from OutSystems, for all their support and help throughout the book's execution process.

Finally, and in a very special way, I wanted to dedicate, in addition to the work of this book, the effort and will, to two very important people in my life who have recently passed away: my grandfather, José Pereira, and my uncle, José Costa Pereira. Thank you for everything you represented to me and for the examples you led that served as a basis for shaping me.

– Ricardo Pereira

Foreword

I have known and worked with Ricardo Pereira for 3 years now. We had the opportunity to work together to deliver OutSystems projects in the banking industry in Portugal and Spain. Being such an important line of business, best practices, solid architectures, and security were always at the top of the requirements list.

Ricardo has been working with OutSystems for quite some time and is now one of the OutSystems Champions worldwide. OutSystems is part of his professional DNA. He breathes it all the time, throughout his professional career.

In *Rapid Application Development with OutSystems*, Ricardo takes you on an amazing journey through all the important aspects of delivering OutSystems applications to the world. From the basic topics to the more advanced ones, you will be able to fully understand what it's like to build an OutSystems application from scratch.

From architecture and data modeling to logic, services, and the UI, you will find the proposed exercises and examples very useful, to better understand how things are put together. Also, business processes and platform monitoring are an excellent complement to get a clear big picture of what the OutSystems platform is all about.

In this book, Ricardo encapsulates the knowledge gained throughout his most recent professional career. With his words, step-by-step instructions, screenshots, examples, and links to additional sources of information, you will learn how to continuously enhance your skills and apps.

Paulo Moreira

OutSystems Expert, Technical Team Leader at Nexllence, Powered by Glintt

Ricardo Pereira is one of the most active members of the OutSystems community. He is a professional developer of reactive web applications and has been active in the OutSystems community since 2016, contributing to us and supporting many developers. He has about 400 Kudos for solving issues and providing information in the forum. Ricardo has been recognized for his work and is now an OutSystems Champion, an officially recognized OutSystems Community Advocate.

This book, written by a man with a real wealth of knowledge and experience, provides an easy-to-understand overview of the know-how needed to develop applications with OutSystems. In this book, you will learn about the basics of the OutSystems platform, the necessary tools and components, application development methods, how to implement your own logic, how to implement server-side and client-side logic, data modeling, exception handling, UI design, debugging, and more. OutSystems is a cool low-code development tool, but using it effectively requires knowledge of software application development as well as OutSystems' own terminology. This book is a must-read for developers who will be using OutSystems to develop applications.

OutSystems has many experts like Ricardo in its user community (OutSystems User Groups). This is a great honor for us. I hope that Ricardo's book will be of help to many developers.

Taiji Hagino

Lead Community Manager, Developer Advocate at OutSystems

Contributors

About the author

Ricardo Pereira is passionate about programming, software, and technology. Coming from a computer science background, he has become, in the last 5 years, a strong bettor on OutSystems learning, holding all existing certifications of the platform. Furthermore, in 2020, he was named OutSystems Champion, participating in several events and following the mentoring program as a mentor. His time is distributed between software projects, learning, studying, and spending time with family.

Ricardo lives with his wife and their two children in Vila Nova de Gaia, Portugal. His greatest influence in the relentless pursuit of continuous improvement and being the best version of himself is his grandfather.

> *This book was driven by Packt's invitation, as I had never considered writing anything. I've always been passionate about what I do, programming, for OutSystems, but only after the invitation did I realize that I could share everything I have learned and experienced in this technology in a much broader way. For all this, I would like to thank Packt and the entire team involved in the process for believing in me, for the fantastic help they gave, and for being the wonderful people they are.*

About the reviewers

João Martins Pereira is an experienced senior developer who works for a large UK company and has been using OutSystems technology since 2016.

His background includes working with Python, SQL, and JavaScript but mainly integrating with the OutSystems platform.

Delivering projects and dealing with different clients around the globe, he has had the opportunity to work with several applications, such as traditional web, web reactive, and mobile applications in several core businesses.

He got the opportunity to attend the NextStep Denver 2019 conference as a speaker, talking about mobile synchronization patterns for large volumes of data.

Mariano Picco is an OutSystems expert, with experience in application architecture, specializing in scalable solutions and integrations. He is particularly interested in the optimization of solutions and the role of low code in the software industry. You can often find him trying to collaborate and participate in the community forums.

Paulo Moreira, born in Portugal's capital, Lisbon, started his professional career with an airline company, back in 1988. While working as an aircraft maintenance technician, this was when IT was first introduced to him as a potential future career. And so it happened.

He bumped into OutSystems a while later, in 2008, and since then it has been a permanent presence in his professional career.

Again, (re)starting as a junior developer, Paulo quickly improved his technical skills with this low-code platform, on all skill sets applicable, including development, delivering, engaging, and more recently, training.

He's currently a technical team leader at Nexllence, where he's also in charge of the OutSystems team's talent and training.

Table of Contents

Preface

Section 1: OutSystems 101

1

Exploring the OutSystems Platform

Platform overview	5	OutSystems factory options	21
Platform server	5	OutSystems platform deployment	
Service Studio	7	options	21
Integration Studio	8		
Service Center	8	**External tools, components,**	
Publishing an application	10	**and support**	**24**
Monitoring and logging	12	Forge and Community	24
Distribution	13	**Summary**	**26**
Cache	15		
SEO – Search Engine Optimization	16		

2

Components, Tools, and Capabilities

Service Studio walkthrough	**28**	The Administration tab	47
The Data tab	33	The Analytics tab	49
The Logic tab	37		
The Interface tab	40	**Managing your infrastructure**	
The Processes tab	42	**with LifeTime**	**51**
Service Center capabilities	**44**	**Managing end users with the**	
The Factory tab	44	**Users application**	**53**
The Monitoring tab	45	**Integration Studio walkthrough**	**54**
		Summary	**56**

3
Starting Work with OutSystems

OutSystems pricing and editions	58	Opening and starting Service Studio	64
Setting up our Personal Environment	59	Opening and starting Integration Studio	66
Installing OutSystems IDEs	62	Summary	68

Section 2: The Magical Path of the Backend

4
Using Your Modules to Simplify and Encapsulate Your Code

Technical requirements	72	Core layer	79
Types of modules	72	End user layer	80
Distributing modules across applications	75	All layers	81
Applying modules to the correct architecture layers	77	Modules and application naming convention	81
Foundation layer	77	Summary	83

5
Modeling Data by Using Entities

Technical requirements	86	Bootstrapping data into Entities from an Excel spreadsheet	93
Exploring database Entities	86		
What are Static Entities?	89	Exercise 1 – creating a data model	95
Modeling data	91	Summary	112

6
Server-Side Logic

Technical requirements	114	Types of variables in Server Actions	118
Introducing logic actions	114		

Taking logic decisions with conditional paths	121	Exercise 2 – Creating server actions	125
Creating loops	123	Summary	141

7

Exceptions Handling

Technical requirements	144	Exercise 3 – raising and handling an Exception	153
Raising Exceptions	144		
Exception handler flows	149	Summary	161
Global Exception handler	151		

Section 3: Create Value and Innovate with the Frontend

8

Reactive UI Development

Technical requirements	166	Screen and block lifecycle events	181
Reactive patterns and templates	166	Events to propagate changes from a block to the parent	184
Reactive widgets	170		
Scaffolding screens	173	Exercise 4 – Creating application screens	185
CSS themes and styles	176		
JavaScript in OutSystems	179	Summary	198

9

Using Mobile Patterns for Fast Mobile UI Development

Technical requirements	202	Target audience	204
Patterns, templates, and widgets	202	Design	204
		Security	204
Mobile design considerations	203	Performance	205
Process and concept	203	Mobile plugins	205

Adding plugins to our applications 208
Native app generation 210

Exercise 5 – Creating mobile app screens 215
Summary 231

10
Client-Side Logic

Technical requirements 234
Screen Client Actions 234
Data actions 235
Client logic actions 238

Exercise 6 – creating Client Actions and using them on the frontend 241
Summary 247

11
Local Storage and Data Synchronization

Creating and using Local Storage entities 250
Fetching data from Local Storage 256

Analyzing data synchronization patterns 260
Summary 273

12
Debugging and Troubleshooting Mobile and Reactive Web Apps

Debugging reactive web applications 276
Debugging native mobile applications 285

Using Service Center logs to support troubleshooting 287
Summary 291

Section 4: Extensibility and Complexity of the OutSystems Platform

13
Designing the Architecture of Your OutSystems Applications

The importance of architecture	296	The architecture design process	299
The 3 Layer Canvas (Architecture Canvas)	297	Summary	306

14
Integrating OutSystems with Your Ecosystem

Creating your own C#/.NET code and using it inside the OutSystems platform	308	Consuming SOAP	320
		Exposing SOAP	323
Connecting with external databases	313	Consuming REST services	327
		Exposing REST	334
Connecting with other systems through web services (REST/SOAP)	320	Summary	338

15
BPT Processes and Timers – Asynchronous Tools in OutSystems

Process BPT overview	340	Monitoring Processes and Timers	363
Timers and how they work	355	Summary	367
BPTs versus Timers	362		

Other Books You May Enjoy

Index

Preface

OutSystems is a software development platform that speeds up the build phase by abstracting code and making almost everything visual – this means replacing textual language with visual artifacts that avoid lexical errors and speed up code composition using accelerators and pre-defined templates.

The book begins by walking you through the fundamentals of the technology, along with a general overview of end-to-end web and mobile software development. You'll learn how to configure your personal area in the cloud and use the OutSystems IDE to connect with it. The book then shows you how to build a web application based on the best architectural and developmental practices, and takes the same approach for the mobile paradigm. As you advance, you'll find out how to develop the same application, and showcase the great potential of reusing code from one paradigm in another and the symbiosis between them. The only application that'll differ is the one used in **BPT** (**Business Process Technology**), with a focus on a common market use case.

By the end of this OutSystems book, you'll be able to develop enterprise-level applications on the web and mobile, integrating them with third parties and other systems on the market. You'll also be able to understand the concepts of performance, security, and software construction and apply them effectively.

Who this book is for

This book is for backend developers, tech leaders, UX/UI developers, frontend developers, (in general, full-stack developers), tech companies, and enterprises looking to learn how to develop web and mobile software quickly and disruptively by leveraging OutSystems, one of the most low-code platforms on the market. An IT background is not mandatory; however, experience in SQL, JavaScript, HTML, CSS, and C# is required to get started with this book.

What this book covers

Chapter 1, Exploring the OutSystems Platform, provides an overview of the base of the OutSystems platform and the characteristics that make it unique. Here, we discover the simplicity with which we can manage our existing development environments and tools.

Chapter 2, Components, Tools, and Capabilities, shows in greater detail the range of features and capabilities provided by the OutSystems platform, from operation and management tools, IDEs, and the strong community component through forums and the Forge.

Chapter 3, Starting Work with OutSystems, introduces the first practical steps so that we can develop our software. We will learn how to register with OutSystems, download the IDEs, and how to initialize them in our personal areas.

Chapter 4, Using Your Modules to Simplify and Encapsulate Your Code, starts with the foundations, as you would for a house, giving an overview of how we should build our software divided into modules and inserted into the layers they correspond to. This step allows us to develop scalable and robust, future-ready software.

Chapter 5, Modeling Data by Using Entities, addresses the fact that applications nowadays live on data. In this chapter, we learn where this data is stored and how we can access and manipulate it. In addition, we learn the terms used to identify each of the components related to the database in OutSystems.

Chapter 6, Server-Side Logic, looks at how modern applications run (in most cases) on the server and on the client (the user's computer browser). In this chapter, we learn what server-side development in OutSystems consists of and how to work on this aspect.

Chapter 7, Exceptions Handling, explains how we should handle anomalous or erroneous behavior in our applications, because things do not always go as expected and it is necessary to predict and deal with cases of failure, such as database errors, access attempts by unauthorized users, or even customized errors.

Chapter 8, Reactive UI Development, explains how to develop the frontend of our web applications within the reactive paradigm. This paradigm is based on the most modern technologies on the market, ensuring safety, performance, and robustness.

Chapter 9, Using Mobile Patterns for Fast Mobile UI Development, looks at the paradigm for mobile application development and how it is very similar to reactive web application development. However, and derived from the characteristics of devices and the use for which they are designed, mobile applications have a different set of points. This chapter focuses on these points in order to allow for an understanding of the differences and why they exist.

Chapter 10, Client-Side Logic, reminds us that we must keep in mind that an application must be composed of not only server-side logic but also client-side logic. This logic allows us to assess the functioning and functionalities of the application, guaranteeing its correct use and always ensuring an excellent user experience. It is in this chapter that we learn about this subject.

Chapter 11, Local Storage and Data Synchronization, deals with a specific case of mobile applications: local storage and how to synchronize data between it and server data. This feature is extremely important these days, as it allows the use of applications even without an internet connection (offline mode) and allows strict management of data that is stored on a less secure device, such as a mobile phone or tablet.

Chapter 12, Debugging and Troubleshooting Mobile and Reactive Web Apps, addresses the questions: Does our application not work? Are we getting errors in certain features? What is up? What is the problem? Calm! The OutSystems platform provides tools to help us! Furthermore, there is a set of basic procedures that are demonstrated in this chapter to facilitate us on this path.

Chapter 13, Designing the Architecture of Your OutSystems Applications, shows us how to create our applications within the standard model recommended by OutSystems: the 3 Layer Canvas, also known as the Architecture Canvas. This model allows the construction of robust, performant, and, above all, highly scalable software. However, we must always remember that architecture is not immutable, and here we understand how easily we can adapt it throughout the life cycle of our applications.

Chapter 14, Integrating OutSystems with Your Ecosystem, looks at how, often in software projects, it is necessary to integrate with other existing systems inside and outside the company's ecosystem. In this chapter, we learn several ways to do this, depending on the technologies of the producer and consumer systems and the planned approach to software development.

Chapter 15, BPT Processes and Timers – Asynchronous Tools in OutSystems, explains what asynchronism is, what tools of this type exist, what they are for, and in what cases we should use them. Here, we understand that we can process logic in programmed time periods and en masse, just as we can control process flows in an isolated and robust way.

To get the most out of this book

You must have installed Visual Studio Community for the C#/.NET native code integrations component discussed in *Chapter 14, Integrating OutSystems with Your Ecosystem*.

In addition, you must have installed the Service Studio 11.50.9 (or above) and Integration Studio 11.10.18 (or above) IDEs. All code demonstrated was tested using these versions. Installation of these IDEs is demonstrated in *Chapter 3, Starting Work with OutSystems*.

Software/hardware covered in the book	Operating system requirements
Service Studio 11	Windows 7 (64-bit)
	Windows 8 (64-bit)
	Windows 10 (64-bit)
	macOS (Catalina)
	macOS (Big Sur)
Integration Studio	Windows 7 (64-bit)
	Windows 8 (64-bit)
	Windows 10 (64-bit)

The use of Integration Studio is only possible in a Windows environment, as this IDE does not exist for the macOS environment.

Code in Action

The Code in Action videos for this book can be viewed at `https://bit.ly/3D1S9bX`.

Download the color images

We also provide a PDF file that has color images of the screenshots and diagrams used in this book. You can download it here:

`https://static.packt-cdn.com/downloads/9781800208759_ColorImages.pdf`

Conventions used

There are a number of text conventions used throughout this book.

`Code in text`: Indicates code words in text, database table names, folder names, filenames, file extensions, pathnames, dummy URLs, user input, and Twitter handles. Here is an example: "Create a new Reactive Web application and name it `Help Desk`."

Bold: Indicates a new term, an important word, or words that you see onscreen. For instance, words in menus or dialog boxes appear in **bold**. Here is an example: "Now, we select the tab **Data**, expand the entity **Ticket**, and drag the CRUD **CreateOrUpdateTicket** to the flow."

> **Tips or important notes**
> Appear like this.

Get in touch

Feedback from our readers is always welcome.

General feedback: If you have questions about any aspect of this book, email us at `customercare@packtpub.com` and mention the book title in the subject of your message.

Errata: Although we have taken every care to ensure the accuracy of our content, mistakes do happen. If you have found a mistake in this book, we would be grateful if you would report this to us. Please visit `www.packtpub.com/support/errata` and fill in the form.

Piracy: If you come across any illegal copies of our works in any form on the internet, we would be grateful if you would provide us with the location address or website name. Please contact us at `copyright@packt.com` with a link to the material.

If you are interested in becoming an author: If there is a topic that you have expertise in and you are interested in either writing or contributing to a book, please visit `authors.packtpub.com`.

Share Your Thoughts

Once you've read *Rapid Application Development with OutSystems*, we'd love to hear your thoughts! Scan the QR code below to go straight to the Amazon review page for this book and share your feedback.

https://packt.link/r/1800208758

Your review is important to us and the tech community and will help us make sure we're delivering excellent quality content.

Section 1: OutSystems 101

In this section, we will find out how an OutSystems framework is composed, how to use it, and what tools we have available to make the most of it.

This section comprises the following chapters:

- *Chapter 1, Exploring the OutSystems Platform*
- *Chapter 2, Components, Tools, and Capabilities*
- *Chapter 3, Starting Work with OutSystems*

1
Exploring the OutSystems Platform

After all, what is OutSystems?

We will provide a quick overview of what their components and tools are and how they work, as well as all the capabilities and potential of the OutSystems platform.

The OutSystems platform enhances and accelerates the development and delivery of enterprise-level web and mobile applications, always with the guarantee of following the best standards of security and performance available on the market.

All of this is possible because it is made available through low-code development environments, while code is generated that will be made available for an enterprise-level, full stack system.

The platform integrates with other systems in a very practical and simple way, namely, existing databases and legacy applications used by the companies themselves or even with existing code.

Out-of-the-box management and analysis tools regarding the applications developed and existing users are made available so that everything can work as expected.

In this chapter, we will have the opportunity to visualize the different features and capabilities of the OutSystems platform at a high level, as well as existing tools and built-in elements such as Service Center, LifeTime, Service Studio, and Integration Studio.

As expected, topics such as connection and integration with existing systems will be addressed using Service Studio, a modern development interface based on the Visual Code paradigm used to create applications in record time, or with Integration Studio, a great interface development that allows us to create our connections to external databases and create our native C#/.NET code to use services from legacy systems. After being created in this powerful tool, applications are then compiled based on standard and optimized code, such as HTML, CSS, JavaScript, and .NET.

These applications are made available on the different OutSystems environments in a continuous approach, following the best CI/CD practices. Code is constantly inspected and analyzed for impacts, and there is zero downtime when promoting applications to the next environment.

In addition to all this, the OutSystems platform can be deployed both in the cloud and on-premises, enabling the availability of applications in any type of infrastructure.

Are you curious? Do you want to take up the challenge? So, let's get started!

We will cover topics from the platform server to development tools, more specifically, the Service Studio and Integration Studio. The administration and operation tools of the framework will also be addressed, namely, Service Center and LifeTime.

As a bonus, we will provide an overview of OutSystems Forge and Community, helping to understand how these resources can be useful in application development.

So let's get started!

The following topics will be covered in this chapter:

- Platform overview
- OutSystems factory options
- External tools, components, and support

Now let's dive deeper into the OutSystems platform and understand the capabilities and features provided by it.

Platform overview

First, we should realize that there are two possible contexts for working in OutSystems:

- **Personal Environment**: OutSystems offers a small software factory free of charge (in the cloud) so that we can do our exercises, tests, and small applications without a productive context.

- **Enterprise**: Licensed software factories for companies. It can exist in the cloud (AWS), private cloud, or on the company's own physical servers (on-premises). Enterprise versions can exist in different types of licensing and are paid.

We will be able to see this issue in more detail in *Chapter 3*, *Starting Work with OutSystems*.

All these tools exist both in personal environments and in enterprise factories. In personal environments, there is a set of restrictions and limitations of services and features, from the number of environments available and the space available in the database to the number of IT users allowed.

Whenever we think of an enterprise environment, we are aware that there must be non-productive and productive environments, the most common model being that of three environments:

- Development

- Quality Assurance

- Production

All existing tools can connect to the environments that make up the OutSystems infrastructure, allowing you to perform any type of necessary task, without, in most cases, the use of external tools.

Platform server

The **Platform server** is composed of a set of servers (which can be installed both in the cloud and on-premises) that perform all the necessary operations so that the developed applications are available to users. These operations are as follows:

- Compile

- Deploy

- Manage

- Run

- Monitor

To develop our applications, we can connect to the platform server using **Service Studio** and **Integration Studio**. After development, we can publish our applications, and the platform server handles the operations necessary to make the applications available to users.

When we publish an application, the platform saves the version of it in its database, thus creating a repository of versions and backups. During publication, the platform will compile, optimize the code, and make it available on the servers for use.

Application servers use traditional databases and conventional external systems to run applications, thereby ensuring uniformity and standardization.

The following screenshot shows the OutSystems environment ecosystem:

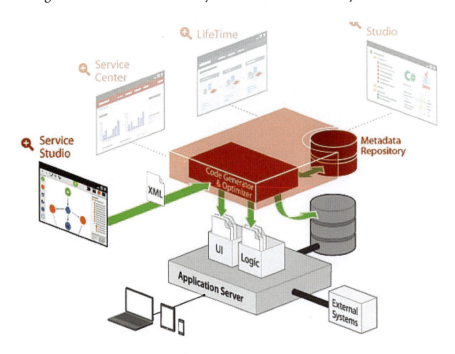

Figure 1.1 – OutSystems ecosystem

As we can see, the ecosystem has all the characteristics of a state-of-the-art model while maintaining simplicity for those who develop applications or manage the platform. To take advantage of this ecosystem, we need to have agile tools at our fingertips, both to develop applications and to manage them and the ecosystem itself. And that's what we've already followed!

Service Studio

Service Studio is the visual OutSystems IDE. Its use is related to the low-code paradigm, reducing the use of textual code as much as possible, reducing the error factor, and thus offering the opportunity for the developer to focus more on the business itself. Using this same tool, we can develop both our web and mobile applications.

This tool addresses four layers of application development:

- Data
- Logic
- Frontend
- Processes

In addition, it provides a section called **TrueChange**, where the entire analysis of the code is reported, providing detailed information on existing errors and warnings.

The following screenshot shows the look and feel of Service Studio:

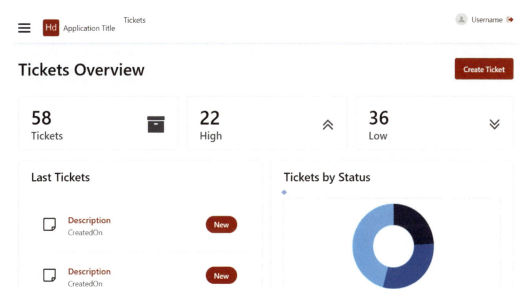

Figure 1.2 – OutSystems Service Studio canvas look and feel

OutSystems main application development tool manages to be super intuitive and provides us with numerous accelerators that we can take advantage of. However, this is not all!

Integration Studio

Do you need to create your own custom C #/.NET code? Do you need to connect with external databases? Do you need to create a connection with your legacy systems? Then this is your tool!

Integration Studio offers a set of accelerators to support our native C # code, as well as integrations with databases external to the platform, making these routines simple and easily scalable.

After creating our code and our integrations, Integration Studio, together with the platform server, creates its representations in the OutSystems universe, thereby being available for use in the same visual paradigm with which we develop our OutSystems applications.

The following screenshot shows the look and feel of Integration Studio:

Figure 1.3 – OutSystems Integration Studio look and feel

With the tools presented, we found out which path to take to develop and make reactive web and mobile applications available at the speed of light. Now, how can we manage and operate the application server? With the next tools!

Service Center

Service Center is a web console that allows you to manage an OutSystems environment, including parameterization, the inspection of logs, and viewing existing applications and the current status of existing services, thereby facilitating the export of generated event reports. The following screenshot shows the look and feel of Service Center:

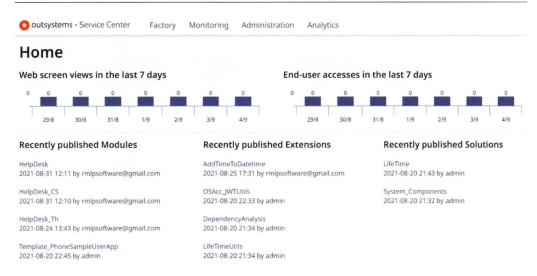

Figure 1.4 – OutSystems Service Center look and feel

Service Center guarantees us a very practical control of each of our environments. However, OutSystems wanted to go further and complemented this tool with the one we'll demonstrate next, taking the power and ease with which we can master our platform even further.

LifeTime

We are going to visualize a kingdom, composed of several layers, and at the top there is someone on a throne. Is it displayed? Whoever is on the throne is called **LifeTime**!

LifeTime, also a web console, allows you to control, monitor, and configure the complete life cycle of our applications between the multiple environments in the framework. With this, this tool allows you to go further than we can through Service Center.

With this console, we are able to deploy the different applications existing in the OutSystems infrastructure, benefiting from multiple integrity checks to guarantee the stability and robustness of the environments. In addition, the deployments made by LifeTime guarantee "zero downtime," translating this into a better experience for the end user since, in this way, applications are never unavailable.

In addition, LifeTime allows you to track versions of our applications, and we can customize their tags at the time of deployment (if we do not, LifeTime does it for us).

Another fantastic feature that exists in LifeTime is the ability to manage the permission levels of each IT user and development team, thus ensuring the ownership of each of the existing workstreams.

The following screenshot shows the look and feel of LifeTime:

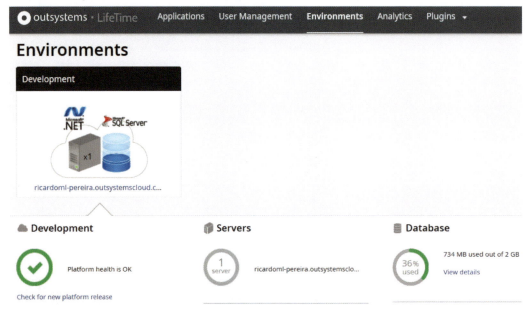

Figure 1.5 – OutSystems LifeTime look and feel

As we can see, OutSystems allows us, in addition to having great power and control over all aspects of the platform, to do so responsibly, with guarantees to maintain the correct functioning and abstracting from the high complexity that a system of this category has. Everything is much simpler, more practical, and more effective.

Next, we will analyze the functionalities and capabilities that the OutSystems platform makes available to us in order to facilitate and accelerate our work, thereby ensuring that we have a greater focus on the business and its needs.

With this information in mind, a pertinent question arises: How do we publish our applications to our servers?

Publishing an application

We know that if we want to have our applications fully available and make the most of our infrastructures, we will want to publish them on all our frontend servers to process all requests coming from browsers or mobile devices in an identical manner. In the example of three frontend servers, did we need to publish the application three times (once on each server)?

The answer is no! OutSystems tools such as Service Studio, Integration Studio, and Service Center provide the **1-Click Publish** functionality, which basically triggers the action of publishing in the corresponding environment. In addition, this feature manages to do it in style: with so-called zero downtime! Applications are never unavailable during the publishing process, minimizing the impact on their users. This feature is achieved by publishing the necessary files in a virtual directory, and when the operation is complete, the old directory is replaced in its entirety by the new one. This whole process is called **hot deployment**.

To obtain this behavior, there is a server called **Deployment Controller Server** that has installed the **Deployment Controller Service** service (it does not need to be a dedicated server; this service can be installed on one of the frontend servers, assuming the same two roles) that communicates with all other frontends through their deployment services.

In summary, we press the **1-Click Publish** button, which saves a new version of our module, generates and compiles optimized code and SQL scripts, and updates the database model until it finally deploys the application.

The following screenshot shows the application publishing flow from Service Studio:

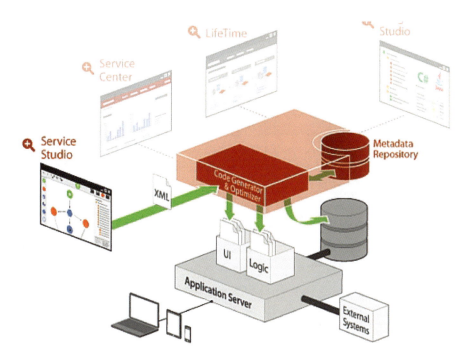

Figure 1.6 – OutSystems application publishing flow from Service Studio

The publishing flow of an application is done in a fully controlled way to ensure that everything is ready and without generating any issues regarding the use of our applications. Even so, it may be necessary to check events to ensure that everything runs smoothly. Monitoring? Logging? Of course these functions are available!

Monitoring and logging

The OutSystems platform provides an automatic monitoring service for our applications. This means that any event is recorded in databases so that we can search for them in the future. To this end, an asynchronous approach was applied to the writing of the logs. If they were recorded in real time, we would have a performance problem because we have lots of logs to be written simultaneously in the database, thereby causing delays and possible locks on the tables. We can imagine an application with hundreds or thousands of users at the same time... anything could go wrong (Murphy's law always comes up).

And how does asynchronous logging work? To this end, each frontend server has a logging service. The logs are transmitted to the **Microsoft Message Queuing** (**MSMQ**) by the service center of the respective server, and they are subsequently captured by the log service from time to time which, in turn, inserts the data in bulk (bulk insert) in the respective database tables. These same tables, to ensure the best possible performance in writing, do not use indexes (indexes are very useful and optimize performance in research, but slow down writing).

Well, throughout this explanation, we have already seen that there are several functionalities for writing data to the existing tables on the database server. For the better segregation of concepts, OutSystems makes it possible (only on on-premises installations, that is, on its own servers and not in the cloud) to create multiple database catalogs in order to facilitate the maintenance and segregation of databases. All of this can be done in a very simple way through the Service Center tool. It is not a topic that it makes sense to go into in too much detail since the focus of OutSystems is to orient the market to the future: the cloud (as a curiosity, OutSystems, when it received its name, did not have the term *cloud* in it because the cloud was not prevalent at that time).

The following screenshot shows the monitoring view (errors) in Service Center:

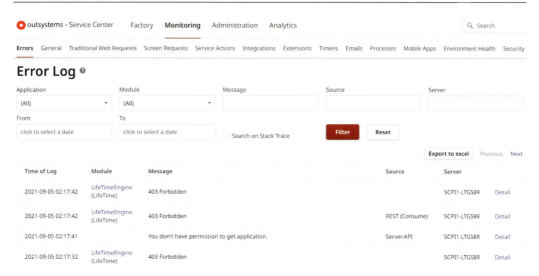

Figure 1.7 – Monitoring View in the OutSystems Service Center

Service Center allows us to make the most of the platform's logs – practical filters, information details, exportability, and everything else – grouped by concept. This is proof that, in addition to OutSystems equipping us with tools, it does it the right way.

Distribution

Another functionality provided by the OutSystems platform is support for **Content Distribution Network (CDN)**. What does this consist of?

Firstly, the CDN is located between the clients' browsers and the frontend servers (on farm installations, from the load balancer).

The CDN is used to distribute content efficiently among end users. Basically, the idea is that, instead of our environment doing the distribution of content for all requests made, there are servers in the various zones where applications are available that do this for them. With this, the distribution of cached resources such as CSS is much more efficient and faster, thereby freeing the environment for other tasks. Note that even with CDN, the frontend servers in our environments continue to process information requested by end users, such as the HTML of the web page for each request. That same HTML has references and links to CSS files, JavaScript, images, and static content, these being loaded from the servers made available by the CDN.

But how do these servers know whether the content should be updated? That is, if we publish a new version of our application with changes to the content stored on the servers made available by the CDN, they must be able to know that such an event has occurred. For this, the platform facilitates this operation with the simple suffix in the resources, and the servers can compare the same with the version existing in themselves. If the suffix is different, the servers obtain the necessary new content and update their versions. The browser's cache works in exactly the same way: if the suffix is different, even in cases of an aggressive cache, the browser obtains the new content from the frontend servers (if there is no CDN) or from the servers provided by the CDN.

> **Note**
> Throughout this book, the term CDN will be used to identify the functionality of the content distribution network.

The following screenshot shows an example of a CDN:

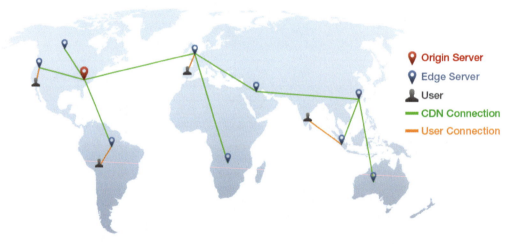

Figure 1.8 – General example of a CDN

While it is difficult to accurately predict what the future of CDNs will be, one thing is certain: this industry will grow exponentially, which means that the technologies used to run them will evolve further.

Cache

The OutSystems platform provides built-in caching capabilities. With this, we seek to obtain substantial improvements in performance (long cache, normally associated with static content, similar to what we saw regarding the CDN) and the prevention of the so-called "peak traffic heavy load" (short cache).

Regarding the long cache, this is something automatic on the part of the platform. For example, if we inspect a web page of an application developed in OutSystems, we can verify in the properties of static content (as in the case of images) that the value of a month is set to a maximum age for cache control in response headers.

In the case of the short cache, it has this name precisely because its period of stay is defined in minutes, seconds, or milliseconds and serves to save computing time on servers. This functionality is used whenever it is guaranteed that the orders are identical and that their result does not vary, otherwise, that same cache would not be used, leading to computational reprocessing.

This short cache can be set to the following:

- Aggregates and SQL nodes (used to fetch data in OutSystems code):

Figure 1.9 – Cache in minutes in Aggregate

- User actions and SOAP methods consumed:

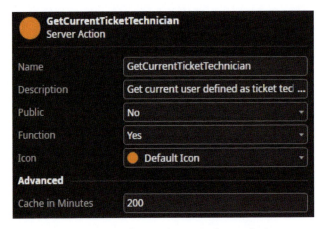

Figure 1.10 – Cache in minutes in Server Action

The value of the cache time is defined in the properties section of each of these components, in the **Cache in Minutes** attribute. When defining the value of the cache, whenever the server is asked for a certain artifact from those mentioned above, instead of recalculating the request, the previously calculated value is returned and made available in the cache. Note the importance of the order having to be exactly the same as foreseen in the multiple scenarios. For example, if we cache an aggregate that has an input defined and is used in the filters, if the value of the different requests is different, the cache will not comply with the forecast, since the previously calculated value does not fit the order in question and it has to be recalculated.

Objectively, to use the short cache, we must carry out a careful analysis of the candidate elements to verify whether their use makes sense. Another scenario to consider, for example, a SOAP service that returns a list, is the fact that we must assess whether the fact that we use the cache and do not have the data in real time can affect the business.

SEO – Search Engine Optimization

The OutSystems platform is already prepared and provides features for the so-called **SEO – Search Engine Optimization**. But what is this?

> **Important Note**
>
> For Reactive web applications, these features are in Technical Preview, so they need to be activated in LifeTime. SEO is a set of techniques used to make web pages more easily indexable by search engines (such as Google). It often involves making the URL of the page more user-friendly or even changing the native URL. With these techniques, the URLs of our applications go up in the indexing ranking, gaining visibility. Basically, the idea is to make the URLs as similar as possible to the search strings entered by users.

> **Note**
>
> Throughout this book, the term SEO will be used to identify the functionality of Search Engine Optimization.

In the service center of each of the constituent environments of the OutSystems platform, four features are available to solve this problem:

- **Module Alias Rules**: This feature allows you to give another name to the module that appears in the URL. For example, if the module is called **AssetsManager** and we want it to be simpler, we define a rule where the alias of that module is **Assets**. From that moment, in the URL, the part of the module no longer shows the initial value showing the value of the alias. With this, it is no longer necessary to rename our modules.

Figure 1.11 – Service Center view for Module Alias

- **Redirect Rules**: This feature allows us to define a URL that, when the call arrives at IIS, informs the browser to make a new request for a URL provided by it. For example, if we call the URL us.acme.com and we have a redirect rule defined so that it is redirected to www.acme.com/us when the call arrives at IIS, it will communicate to the browser to make a new order for this new URL. This is a widely used technique, including by Google.

Figure 1.12 – Service Center view for Redirect Rules

- **Site Rules**: This feature allows you to configure the root application for a given URL. For example, we have an application called **Site** and we set the URL `www.acme.com` so that, when called, this opens the **Site** application. This way, we can optimize the control of our domains in parallel with our applications without needing to access the URL built with the domain and the application to open a specific application. In addition, we were also able to define the **locale** parameter (very useful when working with multiple languages or when we have different versions of our applications based on the language).

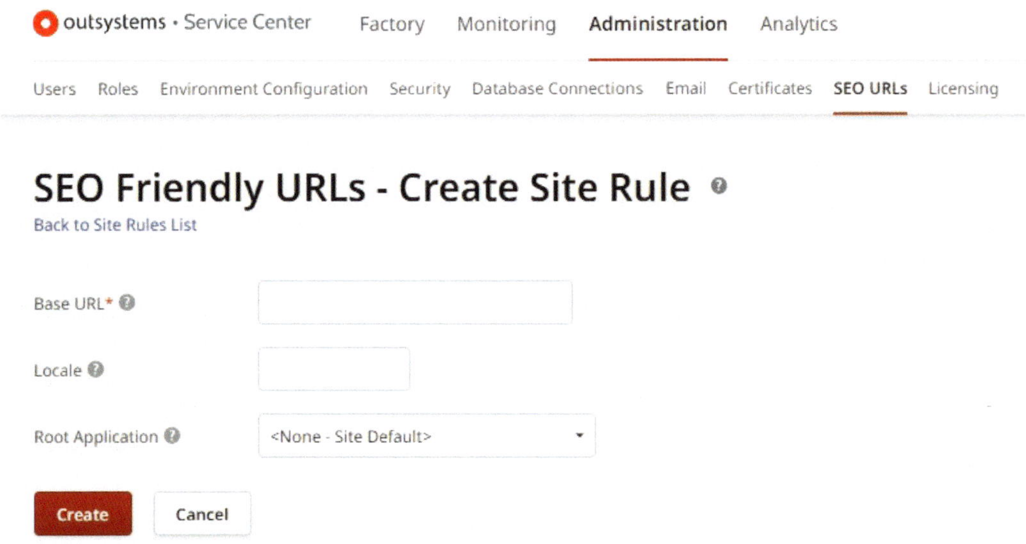

Figure 1.13 – Service Center view for Create Site Rule

- **Page rules**: This feature allows us to configure the trailing part of the URL to be more user-friendly. With this, instead of having something like `/CityBuses/SearchPage? From={From}&To={To}`, we can have something more user-friendly: `/CityBuses/From-{From}-To-{To}` (the values between `{}` are the input parameters for the search). Recently, OutSystems made these settings available in a more understandable way, directly in the page properties in the IDE (Service Studio). With this, as we create and develop our application pages, we can immediately configure our page rules in a simplified and intuitive way. This is the technique that most allows good ranking positions to be achieved in search engines since the trailing part of the URLs is the one that is usually the least human-readable:

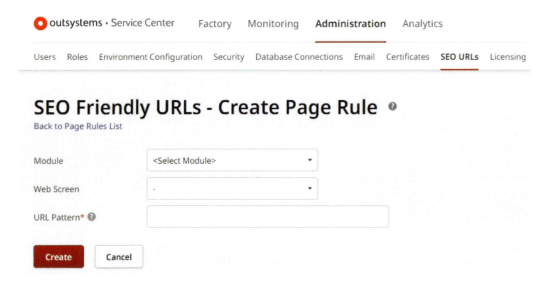

Figure 1.14 – Service Center view for Create Page Rule

With this in mind, we realize that SEO allows us to obtain better results in search engine searches, much more attractive and user-friendly URLs, and a much more understandable use of our applications, always managed in a centralized and simple way.

OutSystems factory options

The OutSystems platform is quite adaptable to the needs of customers and can be configured and installed according to different standards and on different types of installations.

Derived from its construction on native technologies, the way in which all parts complement each other is robust, performant, and safe.

OutSystems platform deployment options

As an example, we will use a typical installation in an isolated environment.

The typical installation has two servers:

- A frontend server, where our applications will live and which browsers will access to receive their pages and content.

- A database server, where our application, system, and log databases will be housed. The OutSystems platform is natively prepared to work with SQL Server, Azure SQL Database, Oracle, and MySQL databases.

The frontend server communicates with the database server to obtain and create/edit/delete the data it needs.

The following screenshot shows the typical OutSystems environment setup:

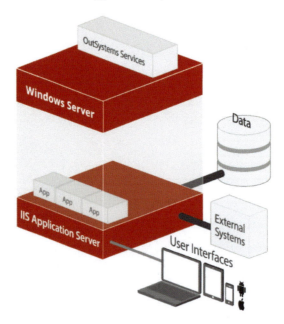

Figure 1.15 – Typical OutSystems environment setup

The OutSystems platform supports horizontal scalability, that is, it allows having multiple frontend servers running simultaneously, and for this scenario, it is necessary to have a load balancer between the browsers and the frontend servers to distribute the charge by them. This same load is distributed based on algorithms such as round-robin or based on some type of metric or measurement.

For this purpose, a tool is used in the Windows environment of the server in question called **Configuration Tool**, where the ports and IP necessary for the correct functioning of the platform are configured.

Following the correct configuration of the frontend servers to the platform, they become visible in the configuration and parameterization console of the respective environment, as well as its services – the service center.

When a user browses our applications, they generate or modify session data. This data is stored on the database server centrally and in a catalog dedicated to that purpose. And this is because? Since requests made by the browser at different times can be processed by different frontend servers, the session data must be in a place that's accessible to all.

In this way, the configuration of the farm type platform (the name given to a platform with multiple frontend servers) becomes much simpler and more robust.

The following screenshot shows the OutSystems farm example:

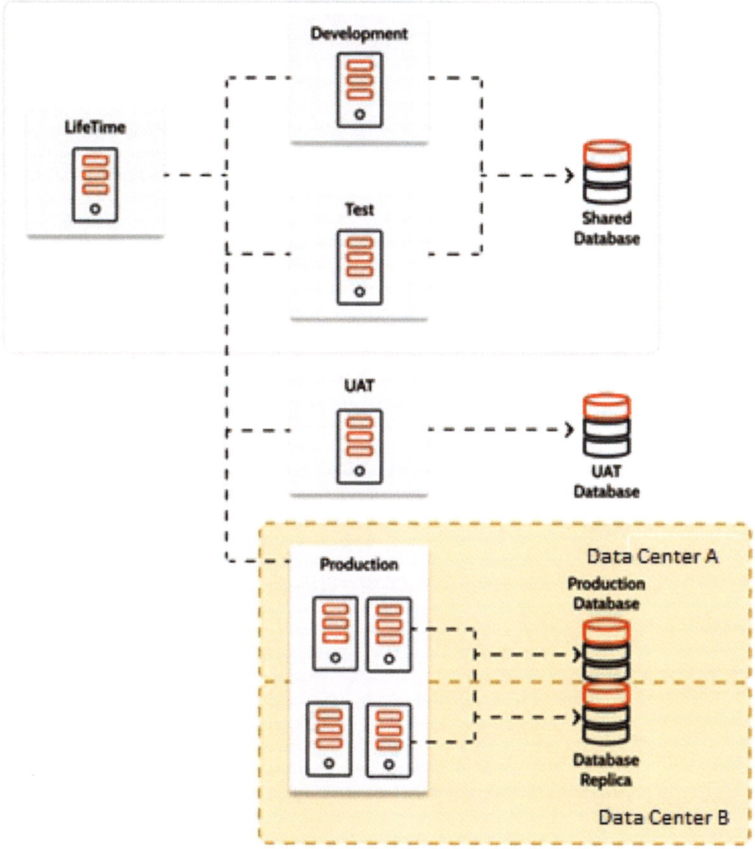

Figure 1.16 – OutSystems setup farm example

The platform is designed to allow different installation and setup configurations in order to adapt to the infrastructure and response needs of the different scenarios imposed by customers. Also, the manner in which we can make these installations and setups is very intuitive, allowing us to have a platform ready for development very quickly.

To get the most out of everything we've seen, OutSystems provides a repository with various pre-designed tools and components, both by OutSystems itself and by members of the community. In addition, OutSystems provides support forums so that we can clear up our doubts and seek help among the members of the OutSystems universe. Let's see how.

External tools, components, and support

As expected, OutSystems offers an extremely attractive help and support ecosystem so that we can leverage our developments and unlock various doubts or problems: the OutSystems Community

In addition, there is a repository of components and plug-ins already built that we can download for free, and that allows us to take even more advantage of our OutSystems software factories: **OutSystems Forge**.

Forge and Community

Forge is a repository of pre-built components and plugins developed by OutSystems and several developers around the world. OutSystems applications are directly supported by the teams that developed them, making the process of using and optimizing them much easier. With this, we can avoid building something we need from scratch, instead reusing something someone has already done, thereby saving time and effort.

The following screenshot shows the look and feel of Forge:

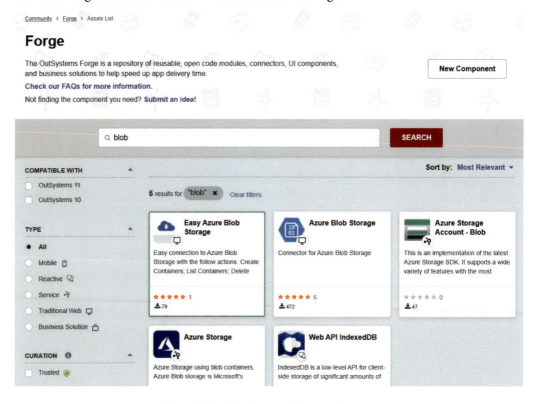

Figure 1.17 – OutSystems Forge main page

The Community is a space for developers (and not just that; it extends to several roles within this huge universe) to share their doubts, help solve problems, and provide feedback and ideas, regardless of the degree of experience of each one.

The following screenshot shows the look and feel of Forums in the Community:

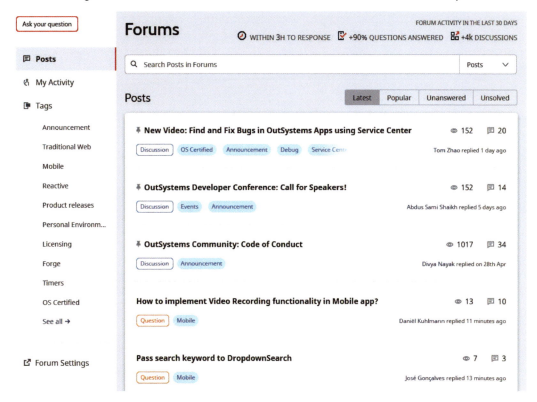

Figure 1.18 – OutSystems Forums (from Community) main page

Community is very useful and always growing and evolving. Therefore, we can always rely on the fact that the OutSystems world is not static but dynamic, simple, fast, and efficient, just like the product available to us.

Summary

In this chapter, we have discussed the enormous size of the OutSystems ecosystem, its enormous potential, and everything we can rely on to ensure that we shine in the development of web and mobile applications.

Basically, the OutSystems platform provides a list of built-in features to help us develop faster, more securely, and with a very low margin of error, including horizontal scalability, hot deployment, asynchronous logging, bulk insert, multiple catalogs (only for on-premises installations), CDN support, traffic optimization, cache, and SEO-friendly URLs.

In addition, under the hood, the platform offers state-of-the-art capabilities, such as automated batch processing scaling, log tables rotation, database connections pooling, unused database connections unloading, optimized field fetching in aggregates, and optimized dataset memory loading.

In the next chapter, we'll take a closer look at the main components, tools, and capabilities used daily to develop our applications quickly, securely, and with high scalability. A work of art, in other words!

Interesting, isn't it? Well, we're just starting out...

2
Components, Tools, and Capabilities

The **OutSystems** platform provides a wide range of tools and components so that we can develop, manage, and monitor our applications in a simple and effective way.

In this chapter, we will learn how we can use the platform's development tools to create our applications, and we will utilize the code integrity verification system, which only allows us to publish our code if it is solid. Furthermore, we will learn how these tools are prepared and optimized to speed up our work by using many pre-existing components. In the case of **Service Studio**, we'll see how OutSystems' visual code development paradigm makes it easier for us to focus on what's important: the business!

We'll also see how the monitoring and configuration tools help us keep the platform healthy and how we can use them to fix our bugs, discover negative application behavior trends, and improve our applications!

This may seem like a lot, but believe me – with OutSystems, everything becomes simpler.

This chapter will cover the following topics:

- Service Studio walkthrough
- Service Center capabilities
- Managing your infrastructure with LifeTime
- Managing end users with the Users application
- Integration Studio walkthrough

Service Studio walkthrough

In order to simplify application development, OutSystems created a highly capable, simple, and intuitive **Integrated Development Environment** (**IDE**), giving it the name Service Studio.

Service Studio is the main tool we use to perform the following:

- Create applications and modules.
- Create **user interfaces** (**UIs**) for our web and mobile applications.
- Define the data model.
- Define business processes and Timers (asynchronous processes).
- Debug our applications (both server-side and client-side).

When we open Service Studio, we must connect to an OutSystems environment (cloud or on-premises) by providing a server URL (or selecting an existing one from the **Environment** dropdown) and our developer credentials.

The following screenshot shows the OutSystems Service Studio **Switch Environment** connection popup:

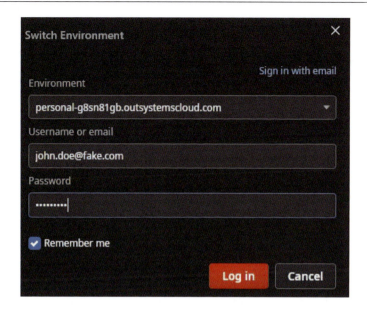

Figure 2.1 – The Service Studio connection popup

After successfully connecting, we will see an overview of the environment we are connected to. Here, we will be able to observe all of the existing applications for which we have permissions (the subject of user permissions for applications will be covered later in this chapter, in the *Managing your infrastructure with LifeTime* section). In the **Environment** tab, we can see options to carry out the following actions:

- Create a new application.

- Install OutSystems Forge applications and components.

- View and access existing applications.

The following screenshot shows the OutSystems Service Studio **Environment** overview:

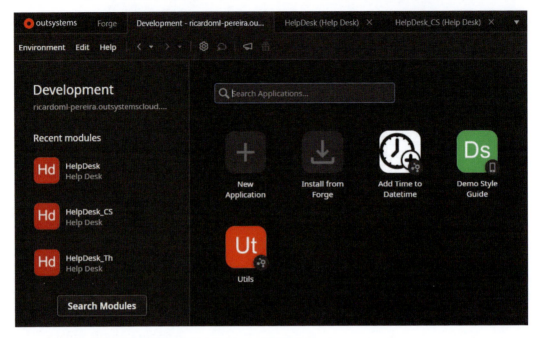

Figure 2.2 – Service Studio Environment overview

We can use the search input field in the **Environment** overview to search for our applications. If we want to open a specific module from an environment, we can use the keyboard shortcut *Ctrl + O*:

Figure 2.3 – The Service Studio Open from Environment popup

In addition, we can install Forge applications and components (predesigned by community members or by OutSystems itself) to leverage our developments. We can do that by selecting the **Forge** tab, next to the **OutSystems** tab as shown in Figure 2.2.

In the **Environment** overview, we can also click the **New Application** link to create new applications.

After creating a new application or accessing an existing one, navigate to the app's details screen:

Figure 2.4 – Service Studio application details screen

On the application details screen, you have the following areas as shown in the preceding screenshot:

- **App details**:

  - The **Edit** button: Click to edit your app's name, description, icon, and main color.

  - The **Delete** button: Click to delete the app from your environment.

  - The **Download** button: Click to download your application as an OutSystems Application Pack (`.oap` file).

  - The **Open In Browser** button: Click to open your app in a browser (only if the application has a frontend module defined as the application's default module).

- **Application tabs**:

  ▪ The **Develop** tab: This is where you manage your application modules. You can also see the application's dependencies (that is, other applications or components used by your application).

  ▪ The **Distribute** tab: In this area, you can generate your mobile app for **iOS** or **Android**. This is also where you can enable **Progressive Web App** (**PWA**) distribution for your application. This tab is only available for mobile apps.

By clicking on one of the modules or creating a new one, we enter its workspace, which is the place where we develop, publish, and debug our code:

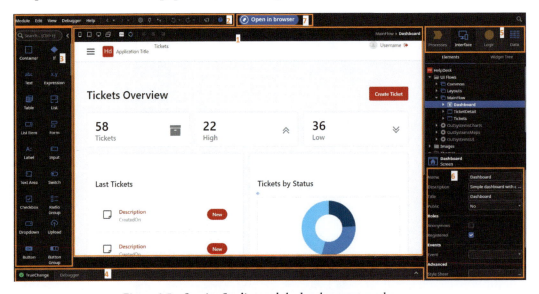

Figure 2.5 – Service Studio module development workspace

The areas of the workspace are as follows (as shown in *Figure 2.5*):

- **1- Main editor**: This is the canvas where we can build our visual code.

- **2- Toolbar**: This is a set of useful shortcuts for tool operations, such as opening Service Center, opening **Manage Dependencies**, merging, undoing and redoing, and changing to the previous or following canvas.

- **3- Toolbox**: This contains all of the existing widgets and patterns to develop the logic and Screens/Blocks of our modules.

- **4- Development tabs**: Here, we have access to the **TrueChange** tab (where we can see and inspect our module's errors and warnings), the **Debugger** tab (where we can start and control the debugging of our module, and whenever it is running, inspect the values that pass through all of the debug scope variables), the **1-Click Publish** tab (where we can view all occurrences of the publication), and a tab with results of performed searches (where we can view all elements found by a search).

- **5- Application layer tabs**: These tabs define the total scope of our module, and are composed of processes, the UI, logic, and data.

- **6- Properties editor**: In this section, we can parameterize and edit a selected element from any of the application layer tabs. Each type of element has its own property characteristics.

- **7- 1-Click Publish button**: This button is only available if there are no errors in our module. When it is available, it triggers the publishing of our module. In modules with a UI, at the end of the publishing process (if the version of the module that we have open does not differ from the one on the server) the button is replaced by a blue **Open in Browser** button that opens the application in the browser.

As we have seen in *Figure 2.5*, Service Studio provides four tabs: **Data**, **Logic**, **Interface**, and **Processes**.

So, let's get to know each of them in more detail!

The Data tab

The Data tab is where everything related to Database Entities, data structures, and variables that support our applications is located, such as Site Properties, Client Variables, and necessary Resources (such as Excel files for bootstrapping, for example).

Entities and Entity Diagrams

In the **Data** tab, **Data Entities** can be defined. These are representations of real database tables, containing all attributes and their respective parameters (data type, size, and requirement), indexes, delete rules, and settings regarding presentation. In the **Data** section, the **Create**, **Retrieve**, **Update**, and **Delete** (**CRUD**) operations that can be carried out on the respective Entities are shown. These operations can be visible in the module itself and in the consumer modules, and we can restrict their use in these modules by defining the Entity as `Expose Read Only`. If we set it to `yes`, the only operation available to consumers is `Get`. To make the other operations available, we must encapsulate them in Server Actions or Service Actions (which are called wrappers), instead of just using the original operations.

In the case of a **Dynamic Entity,** the operations are as follows:

- `Get<Entity name>`
- `GetForUpdate<Entity name>`
- `Create<Entity name>`
- `CreateOrUpdate<Entity name>`
- `Update<Entity name>`
- `Delete<Entity name>`

In the case of a **Static Entity**, the operation is as follows:

- `Get`

But what are Static and Dynamic Entities? Let's remind ourselves.

A **Dynamic Entity** is a representation of a table in a database on which we can perform the different CRUD operations in real time.

A **Static Entity** only allows the definition of records in the development environment, and we can only search for the values inserted in them in real time. The purpose of these tables is very similar to the purpose of the well-known **enum** (the behavior of enumerable, static lists of values that support other pivot data).

In order to facilitate the organization of Entities, we can create folders according to existing concepts and distribute the Entities in them.

During the data model construction process, we can create a data model diagram (or diagrams) and, if necessary, export it.

Structures

In the **Data** tab, we can also define **data Structures**. These Structures are representations to be used in memory and allow data organization according to the intended scenarios (performing Actions, for example). Furthermore, these same Structures are used to avoid exposing the data model to consumers of *Actions* and backend modules (we'll see what *Actions* are later in this chapter).

In order to facilitate the organization of Structures, we can create folders according to existing concepts and distribute Structures in them.

Client Variables

Client Variables allow you to store data of basic types on the client side (browser), both in web and mobile applications. By default, these variables are used for caching purposes, configurations, and application support (for example, to save a certain value of a filter so that, when we return to the same page, the filter remains). The amount of data that can be saved in these variables always depends on the browser.

These variables have the particularity of being shared between several applications in the same environment (with behavior similar to session variables in some characteristics) as long as the following is true:

- The user provider is the same.

- The applications are running in the same browser.

Whenever a user exits the application or when the application automatically closes, the values are reset to their defaults the next time the user logs on.

It is important to note that since these variables are available on the browser side, sensitive data should not be stored in them.

Site Properties

Another type of object that can be defined in the **Data** tab is the **Site Properties** object. Site Properties are supporting variables stored on the server. They are global variables with values that rarely change.

As a rule, it is not advisable to change the value of these variables at runtime, as doing so causes the cache to be invalidated, leading to a drop in performance. The most common practice is to change its value through Service Center, and usually, these values only change between environments (for example, **Development/Quality/Production** environments).

We must always bear in mind that Site Properties affect all users of the application in which they exist.

Multilingual Locales

The OutSystems platform allows us to add extra languages in which the application can be presented to the client. To do this, just add the desired languages in the **Multilingual Locales** section in the **Data** tab. After adding the desired languages, we can define which values we want to translate. We can insert the translations directly in the **Service Studio Multilanguage Editor** or export all the desired values for translation, importing the translations already made later.

The existence of this functionality depends on the platform version and can come in either a technical preview or the final version (for both reactive web and mobile applications).

Resources

In the **Resources** section, we locate all the necessary Resources to support a given application. For example, whenever we use **Microsoft Excel** files to bootstrap data for Entities, the files are saved there, and new ones can be updated or added as needed.

By default, in the modules used for the frontend development, one of the Resources available in this section is the favicon (the icon used in the browser tab to identify our application).

Note that **CSS** and **JavaScript** Resources are saved in their own sections (we'll see this in detail later in this chapter).

The following screenshot shows the OutSystems Service Studio **Data** tab:

Figure 2.6 – The Service Studio Data tab

We must always bear in mind that all the elements present in this tab allow us to preserve the information and data necessary for the correct functioning of our applications.

The Logic tab

The **Logic** tab is where business rules, data manipulation code, engines, and wrappers are defined.

This is where we make our applications work – it's where we put the necessary actions to fulfill an application's requested features.

For this purpose, OutSystems offers six types of elements:

- Client Actions
- Server Actions
- Service Actions
- Integrations
- Roles
- Exceptions

Let's look at these each in detail now.

Client Actions

Client Actions are logic encapsulations that run on the client side (browser). They can be called by other Client Actions, but never by Server Actions. However, Client Actions can call Server Actions. Note that as a matter of good practice, you should only call one Server Action at most. Why? Each Server Action that is called is a **REST** (**Representational State Transfer**) method that is invoked. Note that a Server Action is not a REST API; rather, it is encapsulated in a REST call to the server (that is, if we have two Server Actions to be called in a Client Action, we open two connections to the server using REST). In order to bridge this scenario, it is good practice to encapsulate the Server Actions needed in one Server Action and call this one alone.

Client Actions can have input, local, and output parameters of various types. Furthermore, they can be defined as a function (so they can be used as an argument of a decision logical elements, such as Ifs or switches or by other Client Actions). To be defined as functions, Client Actions must have one and only one output variable. Client Actions can also be defined as public to be consumed by other modules.

Note that these Actions cannot be exposed in the following scenarios:

- An Action has a parameter that is defined through an Entity/Structure that is not exposed.

- An Action has a parameter that is defined from an Entity/Structure that is reused in another module.

Server Actions

Server Actions are simply abstractions and encapsulations of our code. They are similar to **functions** in other languages such as **C#** and **Java**.

Server Actions can have input, local, and output variables. If we want them to be used as functions (so they can be used as an argument of a decision element or other Server Action) they have to present only one output variable. As a rule, when you want to return more than one attribute in a function, Structures are defined in the **Data** tab with their attributes. The attributes of the Structures are defined according to the needs of the Actions. In this way, you can define input variables, output variables, and local variables with their (the variables) types being matched with the Structures that we create in the Data tab.

Service Actions

Service Actions are abstractions of logic that run in a more coupled fashion. They run as separate transactions from the context in which they are called. As they are considered a weak reference, after 1-Click-Publish they are immediately available to all consumers. Note that this type of Action is only available in **Service-type** modules.

Integrations

In this same tab, we can perform Web Services implementations, **Simple Object Access Protocol** (**SOAP**) and REST, consuming or exposing SOAP web services and REST APIs. With OutSystems, the development of methods and configurations and the parameterization of our REST and SOAP services takes only a few minutes.

When consuming REST and SOAP methods, the OutSystems platform can automatically infer and build all the Structures and parameters necessary for the correct functioning of the methods using **Web Services Description Language** (**WSDL**) in the case of SOAP services, or Swagger (a specification for a format describing REST APIs) in the case of REST services.

The platform automatically generates documentation for the exposed SOAP and REST services. This is very useful for developers, who are able to integrate the exposed services and thus save time.

In addition, OutSystems allows the connection to SAP services in a simple and fast way not identical to but as effective as REST and SOAP, inferring SAP Structures and methods (BAPIs) without knowing SAP technology.

Roles

Another out-of-the-box component provided by the platform in the **Logic** tab is the ability to create permission roles for authorization. In this component, we can create roles according to business needs, and Check, Grant, and Revoke Actions are automatically made available for us to use in our server-side code.

Exceptions

At the bottom of the **Logic** tab menu, we have the **Exceptions** folder. Exceptions are used to handle errors or behaviors deviating from the expected flow, taking advantage of native OutSystems error-logging features.

With this feature, it becomes simpler to handle and scale behavior deviations in our application, thus allowing for better control over our code and more efficient tracking of the application flow.

The following screenshot shows the OutSystems Service Studio **Logic** tab:

Figure 2.7 – The Service Studio Logic tab

The content of this tab is essential for the correct functioning of our applications. That is because all data manipulations and information to be saved in the databases in the **Data** tab will be done by the elements in the Logic tab. This is where most of the business rules and features of our applications must be implemented because, even if the frontend layer is poorly designed, the logic artifacts are where we validate and process what goes to the Data Entities. In other words, the **Logic** tab's elements are the gatekeepers of robust and well-formed data.

The Interface tab

The **Interface** tab is where we will develop our application's UI as Screens or Blocks and all the elements they comprise. To do this, we can build two types of visualization components:

- **Screens**: Screens are the pages to be rendered by the browser as the final elements of an application interface.

- **Blocks**: Blocks are reusable abstractions of interface parts and have a life cycle of their own. For example, we could use a Block for a section that we want to show on one screen that can appear on multiple screens, or for a business concept where we want to hide the complexity from the consumer application side.

To define these components in an organized way, Service Studio includes the concept of UI **Flows**. A Flow is the layer where we associate the related Screens and Blocks.

So, the **Interface** tab provides the following folders:

- **UI Flows**

- **Images**

- **Themes**

- **Scripts**

  Note that this tab does not exist in **Service-type** modules.

UI Flows

A UI Flow is made up of a group of Screens and/or Blocks. As a rule, they are organized by their business concept and/or functionality.

When we create a new module, it automatically generates three UI Flows:

- **Common**: This UI Flow contains Blocks, Screens, and Exception Handlers in our module that are reusable and not business related, such as a menu Block, or login and user info Screens.

- **Layouts**: This is where the layout Blocks for use in our Screens are defined. If we create a custom layout, we can add it to this UI Flow.

- **MainFlow**: This is the default UI Flow with which to start creating Screens for our application. However, it can change its designation and we can always create more UI Flows as needed.

Images

The **Images** folder is where we save and insert the images we need to use in our application. It works as a repository, and we can add and delete images, save a copy on our machine, and even change an image for another. We should always pay attention to the size of the images (in bytes) due to the performance impact that their rendering can have on our application.

These elements are cacheable by browsers, and the OutSystems platform automatically resolves this issue, since it is a built-in component.

Themes

The **Themes** folder is where the CSS files that define the look and feel of our applications will be available. CSS files can be edited in Service Studio's Style Sheet Editor, giving us all the potential of the CSS language. However, it is advisable for someone with at least basic CSS knowledge to edit CSS files, as poor editing can have negative impacts on the visual behavior of the application. By default, this CSS file is based on the OutSystems UI, which is a predefined library (with code and classes already made) provided by OutSystems with ready-to-use UX/UI patterns and layouts that follow CSS best practices.

Scripts

The **Scripts** folder is the place to store our JavaScript files!

In this section, we can save our scripts. These scripts can then be used in our Screens or Blocks as required, simply by calling them in the **Required Scripts** attribute. By doing this, we enable the browser to cache the script, simplifying its use and centralizing the availability of the code across the entire application.

When creating a frontend module natively, a JavaScript file is automatically generated to cover performing all the features provided by the OutSystems platform.

The following screenshot shows the OutSystems Service Studio **Interface** tab:

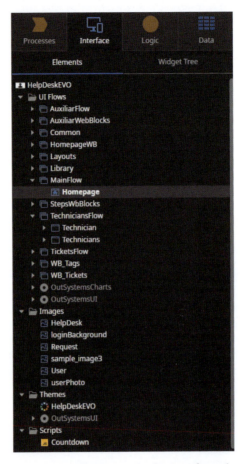

Figure 2.8 – The Service Studio Interface tab

The **Interface** tab is where we will concentrate on the best way to present information, data, and functionality to end users. This is where the *put yourself in the user's shoes* premise comes to the fore. Developing Screens and Blocks can be easy, but the secret is to realize when we should design a Screen and when we should take the Block approach.

The Processes tab

The **Processes** tab is where we set up our asynchronous processes. Here, we can define Timers (batch processes) to run certain predefined business logic (Actions) from the **Logic** tab and send bulk emails, as well as define business process flows (using **Business Process Technology** (**BPT**), which we will discuss in detail in a later chapter).

In this tab, there are two folders.

Processes

Processes are business flows defined by various elements, which could be human activities, automatic activities, waiting points, sub-processes, or decisions. This feature allows us to obtain greater simplicity in the construction and maintenance of our application flows, in addition to isolating their complexity from the rest of the application code.

Timers

Timers are batch jobs in OutSystems. We can define a Timer's periodicity, priority, and timeout. With Timers, we can handle data more efficiently, as we can use them to free up processing time in the frontend of our applications. Instead of running the logic directly in the frontend streams, we can associate it with the logic that runs in a Timer and *wake* that same Timer, passing the logic of that Timer to run asynchronously on the server.

These features allow better optimization of the behavior of our applications, as they prevent unnecessary processing at runtime and allow us to schedule processing for periods of less server usage.

The following screenshot shows the OutSystems Service Studio **Processes** tab:

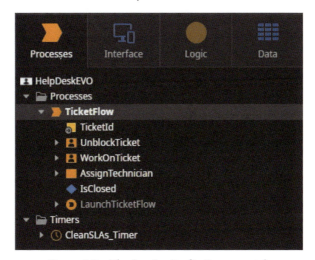

Figure 2.9 – The Service Studio Processes tab

So far we've looked at the four Service Studio tabs, which cover the various layers of our application development.

Additionally, Service Center allows detailed visibility of asynchronous processes, since the platform provides an out-of-the-box intelligent logging system that allows the programmer to view different facets of the asynchronous processes. We will discuss this in more detail in the next section.

Service Center capabilities

Service Center is a management console dedicated to a given OutSystems environment.

In this section, we will see that Service Center is a very powerful tool that allows us to manage settings in OutSystems environments, monitor all events logged by the native logging system (and customized logging systems as well) in a very intuitive way, monitor the state of the infrastructure components that make up the environment, and perform analysis on and export analytical data.

In Service Center, the following features are available:

- **Factory**: This allows us to have an overview of all existing **Applications**, **Modules**, **Extensions**, and **Solutions** in the environment.

- **Monitoring**: This allows us to access the various logs registered on the platform, both for events and errors.

- **Administration**: This allows us to make various configurations for the environment and manage external connections.

- **Analytics**: This allows us to visualize the analytical data of the platform's behavior and export it for external analysis and treatment.

The Factory tab

The **Factory** tab has four further tabs within it:

- **Applications**: In this tab, we can see all the existing applications in the environment and, by clicking on them, we can access their details, such as the modules that are related to them, their dependencies, possible operations, and security settings.

- **Modules**: In this tab, we can view and access all existing modules in the environment that are the component parts of the applications. By accessing their details, we can view their versions (the OutSystems platform has the ability to version our modules automatically, allowing access to previous versions), their dependencies, and their status, single sign-on definitions, deploy solutions which modules are part of, , its integrations, its tenants, its Site Properties (allowing us to configure its effective value if we want to override the default value), existing Timers (also allowing its configuration), and operations.

- **Extensions**: In this tab, we can view all existing extensions in the environment and access their details. In the detail of each extension, we can see its versions, what modules are getting integrated, which solutions refer to it, which Actions, Entities, and Structures it provides, the Resources (files) it uses, and, in the **Operation** subtab, there is an option to activate activity logging.

- **Solutions**: In this tab, we can view all existing solutions and the details of each solution. By accessing its details, we can view its existing versions, as well as the constituent modules of the solution and the status of its last publication. In addition, on the **Solutions** listing screen, there is a link to create a new solution, where we can add the desired modules and either download or publish solutions.

The following screenshot shows the OutSystems Service Center **Factory** and **Applications** tabs:

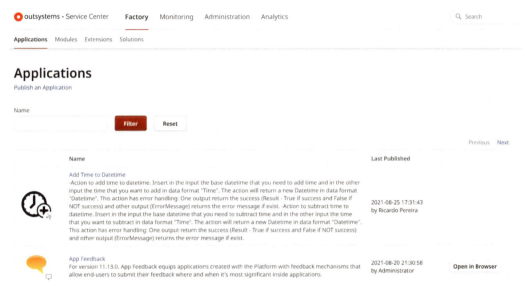

Figure 2.10 – The OutSystems Service Center Factory and Applications tabs

Service Center greatly facilitates the finding, accessing, and configuring of modules and applications that exist in our environment. The filtering capability and the way links appear in associations between elements allow faster and more accurate access to the information we need than normally found in the industry.

The Monitoring tab

In the **Monitoring** tab, we can view events and errors that occurred during the operation of our applications. In addition to the prebuilt logs, we can define our own custom logs and errors, which are also shown on this tab.

The **Monitoring** area is divided into the following subtabs:

- **Errors**: This shows all the errors logged by the platform regarding the applications and the platform's core services.

- **General**: This shows general logs related to the normal functioning defined for the applications and the platform's core services.

- **Traditional Web Requests**: This shows requests made by frontend applications in the traditional paradigm. The traditional paradigm is the predecessor of the reactive paradigm, having in its genesis the native .NET ASPX technology. This paradigm is gradually being discontinued as it is no longer considered to be a cutting-edge technology.

- **Screen Requests**: This shows requests made in the functionalities available on the reactive web and mobile application screens.

- **Service Actions**: This shows Service Action call logs (REST web services abstractions).

- **Integrations**: This shows logs of requests to consumed and exposed web services.

- **Extensions**: This shows logs related to calls to existing extensions in the environment.

- **Timers**: This shows logs related to Timers executed by servers.

- **Emails**: This shows email logs triggered by our applications. If the **Log Content** property is set to Yes in the Action flow in which it is called, the email sent is available for download.

- **Processes**: This shows logs related to existing BPT processes in the environment. The flow and status of each BPT can be analyzed in this section.

- **Mobile Apps**: This shows logs related to the generation of mobile packages for our mobile applications.

- **Environment Health**: This is a dashboard with general information on the different areas covered by Service Center, in addition to the general status of each component.

- **Security**: This shows the logging of blocked addresses and environment security log topics.

The following screenshot shows the OutSystems Service Center **Monitoring** and **Environment Health** tabs:

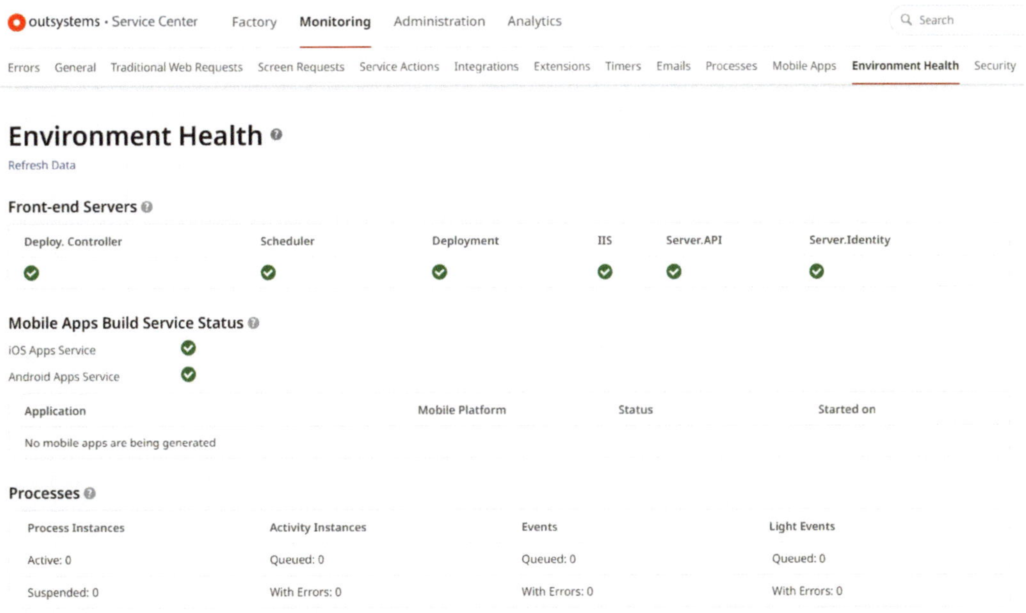

Figure 2.11 – The OutSystems Service Center Monitoring and Environment Health tabs

Whatever metrics we are looking for, we can find everything quickly and fairly comprehensively here. If there is a problem or anomaly, it's easily identifiable thanks to the user-friendly data presentation style (not that it's common for there to be many problems, but the **Monitoring** tab is always accurate!).

The Administration tab

The **Administration** tab is where most of the parameters related to our environment are configured. However, over time, most of these settings have been moved to LifeTime (which we'll see more of later in this chapter).

The following tabs are available in the **Administration** tab:

- **Users**: In this tab, we can see all the IT users registered in this environment (note, these users are not end users; they are all developers, DevOps users, and other profiles related to application development, infrastructure management, and project management). Management of these users is performed in LifeTime.

- **Roles**: Here, we can see the current roles for the IT users. These are also managed in LifeTime.

- **Environment Configuration**: This is where we configure important settings for our environment. We can set the environment name, whether it is productive or not, whether it allows debugging, the date format, the administration email, the number of retries for Timers in case of failure, along with enabling/disabling deployment and reporting features.

- **Security**: This is where we check and enable/disable security features, such as the use of SSL/TLS, **HTTP Strict Transport Security** (**HSTS**), cookie security, and **content security policy** (**CSP**) management.

- **Database Connections**: Remember we said we can connect our platform to external databases? This is where we configure, create, and visualize the connection points.

- **Email**: To send emails through our applications, it is necessary to configure an email account (sender). In this tab, we configure the email sender data so that the platform can take advantage of this feature.

- **Certificates**: Here, we can insert and activate the certificates that are necessary for the given environment (for example, authentication certificates).

- **SEO Friendly URLs**: Here, we can configure our aliases, site rules, and redirects to obtain more user-friendly and intuitive URLs for search engine optimization.

- **Licensing**: Here, we can check all the attributes related to the licensing of our environment, including the users, application objects, serial numbers, activation codes, license types, end dates, organization names, and editions.

The following screenshot shows the OutSystems Service Center **Administration** and **Environment Configuration** tabs:

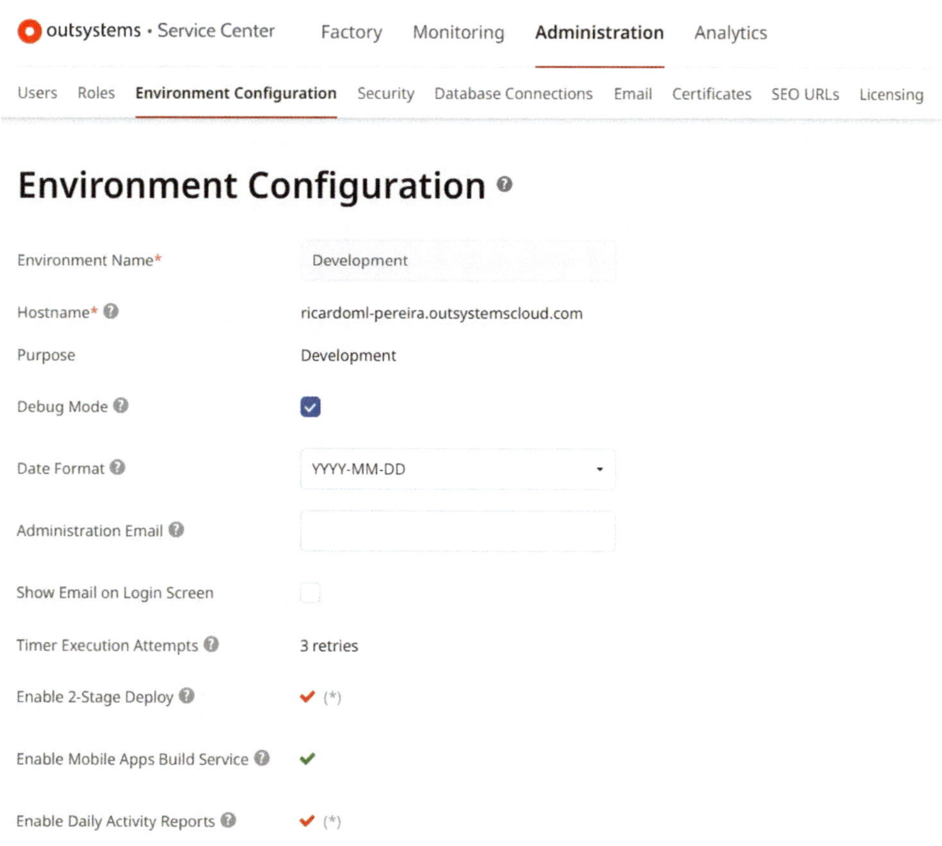

Figure 2.12 – The Service Center Administration and Environment Configuration tabs

Note that the available configurations vary with the type of platform we are parameterizing. By default, Personal Environments have fewer parameterizable fields and, in enterprise accounts, only those who have permissions to do so can configure the environment (that is, the permissions assigned to the IT users in LifeTime).

The Analytics tab

In the **Analytics** tab, we can obtain or create various reports on the behavior of the environment, such as daily history, or modules that have not been used for a specified period of time.

In the **Reports** tab, we can generate or obtain the following report types:

- Activity per hour
- Activity per day

- Extension performance

- Screen performance

- Performance of database queries

- Performance of Timers (batch jobs)

- Service Actions performance (internal abstractions of the REST API's platform)

- Integration performance

- Top errors

Typically, much of the analytics data is shown in both Service Center and LifeTime.

The following screenshot shows the OutSystems Service Center **Analytics** and **Reports** tabs:

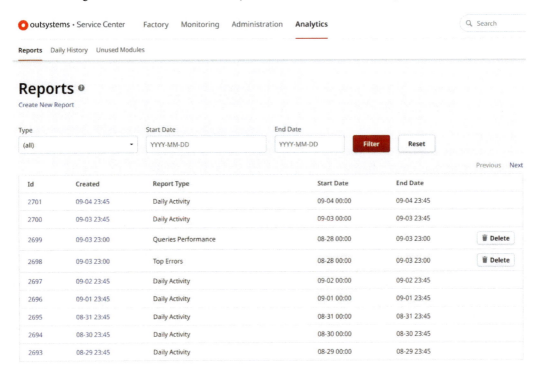

Figure 2.13 – The Service Center Analytics and Reports tabs

However, for a more detailed analysis of the level of performance and trends relating to the frontend layer, OutSystems recommends the use of external tools and, in the Forge, there are already connectors for this.

OutSystems wanted to go further and provide more power to manage DevOps within the platform, such as managing teams and IT users, quick deployment management, and efficiently performing deeper configurations on the platform. So, in the next section, we'll look at a worthy tool for this purpose: LifeTime!

Managing your infrastructure with LifeTime

LifeTime is a centralized console that allows the end-to-end management of the OutSystems infrastructure, including the configuration of its constituent environments, the management of IT users and their roles, application deployment, and security.

In this console, we are able to add plugins such as **Architecture Dashboard**, a very useful tool in the context of OutSystems architecture.

LifeTime provides the following tabs:

- **Applications**: In this tab, we can manage the complete life cycle of our applications across environments, check versions, perform deployment plans across environments, and inspect past deploys. Also, it allows you to check whether we have any outdated or broken applications.

- **User Management**: Here, we can manage IT users and teams and their access profiles across all environments. Roles are highly configurable – that is, we can create custom profiles. In addition, the platform provides the ability to create teams and assign profiles to users based on the teams to which they belong, facilitating the management of permissions within the infrastructure.

- **Environments**: In this tab, we can view and access the configurations of all the environments that make up the infrastructure. Settings can be modified in an intuitive and practical way related to secure endpoints, adding and removing environments, and creating database users. In addition, access to Service Center for each environment is provided so that we can check the environments' logs.

- **Analytics**: In this tab, we can inspect performance issues in several layers, and for reactive web and mobile applications, we must use external monitoring tools that integrate with the OutSystems platform via APIs, such as, for example, **Elastic RUM** (note that this is only available for traditional applications, which are out of scope for this book). In the Forge, there are already connectors to monitoring Reactive web and Mobile applications existing in our platform,, simplifying the integration and adaptation process.

- **Plugins**: In this tab, we can install existing components (such as Architecture Dashboard), as well as create our own plugins. These tools allow us to extend the capabilities of LifeTime to third parties and/or acquire capabilities for LifeTime itself.

The following screenshot shows the OutSystems LifeTime **Environments** tab:

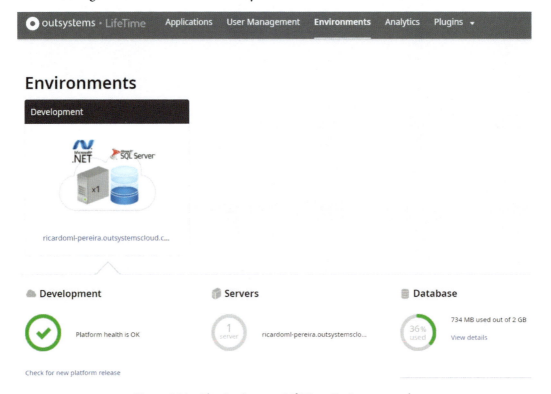

Figure 2.14 – The OutSystems LifeTime Environment tab

The OutSystems platform was designed to make it easier to access relevant information about the life cycle of our applications and all kinds of events that allow us to monitor and control the status of our environments, with LifeTime being a perfect example of this. In each of the aforementioned tabs, we can immediately find what we are looking for.

There is a concept that is so important that it is dealt with in a separate application: the end users. We can create and edit them, and assign and remove their roles. Let's see how to do this in the next section!

Managing end users with the Users application

The **Users** application is where we manage the end users of our OutSystems applications. Here, we can create and edit users, manage their status and role assignment, and unlock them.

To perform these operations, the current user must have the **UserManager** role, otherwise, they will not have access to the features of this application.

In order to facilitate the assignment of roles to multiple users, we can create teams, where we assign the team its given roles, and every end user added to that team will inherit those roles. This way, we can manage the roles that each user must have in a more practical and streamlined way.

Roles created in our applications through Service Studio are automatically visible in the Users application and can be assigned here or programmatically through code in our own applications.

The Users application provides three tabs:

- **Users**: In this tab, we can view existing users, access their details (and edit them), view inactive users (and activate them), and export user lists as Excel files. Additionally, there is a link to create new users, redirecting the application to a **Create New User** screen.

- **Groups**: Here, we can create groups based on business or permissions concepts. After creating them, we can add the desired roles and their permissions, and associate users with them. This way, it becomes easier to manage the assignment of roles, allowing to add or remove roles to multiple users simultaneously. On this page, we can see all existing groups.

- **Applications**: Here, we can see all the applications that use OutSystems as user providers and the number of active users with roles related to each application.

The following screenshot shows the **Users** tab of the OutSystems Users application:

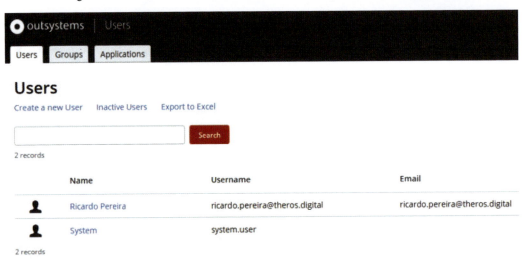

Figure 2.15 – The Users tab of the OutSystems Users application

Note that this application makes all these features available to users registered in the OutSystems default user provider. In more specific and customized cases, we can have applications that use another user provider, and its users are not listed in the Users application.

It is possible to configure delegated authentication methods in this application, including Microsoft **Active Directory** (**AD**) and **Azure AD**.

All this makes a lot of sense if we want to extend our platform and create custom code in **C#/.NET**, or even integrate with third parties and legacy systems. For this, we use a development tool that, despite being very simple, is extremely powerful, and even allows connection with **Microsoft Visual Studio** (for custom native code development). We present, in the next section, Integration Studio!

Integration Studio walkthrough

Integration Studio is a tool that allows us to create extensions to our platform, such as creating functionalities in native C#/.NET code. Functions made in C#/.NET are transformed by Integration Studio into Server Actions. In this way, our custom code is available similarly to our application code for consumer modules.

Furthermore, with this tool, we can configure our connections to external databases (after the given connection has been configured in Service Center).

In a way, it's a simpler tool than Service Studio since it offers much less functionality; Integration Studio works in parallel with Microsoft Visual Studio to help us develop our code.

The following screenshot shows the OutSystems Integration Studio popup where we configure the Visual Studio connection:

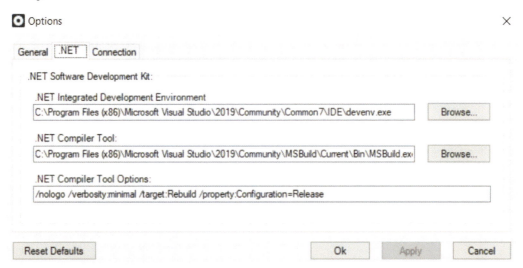

Figure 2.16 – The Integration Studio popup to configure the connection with Microsoft Visual Studio

Integration Studio has fewer layers and features than Service Studio:

Figure 2.17 – The Integration Studio main screen

All sections of the main screen are designed to be visually intuitive and easy to find according to context. In addition, it maintains a pattern similar to (albeit simpler than) Service Studio, so developers won't have difficulty adapting.

Therefore, Integration Studio's main screen is divided into the following sections:

- **Toolbar**: In this area, you can create new extensions, verify and publish an extension, connect to the Platform Server, and download your extensions.

- **Multi-tree Navigator**: In this area, you can add and select your **Actions**, **Structures**, and **Entities** (in the Extension tree), and add and select your **Resources** (in the Resources tree).

- **Status bar**: This area contains information about the extension, including the folder where the **Extension and Integration Framework** (**XIF**) is saved.

- **Multi-tab editors**: This area contains all the elements (extension, Actions, Structures, Entities, and Resources) that you have selected in the Multi-tree Navigator.

- **Specific Editor**: In this area, you can edit the extension and its elements: Actions, Structures, Entities, or Resources.

- **Server Info**: In this area, you can find information about which Platform Server you are connected to and which user established this connection.

In order to facilitate the use of Outsystems IDEs and maintain uniformity between the tools, after completing our development, Integration Studio also provides the **1-Click Publish** button seen elsewhere in OutSystems. When **1-Click Publish** is clicked, it triggers the entire compilation process and the verification and publication of the code we have developed.

Summary

OutSystems provides a set of tools that covers all the necessary requirements for the easy, fast, and secure development, monitoring, and configuration of infrastructure and applications.

We have two development tools: Service Studio and Integration Studio.

OutSystems also provides three out-of-the-box management tools: Service Center, LifeTime, and the Users application.

Comparing OutSystems tools to native technology tools makes it seem too easy! But that's the way it is – easier to learn, easier to use, and faster to develop with!

In the next chapter, we will learn how to register with OutSystems in order to obtain a Personal Environment and the necessary tools for application development.

Let's get to work! Now it will be even more fun!

3
Starting Work with OutSystems

In this chapter, we'll see how OutSystems offers a free account option. This means we can learn how to develop projects, test our code, and even make small personal applications for free!

In order to start enjoying all the OutSystems features, we need to purchase an environment and register.

In this chapter, we will learn how to scale our application according to our needs. We will also learn what OutSystems platform capabilities and features are, and what we have to gain by adopting it.

OutSystems offers a set of solutions with simple mechanisms for registering and downloading tools. Let's look at them in more detail!

This chapter will cover the following main topics:

- OutSystems pricing and editions
- Setting up our Personal Environment
- Installing OutSystems IDEs
- Opening and starting Service Studio
- Opening and starting Integration Studio

Let's get started!

OutSystems pricing and editions

The first thing to do is identify the best solution for our business needs regarding the available OutSystems editions. There are currently four different editions, and each edition can be customized in different ways:

	Free	Basic	Standard	Enterprise
Capacity				
Unlimited applications	✓*	✓	✓	✓
Internal end users included	100	100	100	100
Internal end user limit	100	1,000	No limit	No limit
External end users (in packs of 10,000)			✓	✓
Deployment Options				
OutSystems Cloud	✓	✓	✓	✓
Option to upgrade to the high-compliance OutSystems Cloud			✓	✓
On-premises or private cloud			✓	✓
Platform Configuration				
Environments	1	3	3**	5**
Pipelines		1	1	2**
Continuous integration and deployment		✓	✓	✓

* Shared infrastructure and database limited to 2 GB

** Option to upgrade

Figure 3.1 – OutSystems editions, and features

For the most up-to-date details on OutSystems pricing and editions, refer to the OutSystems website:

`https://www.outsystems.com/pricing-and-editions/`

To begin working through the developments in this book, we will use the free version.

This version allows us to learn for free, and OutSystems itself encourages us to use it to test our code before progressing to the paid versions. It's also extremely simple to set up our free Personal Environment, as we'll see now!

Setting up our Personal Environment

To set up our **Personal Environment** (that is, the free OutSystems version), we must follow some simple steps:

1. To start, we must go to the OutSystems website (`www.outsystems.com`) and click on the **Start Free** button:

Figure 3.2 – The OutSystems home page

2. Then we need to provide the required information:

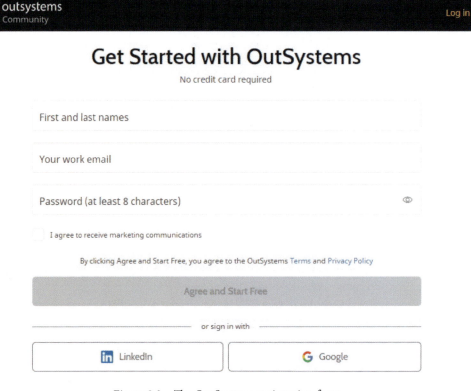

Figure 3.3 – The OutSystems registration form

After submitting your details, an activation email will be sent to the provided email address.

3. To continue the process, we need to open the email just received from OutSystems and click on the **CLICK ME!** button. We are then redirected to the creation page for our Personal Environment, where we set our password. After setting it, click on the **CREATE YOUR CLOUD ENVIRONMENT** button:

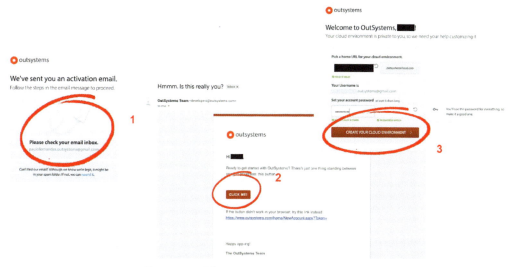

Figure 3.4 – The OutSystems registration steps

> **Tip**
>
> Make a note of the cloud environment address, username, and password. You will need this in the next steps to connect to the cloud environment through the OutSystems tools.

4. After this process, our Personal Environment is ready. We just need to answer some questions from OutSystems and then click on the **CONTINUE** button:

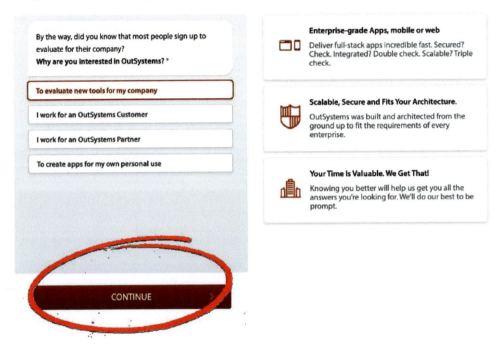

Figure 3.5 – Finalization of the registration process

Now that we have our Personal Environment, we need to set up the tools to develop our applications in it.

Installing OutSystems IDEs

In order for us to develop applications, we need tools. OutSystems makes these tools available to us free of charge, we just download and install them and we can connect to the desired environment. So let's see how!

The first step is to download the required **integrated development environments** (**IDEs**) and install them on our computer. This is similar to the process of setting up our Personal Environment:

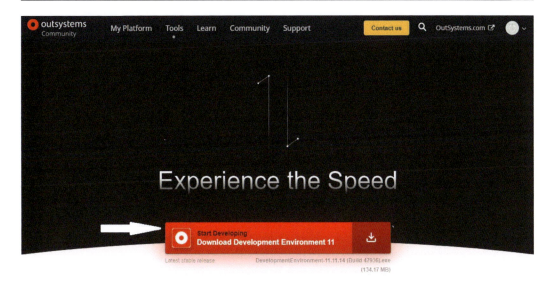

Figure 3.6 – The OutSystems Tools screen

You can download the development tools directly through this link: `https://www.outsystems.com/downloads/`.

After downloading the package, we must run it, press the **INSTALL** button (**1**) and, if we want, launch the tutorial at the end of the installation (**2**):

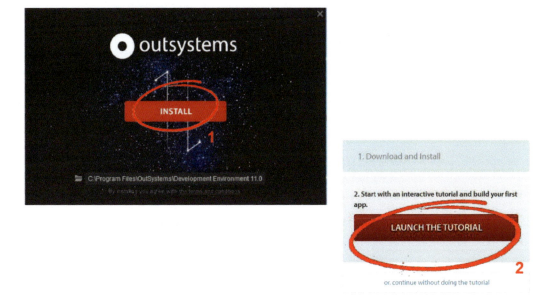

Figure 3.7 – The OutSystems popup for the development tools installation

Now we have our Personal Environment and the necessary tools set up to develop our applications. So now let's open our tools and start our work!

Opening and starting Service Studio

The main tool for developing OutSystems applications is Service Studio, a very easy-to-understand IDE completely oriented toward the visual development paradigm.

Shall we start our adventure? Okay!

1. In the **Windows Search** field, type `Service Studio`:

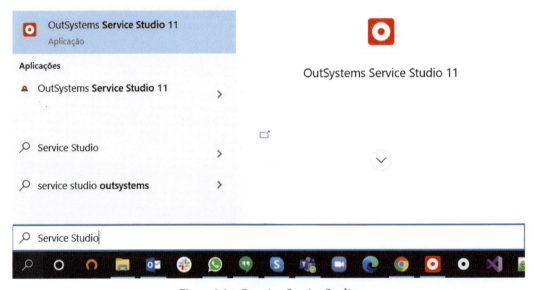

Figure 3.8 – Opening Service Studio

2. Then, open the application by clicking on the **OutSystems Service Studio 11** icon.

> **Tip**
> We can add a shortcut for Service Studio to the taskbar by right-clicking on the application icon and selecting **Pin to taskbar**.

3. After opening the application, enter your user credentials and the URL of your Personal Environment (that is, the details we advised you to make a note of in the previous section), and then click **Log in**:

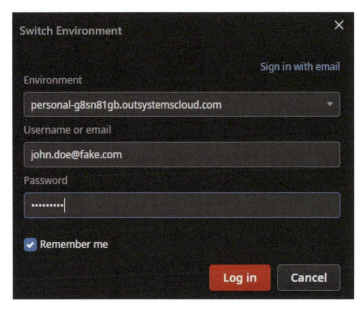

Figure 3.9 – Connecting to our Personal Environment in Service Studio

After successfully connecting, we will see an overview of all the existing applications in our Personal Environment, with access to all of the functionalities that Service Studio provides:

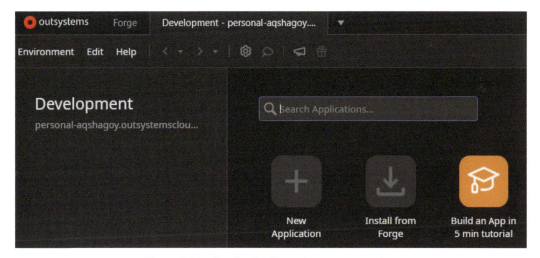

Figure 3.10 – Service Studio environment overview

We've already figured out how we can start Service Studio and create OutSystems applications (but this is something we'll start doing in the next chapter).

But what if we want to extend our platform with external database connections or create our **C#/.NET** code? For that, we have to learn how to open and start the second IDE from OutSystems: **Integration Studio**!

Opening and starting Integration Studio

OutSystems provides a tool that allows us to extend the platform with custom C#/.NET code and to carry out more complicated and non-standard integrations. It doesn't offer as many features as Service Studio, but it manages to be as powerful nonetheless.

To start Integration Studio, follow these steps:

1. Just like we did to open Service Studio, in the Windows Search field, type
    `Integration Studio`:

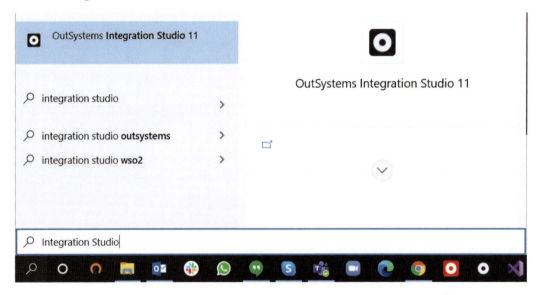

Figure 3.11 – Opening Integration Studio

2. Then, open the application by clicking on the **OutSystems Integration Studio 11** icon.

> **Tip**
> We can add a shortcut for Integration Studio to the taskbar by right-clicking on the application icon and selecting **Pin to taskbar**.

3. After opening the application, enter your user credentials and the URL of your Personal Environment (yes, the same URL as before), and then click the **Connect** button:

Figure 3.12 – Connecting to our Personal Environment in Integration Studio

After successfully connecting, we will find an empty main screen where we can start creating our extensions, custom code, and connections to external databases:

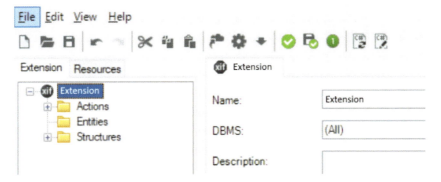

Figure 3.13 – The Integration Studio main screen

From here, we can start creating our code, such as C# native code abstractions or database integrations. In the end, everything we create here is available for consumption in Service Studio as dependencies.

Summary

We have now learned all the necessary steps to start creating our applications: registering to set up a Personal Environment, installing the OutSystems development tools, and connecting both of these parts.

From this moment on, we will learn everything that is necessary to develop state-of-the-art applications, making the most of the features provided by the development tools and by the OutSystems platform itself.

In the next chapter, we will learn the fundamentals for correctly developing our applications – that is, the types of modules that exist, when we should use them, and how we should use them.

We will also learn about naming conventions and how to apply this concepts in OutSystems software development.

Now, let's roll up our sleeves and get to work!

Section 2:
The Magical Path of
the Backend

In this section, we will learn how to develop modules based on segregation, how to create, manage, and handle databases, how to create and develop server-side-oriented logic and code, and how to manage exceptions and errors.

This section comprises the following chapters:

- *Chapter 4, Using Your Modules to Simplify and Encapsulate Your Code*
- *Chapter 5, Modeling Data by Using Entities*
- *Chapter 6, Server-Side Logic*
- *Chapter 7, Exceptions Handling*

4
Using Your Modules to Simplify and Encapsulate Your Code

The OutSystems platform was designed to simplify technical and architectural issues as much as possible. Thus, it offers different types of modules according to the needs and features that we want to develop. All just a few clicks away.

Here, we will learn what types of modules exist, their characteristics, and their purposes, as they relate to each other. We will also notice that the standardized nomenclature allow us and the platform itself to catalog the modules and applications in the correct layers of **Architecture Canvas** (also known as **3 Layer Canvas**).

This chapter covers the following topics:

- Types of modules
- Distributing modules across applications
- Applying modules to the correct architecture layers
- Modules and application naming conventions

In the end, we will be able to identify where we should place our developments based on the role and purpose they fulfill.

Technical requirements

In this chapter we will cover how to create modules based on their types and name them in Service Studio, this being the base software for us to apply the knowledge that we will acquire here.

Types of modules

For a better understanding of this topic, we must make the following analogy: the application is the molecule and its modules are the atoms. Atoms can be of different types, according to their purpose. To this end, when creating modules within the application, five types are natively available:

- **Reactive web app/phone app/tablet app**: These are the modules that provide the final user interface for our applications. These are used to build and develop everything related to the frontend, from widgets and patterns to blocks and web screens. These modules can be used in the frontend layer to provide the pages and blocks that users will access for the foundation layer, to create themes, templates, custom patterns, and business-agnostic widgets.

- **Blank**: These modules are a blank screen. Here, the prebuilt components are initially minimally used, leaving the programmer the possibility to go their own way.

- **Service**: These modules are used from a Core Services perspective. These are the modules used for the backend code, where we create and manage our own databases and manage the code that ensures compliance with business rules.

- **Library**: As the name implies, these modules are business-agnostic libraries that are used to support mainly non-functional requirements. These modules usually belong to the foundations layer.

- **Extension**: Although we can invoke their creation through Service Studio, these modules are created and developed in Integration Studio. These serve to extend our platform, such as creating our C#/.NET code and abstracting it in OutSystems, creating connections with non-standard external systems, and connecting with external databases.

Service Studio's way of selecting the module type at the time of creation is as simple as a selection dropdown, as shown in *Figure 4.1*:

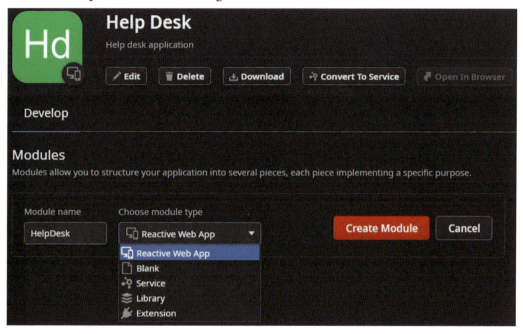

Figure 4.1 – Module types for web applications

In the previous case, the application is for the web, with the first type appearing as **Reactive Web App**. If it is a mobile application, the first type becomes **Phone App**, as shown in *Figure 4.2*:

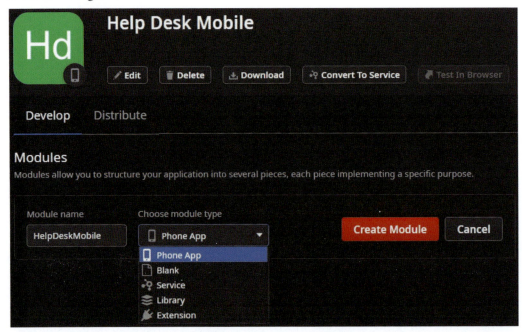

Figure 4.2 – Module types for mobile applications

Note that, depending on the type of module, certain tabs may appear or disappear in Service Studio. For example, a module of the **Service** type does not have an **Interface** tab as it is not intended to contain frontend elements, just as modules of the **Library** type do not have a **Processes** tab, as it is not its purpose to make asynchronous processes available.

The types of modules allow us to distinguish their purpose, just as Service Studio characterizes with the right tabs and tools for each of them. This makes it more intuitive and easier to follow the concepts of our developments. In addition, it makes it easier to identify any relationship that exists between modules and applications and how they are distributed, which is what we will see next.

Distributing modules across applications

Modules must be organized within applications according to the layer to which they correspond. For this, we will be based on OutSystems Architecture Canvas, also called 3LC or 3 Layer Canvas.

> **Tip**
> The OutSystems architecture model from now on will simply be called 3LC.

This model is applied on two levels: the applications level and the modules level. What does this mean? Both applications and modules correspond to certain layers, and applications adopt the topmost layer of the module that constitutes it, which has the upper layer. For example, an application that contains a foundation layer module and a core layer module is from the core layer, since the top module that composes it belongs to this layer. If this application contains an end user layer module, it will assume the end user layer.

The typical OutSystems framework architecture layers and their properties are as shown in *Figure 4.3*:

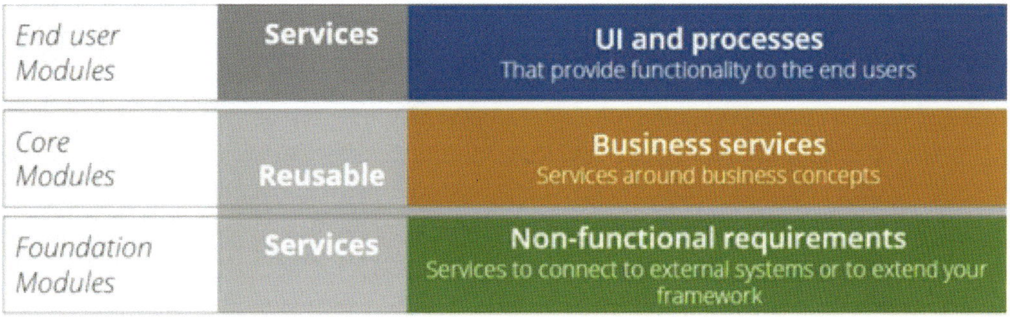

End user Modules	**Services**	**UI and processes** That provide functionality to the end users
Core Modules	**Reusable**	**Business services** Services around business concepts
Foundation Modules	**Services**	**Non-functional requirements** Services to connect to external systems or to extend your framework

Figure 4.3 – Framework layers and their properties

> **Info**
> We'll learn more about architecture issues in *Chapter 13, Designing the Architecture of Your OutSystems Applications*.

Although modules belong to a given application, they can be consumed as dependencies in other modules of other applications in order to reuse features and data models, thus preventing data and code replication.

To do so, Service Studio's **Manage Dependencies** functionality is used, as shown in *Figure 4.4*:

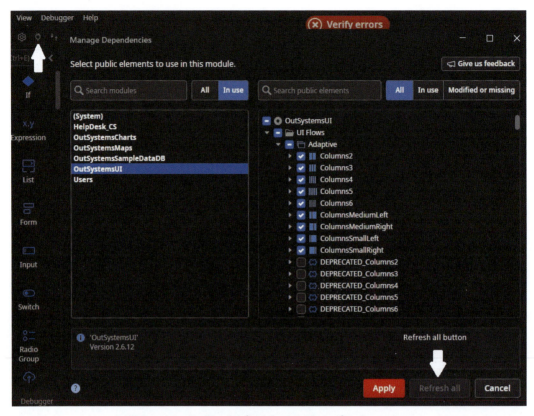

Figure 4.4 – Service Studio Manage Dependencies popup

Clicking on the **Manage Dependencies** link opens a popup with all modules that have public elements (otherwise they will not appear as available, as they are only from the context of the module in which they exist) where we can search for the desired module and the elements we are looking for. Finally, we just select the elements we want to reuse in the right column, click **Apply**, and that's it! It is available for use!

> **Tip**
>
> When a certain consumed element is updated or changed in its producer, we must open the **Manage Dependencies** console and refresh it (only in strong references or when a weak reference updates its signature). We can update the producer modules individually (those that have changes are identified with a refresh icon) or we can use the **Refresh all** button shown in the previous screenshot. If we are opening the module after these changes, Service Studio detects them and asks whether we want to open the **Manage Dependencies** console to refresh. If we do not perform this operation, we may have problems at runtime.

In this section, we can see that for our applications to be scalable, sustainable, and well organized, they must be built on a proven architectural template, the 3LC. This turns out to be like libraries; each book must be in the right place based on its content and subject in order to make your search simpler and allow the library to grow in the right way. It's the same with applications: the more organized, the easier it is to grow, scale, and maintain.

For this to work, we have to know how to catalog and apply modules to their layers correctly. Let's go see how to do that!

Applying modules to the correct architecture layers

In order to define our modules in the correct layers, we must know their purpose at the time we create them. For this, they can be categorized in different ways and depending on the layer they belong to.

Foundation layer

In this layer, we can have specific types of modules to support our applications; that is, they are like the foundations of a house. They serve to ensure that foundations are present, well organized, and reusable wherever they are needed.

Library modules

Library modules are business-agnostic modules that are a perfect match for the foundation layer, as they are intended to support non-functional or foundation functionalities of our applications, like the foundations of a house.

These modules can support the following types of artifacts:

- **UI Flow**: Group of screens or blocks

- **Blocks**: Set of sections for reuse on screens

- **Images**: `jpg`, `jpeg`, `bmp`, `png`, or `diff` files

- **Themes**: CSS file abstractions to use in screen customization

- **Scripts**: JavaScript code encapsulation

- **Data Actions**: Encapsulation of data handling for data that comes from external sources

- **Server Actions and Client Actions**: Encapsulation of handling and implementing components behavior

- **Consumed and exposed integrations (SOAP, REST, and SAP)**: Abstractions of standard web service integrations

- **Exceptions**: Abstractions for handling errors or unexpected behavior

- **Structures**: Representations of in-memory data models

- **Resources**: Files used as a resource in our applications, such as Excel for data bootstrapping

> **Tip**
> If you are curious, you can see the official documentation on libraries here:
> `https://success.outsystems.com/Documentation/11/`
> `Developing_an_Application/Reuse_and_Refactor/`
> `Libraries`.

Extension modules

As the name implies, these modules are used to extend our platform. These modules work with Integration Studio, and we can create our own native C#/.NET code to integrate its functionality in our applications. We can create custom integrations with third parties and we can also connect our platform with external databases.

For this, these modules provide four types of elements:

- **Actions**: Encapsulation of handling and implementing business rules
- **Structures**: Representations of in-memory data models
- **Entities**: Representation of database tables in OutSystems
- **Resources**: Files used as a resource in our applications, such as Excel for data bootstrapping

When these elements are used by consumer modules, their visualization will be identical to elements from other types of modules generated and developed in Service Studio. This guarantees the standardization of OutSystems' low-code paradigm, in addition to abstracting the complexity of developing the code provided by the producer module.

> Tip
> If you are curious, you can see the official documentation on extensions here:
> ```
> https://success.outsystems.com/Documentation/11/
> Extensibility_and_Integration/Extend_Logic_with_
> Your_Own_Code/Extensions.
> ```

Core layer

In this layer, the modules that define the data models and business operating rules will be present. Here, we can find database Entities and Actions to manipulate them, synchronize them with external databases, and batch process information standardization.

Service modules

In our applications, we have to process, treat, and manage the concepts and business rules related to the problem we are solving. We often have to offer an extension of our application to third parties, both internal and external. Well then, service modules are meant to abstract, centralize, and guarantee this. These modules have core characteristics of our applications; they govern and process what the business needs, thus being directly associated with the core layer.

These modules can support the following types of artifacts:

- Service logic, using server Actions and service Actions
- Integrations (SOAP, REST, and SAP)
- Processes and Timers
- Database Entities

These modules have a very well-defined purpose at the backend level and, due to this context, they do not have frontend-related functionalities, such as the **Interface** tab and any kind of logic or artifacts related to that theme.

> Tip
> If you are curious, you can see the official documentation on services here:
> `https://success.outsystems.com/Documentation/11/`
> `Developing_an_Application/Reuse_and_Refactor/Use_`
> `Services_to_Expose_Functionality`.

End user layer

In this layer, the modules where we define our frontend will be present. Here, we will be presenting the screens that we will show our users, separated by the application concept in order to simplify and facilitate the segregation in the development for the future.

Reactive web/phone app/tablet app modules

Reactive web modules are nothing more than the modules where we develop our frontends for web applications (Reactive web app modules) and mobile applications (phone app or tablet app).

> **Note**
> In these modules, we create blocks and web screens that we show to the
> end user. By default, the only logic and Entities that exist in these modules
> are just frontend support and not related to the business. These modules can
> also be used to develop foundation layer features, more specifically, themes
> and UI templates.

All layers

There are types of modules that can be used in any of the layers, and they are presented as **blank sheets**, making available all of the existing features in Service Studio so that we can create our code freely and according to our needs without limit on customization.

Blank modules

Blank modules can be used transversely. What does this mean? Basically, it's a blank sheet that we can use to create whatever we want, in the context we want, with the necessary customizations.

By default, these modules are used in cases where the application's needs do not take great advantage of the prebuilt components of the previous types of modules.

In summary, for each of the existing 3LC layers, OutSystems provides different types of modules characterized and enhanced by the tools necessary for the characteristics of each one of them, thus ensuring greater robustness in the modular construction of applications and a more refined and precise architecture according to best practices.

However, we also show that this does not in any way remove the customization capacity or borders regarding what we need to do, as everything was designed to leave us free, but always with maximum security and prevention in order to avoid unnecessary mistakes and allow a greater focus on what matters: success!

Modules and application naming convention

To better identify the modules and applications we create, there is a convention advised by OutSystems for their names. This convention involves the use of suffixes, and although the suggestion is not mandatory (each one can follow its own normalization, as long as it is adequate), it is heavily used in the OutSystems world.

This convention is based on two attributes of modules and applications: their layer and their sub layer.

The following table explains the convention used today:

LAYER	SUB LAYER	SUFFIX	EXAMPLE	DESCRIPTION
Frontend modules	End user	_UI*	Clients_UI	Interface modules that contain the screens made available to the user.
Core modules	API	_API	Clients_API	Wrapper that exposes an API for external consumers (REST/SOAP) to the OutSystems platform, supporting multiple versions.
		_OAPI	Clients_OAPI	Wrapper that exposes an API for internal consumers (service Actions) to the OutSystems platform, supporting multiple versions.
	Core widgets	_CW	Request_CW	Modules that contain reusable interface blocks that have their own life cycles and manage to abstract business complexity.
	Composite logic	_BL**	Invoices_BL	Modules used to manage and work logical business complexity, with its own life cycle, isolated and abstracted from consumers.
		_Eng	Invoices_Eng	Modules used to manage high business complexity, such as calculation engines. They can be versioned and, as a rule, can originate from "_BL" modules that have gone up in complexity.
		_Sync	Clients_Sync	These modules use connections to external systems to synchronize OutSystems data Entities. From this module, we remove the unnecessary complexity of the modules that contain the Entities and make the synchronization logic isolated.
	Core Services	_CS**	Clients_CS	Core modules with business Entities and respective Actions for data manipulation within the same architectural domain.
Foundation modules	Style guide	_Pat**	Portal_Pat	Module for reusable and business-agnostic UX/UI patterns.
		_Th	Portal_Th	Module with the applicational theme, that is, the look and feel to be presented in a given application.
	Foundation services	_IS	Clients_IS	Wrapper module for external services integration and standardization.
		_Drv	Sponsors_Drv	Module for several integration services to different systems, performing the same type of operation by several drivers that expose the same API.
		_Lib	MathUtils_Lib	Module with generic and cross-cutting, business-agnostic libraries (for example, date formats).
		_Plug	Camera_Plug	Module with third-party plugin integration. Widely used in the mobile context.

Figure 4.5 – Module naming conventions in OutSystems

* Nowadays, in frontend modules, suffixes are no longer used, because it is presented in the URL and is unfriendly if it has one.

** If they are modules dedicated to mobile, add an M before, such as _MCS or _MPat.

Based on the suffixes shown, the platform can correctly infer (in most cases) which layer and sub layer each module/application belongs to. This makes it easier to understand the general state of the architecture in our OutSystems software factory and what types of violations may or may not be occurring.

Summary

In this chapter, we get to know the various types of modules that exist, which layers they fit into, and what the conditions for this are.

In addition, we understood how to perform the naming in order to easily identify the purpose of each of the modules and respective examples.

Basically, if we adopt this kind of approach, development becomes much simpler, following one of the best software development practices: divide and conquer!

The next step, which we will cover in the next chapter, will be learning what types of Entities exist to store our data, how they are related, how to model them, and how we can populate them in a simple and fast way.

Ready, set, go!

5
Modeling Data by Using Entities

All applications are based on data. We use them to view, create, edit, and delete information relating to the business context in which we work. For everything to work as smoothly as possible, we must design a good data model. All this in OutSystems is supported by Entities, which are representations of native SQL tables.

This chapter focuses on explaining how we can create our data models and what their foundations are. With this, we can start building a scalable and easy-to-maintain application from scratch.

The chapter covers the following topics:

- Exploring database Entities
- What are Static Entities?
- Modeling data
- Bootstrapping data into Entities from Excel spreadsheets
- Exercise 1 – creating a data model

By the end of the chapter, you will understand the concept of Entities, their purpose, and how we can relate them in order to obtain a robust, performing, and coherent repository of data and information for use in our applications.

> **Note**
>
> To best illustrate how to build a data model, we will start the development of our demo application from here.
>
> The application will be to support the help desk of a conventional company with an IT department.

Technical requirements

Check out the following video to see the code in action: `https://bit.ly/3xoANVs`.

Exploring database Entities

As said before, database Entities are representations of tables that support our applications.

> **Note**
>
> A table is a structure for organizing and displaying information, with data arranged in columns and rows. Information is displayed as text, using words and numbers, and grid lines may or may not be present.

To this purpose, they have the following characteristics:

- **Attributes**: Attributes are the fields where we store data. They can be of several simple types. We can define some properties, varying according to the configured type, and one of the common properties is the mandatory configuration. The possible attribute types are as follows:

  - Text
  - Integer
  - Long Integer
  - Decimal
  - Boolean
  - Date Time
  - Date
  - Time
  - Phone Number
  - Email

- Binary Data

- Currency

- Identifier

- **Primary keys**: The primary key in OutSystems is called the **Entity Identifier**. This is created automatically at Entity creation time and cannot be a composite key. The Entity Identifier can only be of the Long Integer, Integer, Text, or other Identifier (from another Entity, making a one-to-one relation) type. It is a mandatory field. Although not a good practice, an Entity Identifier attribute can be deleted, but with the downside that from that moment on, that Entity cannot be related to others.

- **Foreign keys**: Foreign keys are attributes that define the relationships between Entities. A foreign key in an Entity refers to a primary key of the Entity to be related.

- **Indexes**: As is common in relational databases, Entities allow the creation of indexes. These are used to optimize searches. By creating an index for an attribute often used in obtaining information, it is easier and faster for the SQL engine to return the expected result. We have to be aware that indexes affect performance for data insert and update operations. Those indexes are also very useful to create unique constraints on an Entity, ensuring a more robust data model.

Foreign keys have a very useful parameter called **Delete Rule**. This parameter is used to guarantee referential integrity between main Entities and referenced Entities.

For this purpose, this attribute can have one of three values:

- **Protect**: With this value, the platform does not allow deleting the record in the main Entity while there are records in the referenced Entity associated with it.

- **Delete**: In this case, the platform deletes the records in the referenced tables that are associated with the record we want to delete in the main Entity. This is the **cascade** effect.

- **Ignore**: This last value has to be used very carefully and after we ensure that there is no impact on data integrity. If we choose **Ignore**, the platform will ignore the records in the referenced tables associated with the record that we deleted in the main Entity, leaving them **orphaned**. This is the advised type of delete rule by best practice standards since as the database engine will not need to perform any operation regarding the removal of child records or verification of their existence, the operation in the Entity that we want is faster.

> **Tip**
>
> If you are curious, you can see the official documentation on Delete Rules here:
> `https://success.outsystems.com/Documentation/11/`
> `Developing_an_Application/Use_Data/Data_Modeling/`
> `Entity_Relationships/Delete_Rules`.

The view of an Entity is as shown in *Figure 5.1*:

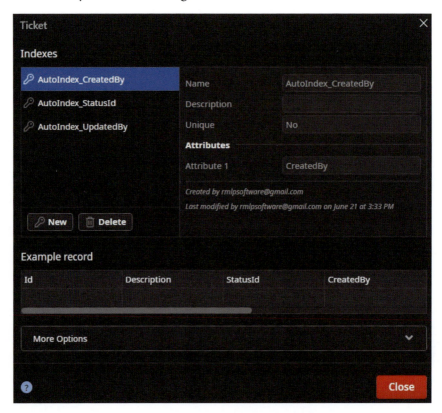

Figure 5.1 – Entity view in Service Studio

> **Tip**
>
> If you are curious, you can see the official documentation on Entities here:
> `https://success.outsystems.com/Documentation/11/`
> `Developing_an_Application/Use_Data/Data_Modeling/`
> `Entities`.

Many of the business rules can be more robustly guaranteed by taking advantage of all the mentioned parameterizable attributes of Entities. At a later stage, we must take care to make the visibility of these rules as user-friendly as possible, considering that the end user does not need to understand the technological complexity imposed in this part of the development.

In order to visualize and manipulate the data of our Entities, when we create them, the platform automatically provides the following operations:

- **Create**: Create a new record in the Entity.
- **CreateOrUpdate**: Create a new record or update an existing one (if the Identifier is null, it will be seen as new).
- **Update**: Update an existing record in the Entity.
- **Get**: Get a record from the Entity.
- **GetForUpdate**: Get a record from the Entity and lock it, preventing someone from changing it until we make a change.
- **Delete**: Delete a record from the Entity.

These operations are called **CRUD** operations (**Create, Read, Update, Delete**).

In summary, Entities allow us to store our information with different types, thus guaranteeing the robustness of the information. They can be related and organized through the use of foreign keys, thus facilitating the design of the data model.

In addition, we can use a special Entity type that simplifies many cataloging and typing issues: the Static Entities that we'll look at in the next section.

What are Static Entities?

Static Entities can be seen as literal values stored in the database and with global context between environments (such as typical enumeration).

These Entities only provide the Get Entity method, and any record to be added, edited, or deleted has to be done in Service Studio (it is not possible to programmatically perform these operations).

Natively, when creating a Static Entity, four attributes are created automatically, and we can edit, delete, or create new ones in our IDE. The four attributes created automatically are as follows:

- **Id**: Identifies a record and is always unique. It is the only attribute on the Static Entity that can be automatically numbered.

- **Label**: Contains a value to be displayed in an application.

- **Order**: Defines the order in which records are displayed to the end user.

- **Is_Active**: Defines whether a record is available at runtime. For example, records with `Is_Active` set to `false` are not used when scaffolding uses the Static Entity.

> **Tip**
>
> If you are curious, you can see the official documentation on Static Entities here: `https://success.outsystems.com/ Documentation/11/Developing_an_Application/Use_ Data/Data_Modeling/Static_Entities`.

The view of a Static Entity is as follows:

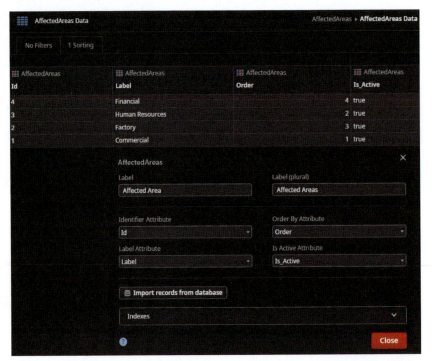

Figure 5.2 – Static Entity view in Service Studio

This type of Entity is often used when we have values that do not change over time, such as state machine statuses. Static Entities greatly facilitate development, as their structure is so robust that we can invoke certain records without having to resort to a bad practice called **hardcoded values**.

As we can easily understand, these types of Entities are less parameterizable and should only be used on data types that are not mutable. However, they allow much simpler robustness and maintenance of our data models.

Speaking of data models, how can we relate all these concepts? How can we relate this technical component to the application's needs? This is the focus of the next section: modeling data!

Modeling data

In data modeling, we deal with the relationships between Entities. As an example, a support ticket request from a help desk application (already setting the tone for the application that we are going to develop in the exercise) will have several fields, and not all of them will be in the same Entity. The Entity that supports the ticket must have its primary key, description, who created it, when it was created, who updated it, when it was updated, and its status. If we analyze it carefully, we can model this data through relationships with other Entities. For example, who created and who updated the record in the Entity can be foreign keys that refer to a user Entity (which the platform already makes available automatically, synchronized with the user provider). The state can be a foreign key that references a Static Entity where we will have all the states. These are examples of **one-to-many** relationships:

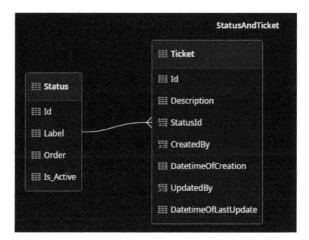

Figure 5.3 – One-to-many view in Service Studio

Now let's consider the following scenario: for each help desk support ticket, we will be able to enter the affected areas, and we can have several at the same time. In this case, we can have a Static Entity with the areas and a helper Entity that will store the ticket ID and the affected area, thus allowing multiple tickets to have multiple affected areas. This is an example of a **many-to-many** relationship:

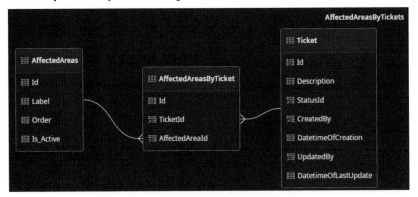

Figure 5.4 – Many-to-many view in Service Studio

There are certain cases where we only need to extend a certain Entity. Let's assume the situation where we need to add user data that is not foreseen in the original table. In this case, we can create a **UserExtended** Entity where its Identifier is the Identifier of the native Entity of users. This is an example of a **one-to-one** relationship:

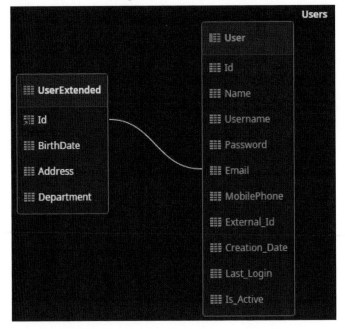

Figure 5.5 – One-to-one view in Service Studio

> **Tip**
>
> If you are curious, you can see the official documentation on data modeling here: `https://success.outsystems.com/ Documentation/11/Developing_an_Application/Use_ Data/Data_Modeling`.

Based on this type of relationship, we must think and design our data model well, always bearing in mind performance, security, and scalability. We must always build our Entities and relationships so that they can evolve and avoid the replication of Entities with the same purpose (avoiding replication and data synchronization).

The ways we can model our data is always adjustable and must be thought of in order to respond to the needs of the applications. We could see that the types of existing relationships allow for creativity and the search for the best balance between performance, security, robustness, and maintenance.

However, sometimes we need to massively populate our Entities with external data (often in cases of demos, proofs of concept/value, or data imports from other applications that do not have a service interface). For this, Service Studio provides accelerating features, where we can populate our Entities and even create new Entities from a given Excel file. And that's what the next section will focus on!

Bootstrapping data into Entities from an Excel spreadsheet

We often need to populate our Entities with pre-existing data, either for testing or for a production environment context. For this, the platform provides a feature (with two alternatives) to bootstrap from Excel files:

- **Populate the data into an existing Entity**: In this case, we will have to be careful to match the Entity's fields to the Excel columns. The platform automatically creates the necessary code for this purpose and a timer to load the data in the next module publishing process (the file will later be in the resources section of the module).

When we use this functionality, Service Studio, in order to ensure that the fields are correctly mapped, asks the developer about the match between the Excel fields and the Entity's attributes, as we can see in *Figure 5.6*:

Figure 5.6 – Mapping fields from Excel to an Entity in Service Studio popup

- **Create an Entity from an Excel sheet**: In this case, the platform creates an Entity in which the attributes will be the fields of the Excel sheet and adds the Identifier. The platform automatically creates the necessary code for this purpose and a timer to load the data in the next module publishing process (the file will later be in the resources section of the module).

This is an example of an automatically created Action for a data bootstrap:

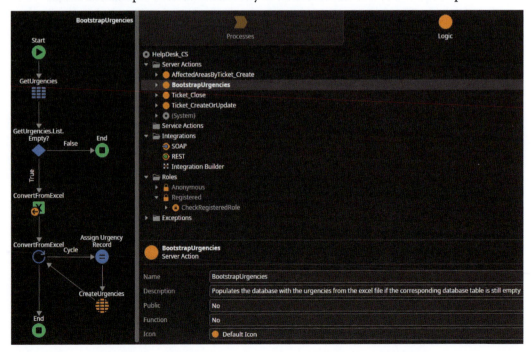

Figure 5.7 – Code example for an Entity bootstrap in Service Studio

> **Tip**
> If you are curious, you can see the official documentation on bootstrapping data here: `https://success.outsystems.com/Documentation/11/Developing_an_Application/Use_Data/Bootstrap_an_Entity_Using_an_Excel_File`.

Often, one of the requirements that exists for new projects is to migrate historical data of existing applications into new applications. One of the most commonly used methods (especially because new applications often replace jobs executed in Excel sheets) is bootstrapping from Excel, making this feature a great asset to the platform.

In this section, we understood how we can populate our database Entities in a simple and efficient way, and how Service Studio automatically generates code to accomplish this task, allowing us to speed up development.

We also realized that we can populate existing Entities with data from an Excel sheet, as we can even create an Entity that replicates the Excel sheet itself.

This is all very interesting, but the best thing is when we put into practice what we've learned.

The next section is an exercise where we will create our Entities and relate them to support our own application.

Exercise 1 – creating a data model

This section will focus on developing a data model that supports an application. We'll be able to put into practice what we've learned in previous topics in this chapter about creating Entities and setting up relations between them to support an application.

To better understand how all this works, there is nothing better than practicing.

For this, we will do an exercise that is basically the initial part of the application to be developed while working through the rest of this book.

So, to start the exercise, we must follow these steps:

1. Create a new Reactive web application and name it `Help Desk`:

    I.   To do this, open Service Studio and click on the **New Application** button:

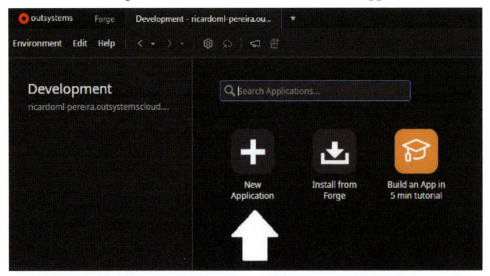

Figure 5.8 – New Application button in Service Studio

    II. Next, we select the **Start from scratch** option and click on the **Next** button:

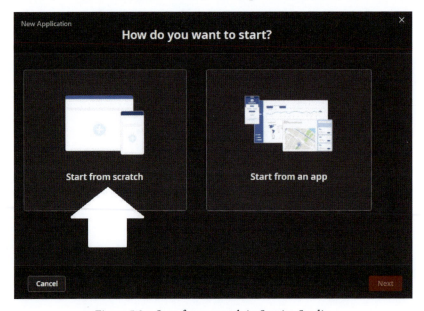

Figure 5.9 – Start from scratch in Service Studio

III.   Next, select the **Reactive Web App** option and click on the **Next** button:

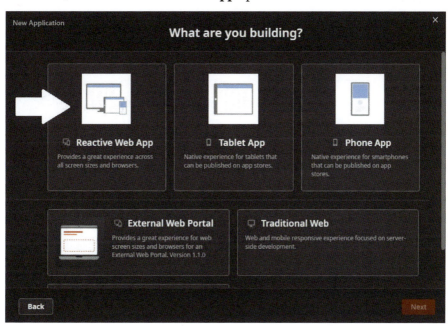

Figure 5.10 – Selecting the type of application in Service Studio

IV.   Now, we set the name as Help Desk, fill in a brief description of the application purpose, select the main color of the theme in the color picker (or upload an icon file), and click **Create App**:

Figure 5.11 – Filling in details for a new application in Service Studio

2. Create a Core Services module to support the data model:

    I.   In the **Module name** field, we put `HelpDesk_CS`, set the module type to **Service**, and click **Create Module**:

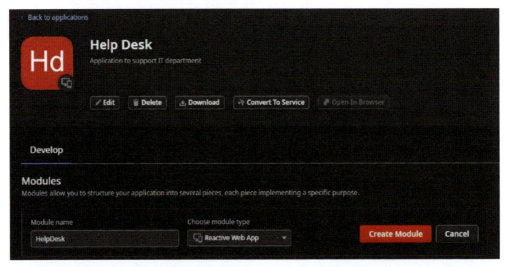

Figure 5.12 – Creating a new module in an application in Service Studio

    II.   To save the module permanently before we start implementing the data model, click on the **Publish** button:

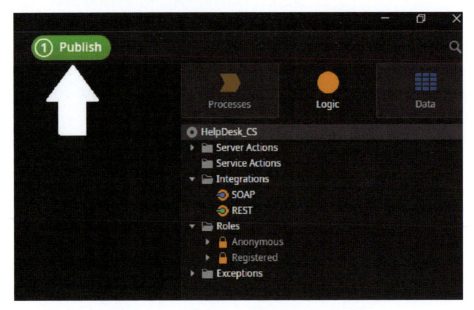

Figure 5.13 – Publishing a module in Service Studio

3. Create a data model inside our new module:

    I.   Click on the **Data** tab, then right-click on **Database** and select **Add Entity**:

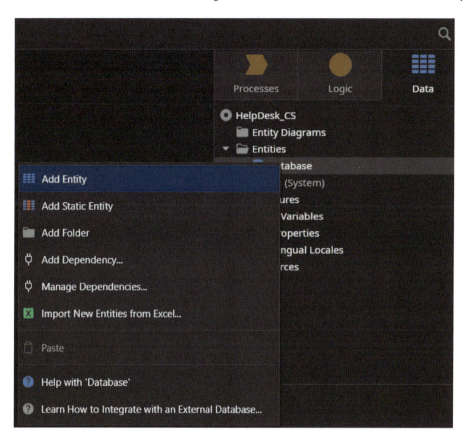

Figure 5.14 – Adding an Entity to the database

II.   Name the Entity `Ticket`. Then, right-click and select the **Add Entity attribute** option. Name this new attribute `Description`:

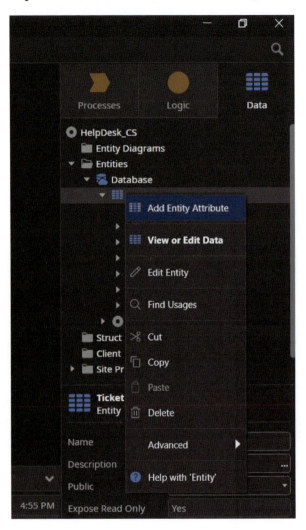

Figure 5.15 – Creating an attribute on an Entity

III. Now, we right-click on **Database** and select **Add Static Entity**. Name the new
Static Entity `Status`:

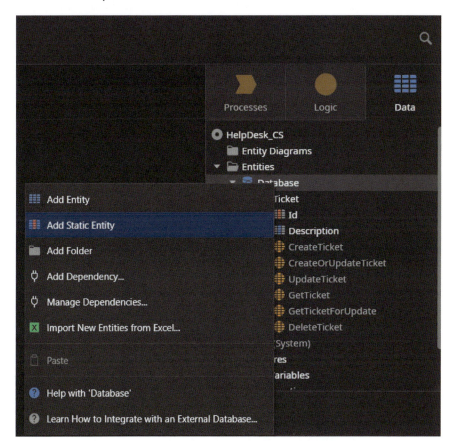

Figure 5.16 – Adding a Static Entity to a database

IV.   Expand the newly created **Status** Static Entity, right-click on the **Records** folder, and select the **Add Record** option. Name it New. Repeat the process of adding records to create the **Open**, **Discarded**, and **Closed** records:

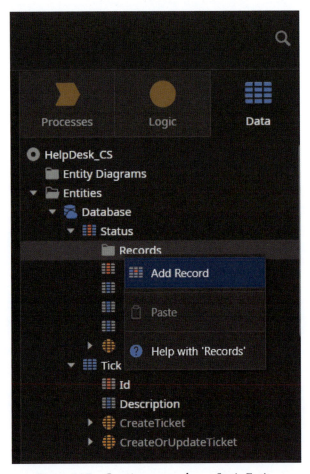

Figure 5.17 – Creating a record on a Static Entity

The new Static Entity should look like this:

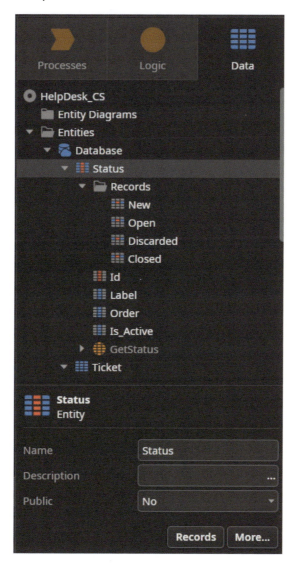

Figure 5.18 – Status Static Entity with records view

V.   The next step is to use the same technique for creating a new Static Entity but for **AffectedAreas**. This Entity must have the **Commercial**, **HumanResources**, **Factory**, and **Financial** records. In the end, the Entity must have the following structure:

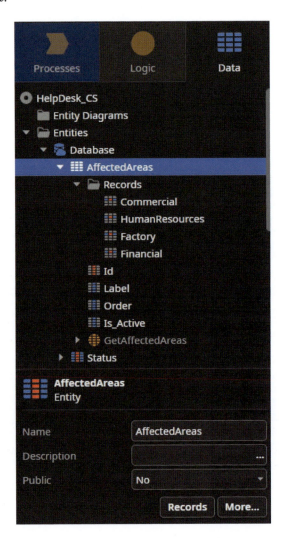

Figure 5.19 – AffectedAreas Static Entity with records view

> **Tip**
> The label that is shown later can be edited directly in the record. To do this, we just click on the record in question, go to the properties, and customize the label's value. This can be very useful to make the value more human-readable.

VI.   Now, we are going to create an auxiliary Entity that allows us to implement a many-to-many relationship between the tickets and the affected areas. To do this, right-click on **Database** again and select **Add Entity**. Name this Entity `AffectedAreasByTicket`. Next, drag and drop the **Ticket** Entity on top of the newly created Entity. Do the same with the **AffectedAreas** Entity. We will see that Service Studio automatically creates the foreign keys for these two Entities in our new Entity, thus making the many-to-many relationship:

Figure 5.20 – Affected areas by ticket auxiliary Entity with their foreign keys

VII. Both foreign keys must be mandatory. To do this, click on the attributes sequentially and change the **Is Mandatory** parameter to true in the properties section, looking like this:

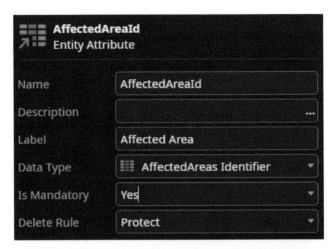

Figure 5.21 – Foreign key properties and focus on the Is Mandatory attribute

VIII. The next step is to add the missing attributes to the **Ticket** Entity. Foreign keys relating to the **Status**, **CreatedBy**, and **updatedBy** attributes can be created by simply dragging the Entity to be related on top of the **Ticket** Entity, but let's see another way to do it. Let's create the **StatusId**, **CreatedBy**, and **UpdatedBy** attributes, as explained in the previous steps for creating attributes in Entities. Let's confirm that the platform automatically inferred the attribute types for the intended foreign keys:

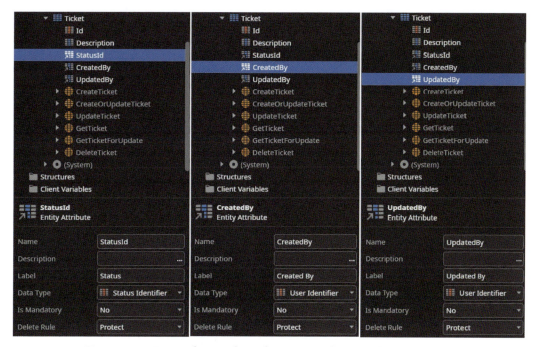

Figure 5.22 – Foreign keys in the Ticket Entity with Is Mandatory set to No

> **Tip**
>
> The platform infers the attribute type based on the name we give it. If we want something more personalized and the platform cannot infer the correct type, clicking on the attribute, in the same properties box, we can change the type in the **Data Type** dropdown.

IX. Now we must make these three new attributes mandatory using the method explained in the previous steps. It should look like this:

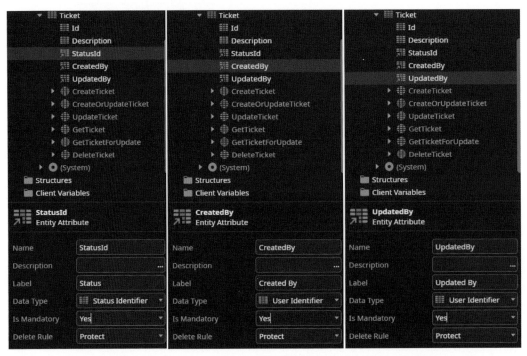

Figure 5.23 – Foreign keys in the Ticket Entity with Is Mandatory set to Yes

X. Finally, let's create the last two attributes needed for this phase: **CreatedOn** and **UpdatedOn**. Right-click on the **Ticket** Entity and select **Add Entity Attribute** for each one of them. In the properties section of each of these attributes, we must set the **Is Mandatory** parameter to **Yes**. It should look like this:

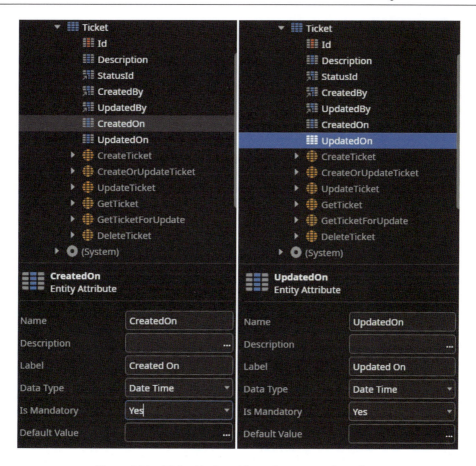

Figure 5.24 – Ticket Entity with attributes to audit updates

> **Tip**
>
> In the section with the properties of Entities and their attributes, there is a parameter called **Description**. Here, we can write a brief explanation of the concept of the respective Entity or attribute. With this, we facilitate future interpretations of the implementation of our applications.

4. Create our data model inside our Entity diagram:

I.   In order to have an overview of how our Entities are related, we can create a diagram of the data model. To do this, right-click on the **Diagrams** folder in the **Data** tab and select the **Add Entity Diagram** option. Name it `HelpdeskDiagram`:

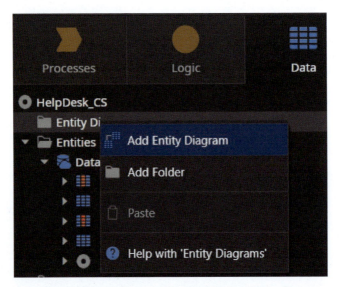

Figure 5.25 – Add Entity Diagram in Service Studio

II. To finish the diagram, we drag and drop all the necessary Entities to the canvas. The end result will be the visualization of Entities and their relationships in our data model:

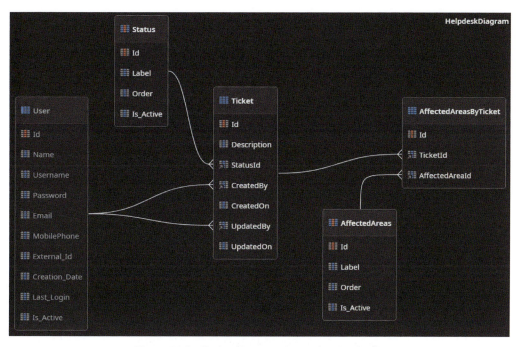

Figure 5.26 – Entity diagram view in Service Studio

III.   Finally, just click on the **Publish** button and our module is compiled and saved in our environment:

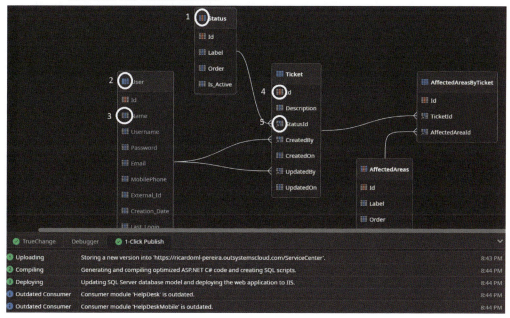

Figure 5.27 – Publishing new developments in Service Studio

Graphically, the representation of the various components of Entities are numbered in *Figure 5.27 as follows*:

1. Static Entity symbol

2. Entity symbol

3. Symbol of a regular attribute (not primary or foreign key)

4. Primary key symbol

5. Foreign key symbol

With this exercise, we understood how to create our Entities and how to set up relations between them in order to store all the necessary information efficiently.

Although simple, we have an efficient data model capable of supporting the needs of our application. All this is done in just minutes, unlike native technologies. Fantastic, isn't it?

Summary

In this section, we learned how to build our relational database and the importance of this topic for the development of a functional application.

The topics discussed here that are of great importance were Entities, Static Entities, Entity diagrams, and how to bootstrap our Entities with data from Excel files.

The quality of our data model will largely dictate how easy, quick, and scalable our application can be in the future.

Furthermore, we were able to carry out this type of development very quickly and safely. But beware, the fact that we develop very fast can also make us fail faster!

In the next chapter, we will learn how to manipulate and use our data through logic Actions and variables, using a set of decision and iteration artifacts provided by our IDE, Service Studio. We'll also continue with exercises so we can put into practice what we've learned!

6
Server-Side Logic

Our applications don't live only on data and beautiful screens. For all this to work, there has to be the glue that connects all the parts: logic! For this, at the backend level, the platform provides abstraction artifacts known as **Server Actions** that allow us to create functionalities and business logic. Through them, we are able to ensure the robustness of our data, efficiently follow business rules, and abstract complexity from our application.

This chapter focuses on developing our Server Actions in order to build and abstract our business rules and data handling in a robust and non-compromising way, thus facilitating the logical operation of our applications.

In this chapter we will cover the following topics:

- Introducing logic actions
- Types of variables in Server Actions
- Taking logic decisions with conditional paths
- Creating loops
- Exercise 2 – Creating Server Actions

By the end of this chapter, it is intended that you are able to create your own Server Actions, using different variables and techniques, in order to abstract the creation and updating of data in the Entities that support the applications.

Technical requirements

Check out the following video to see the code in action: `https://bit.ly/3DRBcSF`.

Introducing logic actions

Logic actions are the artifacts we use to manipulate data, perform calculations, and abstract the complexity of our application. In the backend, the actions used in logic are the *Server Actions*. This name is derived from the fact that actions are only run on the server side, and never on the client side.

> **Info**
>
> For the client side, we have Client Actions that are used in reactive web and mobile. This is the main topic of *Chapter 10, Client-Side Logic*.

These actions have a set of properties that allow a quick and accurate parameterization for your objective:

PROPERTY NAME	DESCRIPTION	IS MANDATORY?	DEFAULT VALUE	IMPORTANT NOTES
Name	Identifies an element in the scope where it is defined, such as a screen, action, or module.	✓		
Description	Text that documents the element.			Useful for documentation purposes. The maximum size of this property is 2,000 characters.
Public	Set to Yes to allow the element to be added as a dependency by other modules.	✓	No	
Function	Set to Yes to define the action as a function. Functions must return a value and can be used in expressions.	✓	No	This property is only available in global scope actions. Server Actions set as functions can only be used in Server Action expressions.
Icon	Picture to be displayed to help identify this element.	✓		The recommended dimensions for the icon are 32×32 pixels.
Original Name	Name of the element as defined in the module that implements it (producer module). This property is read only.	✓		This property is only visible for referenced elements.
Cache in minutes	The maximum time that content or results are stored in memory. When undefined, nothing is cached.			

Figure 6.1 – Server Actions properties (based on official documentation)

A **Server Action** can have input variables, local variables, and output variables. These can be of any available type, including text, entity, and structure records, lists of records or structures, and even a composition of several types.

These variables allow us to manipulate information in isolation and with context abstraction, since the **Server Action** alone has visibility of the code it contains. That is, some value whose context we want to pass must be sent by an input variable, and for any result that we want to pass to another context, we must pass it through an output variable. Note that local variables used and defined within Server Actions only have context within themselves.

In Service Studio, **Server Actions** are developed under the **Logic** tab and they look like this:

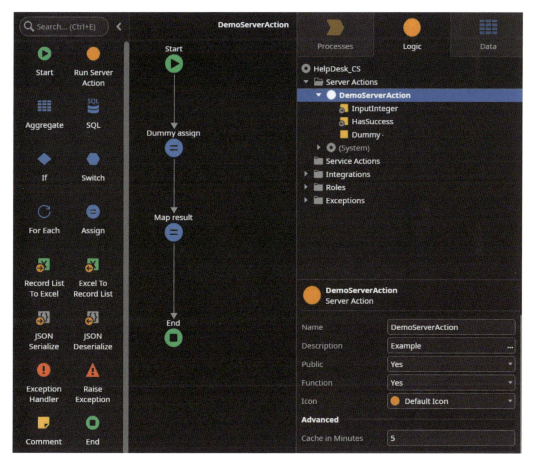

Figure 6.2 – Service Studio canvas for a Server Action

If we want a certain action to be public and consumable by other modules, we must be careful that any input or output variables of a compound type or local structure are made public as well. That is, if an input variable is of record type of an entity or structure that is not public, then when we set the **Server Action** to public, we will get an error. To solve this, either the action cannot be public, or we need to set the input type (in this case of the entity or structure) to public itself.

> **Tip**
>
> If you are curious, you can see the official documentation on Server Actions here: `https://success.outsystems.com/` `Documentation/11/Reference/OutSystems_Language/` `Logic/Implementing_Logic/Logic_Elements/Server_` `Action`.

Note that we can create **Service Actions** instead of **Server Actions**. The development principle is the same between both, and, natively, they work a little differently, since a **Service Action** is an abstraction of a web service and its behavior and error handling must be approached from this perspective. Service Actions are executed in a different transaction context than the caller modules, and therefore additional precautions and logic have to be implemented to properly roll back something if an error occurs. Server Actions, on the other hand, are always executed in the same transactional context that the caller, so everything is properly rolled back in the event of errors or Exceptions.

The advantage of these actions is that, when referenced, they are performed as weak references, which leads to a microservices architecture. These types of actions and artifacts will be referenced in *Chapter 13, Designing the Architecture of Your OutSystems Applications*.

In order to develop our logic in the server and Service Actions, the platform makes the following nodes available:

- **Start** – sets the beginning of a flow
- **Run Server Action** – executes logic on the server side
- **Aggregate** – fetches data from database
- **SQL** – executes your SQL statement in the database to read or write data
- **If** – executes a flow based on a single condition
- **Switch** – executes a flow based on multiple conditions
- **For Each** – executes the same logic for each element on a list
- **Assign** – sets the value of a variable
- **Record List to Excel** – converts a Record List content to an Excel spreadsheet
- **Excel to Record List** – converts an Excel spreadsheet content to a Record List
- **JSON Serialize** – converts an OutSystems object to a JSON string
- **JSON Deserialize** – converts a JSON string to an OutSystems object
- **Exception Handler** – catches an Exceptions or set of Exceptions
- **Raise Exception** – throws a user Exception, interrupting the logic flow, and causing an application runtime error if the Exception isn't being handled
- **Comment** – adds a development note that is only visible in the flow and can be set as a reminder (notification appears in the TrueChange window)
- **End** – sets the end of a flow

But, in order to get the full potential out of our **Server Actions** we will need representations of information that can be used as input, output, and for local use. These are called variables, which is what the next section is about.

Types of variables in Server Actions

In the backend, variables are used to transport and manipulate data. We normally use three types of variables in our Server Actions:

- **Input variables** – These are variables that are outside the context of the action itself and are necessary for the operations to be performed on it. These variables can be defined as mandatory and can be of basic types, identifiers, records, and lists. These variables do not allow defining their default value if they are mandatory:

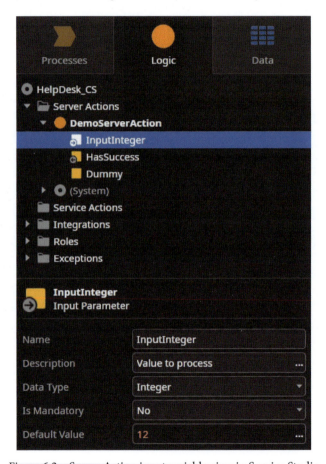

Figure 6.3 – Server Action input variable view in Service Studio

- **Output variables** – These variables are, by default, results of processing that takes place within our Server Actions or error handling (if it was successful and any notification message that is necessary). These variables can be of **basic types**, **identifiers**, **records**, and **lists**. These variables allow the definition of a default value:

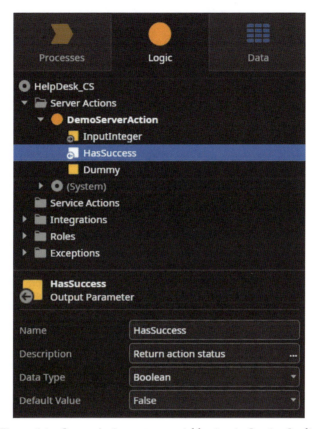

Figure 6.4 – Server Action output variable view in Service Studio

- **Local variables** – These variables are a particular case, as they only exist in the context of the Server Action where it is defined. These variables are not visible in the context of actions or modules that consume the action where they are defined (closed scope). These variables can be of **basic types**, **identifiers**, **records**, and **lists**. These variables allow the definition of a default value:

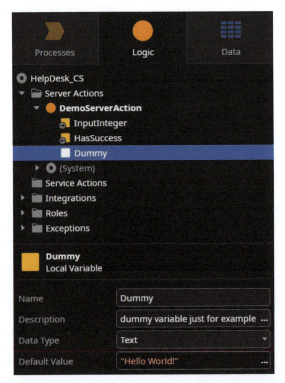

Figure 6.5 – Server Action local variable view in Service Studio

Server Actions do not limit the number of variables to be defined. However, for reasons of simplicity and performance, we should always evaluate the development scenario in question to minimize their use and the types of data to be transported and manipulated. The greater the complexity, the worse the performance, the worse the maintenance of the code, and the more computational resources will be allocated.

> **Tip**
> If we need a **Server Action** to be defined as a function, it will have to have one and only one output variable. If we want the output of this **Server Action** to return more than one value or attribute, we can define this output variable to be of a structure type that by definition returns all the necessary attributes. This structure can be created by us in the **Structures** section under the **Data** tab.

Variables are extremely important for data manipulation and facilitate the creation of logic, even for the reason of changing the scope whenever a **Server Action** is called. But how can we make decisions about what values to assign to variables? With conditional paths, as we'll see in the next section!

Taking logic decisions with conditional paths

In this part of the chapter we will learn how to code decisions based on data criteria and conditions.

Often, in our actions, we need to make decisions. This decision-making can be done through two artifacts:

- **If** – In the case of **If**, there are two possible outputs: true or false for the condition being tested. An interesting feature is that we can change the branch from true to false (false is automatically changed to true). Just right-click on **If** and select **Swap Connectors**. The Ifs can be nested (putting Ifs inside each other in branches when required), although when increasing complexity is an issue, it is advisable to use the **Switch** artifact:

Figure 6.6 – Example use of the If artifact in a Server Action

- **Switch** – With **Switch**, we have multiple outputs (which allows us to test multiple conditions), and we can define how many we need. The operation consists of cases (**if case A**, **output 1**, **if case B**, **output 2**, otherwise **default**). One of the outputs that always exists is the **Otherwise**, for cases where none of the tested conditions are met.

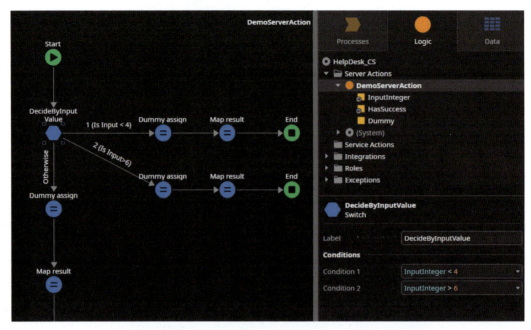

Figure 6.7 – Example use of the Switch artifact in a Server Action

Decisions are a mandatory part of application development, since we use them to enforce business rules precisely. One of the precautions to be taken (since it is one of the most recurrent errors) is always to confirm that the branches respect the necessary conditions, both If and Switch.

With conditional paths, we can already configure decisions to be taken in the context of certain scenarios encountered during the course of our logic. However, what if we want to iterate through a set of information? Can we create loops? Yes, of course! Let's analyze this topic in the next section!

Creating loops

In this section, we will learn techniques for performing process iterations and multiple iterations of data lists.

Loops are used when we want to iterate something. For example, if we have a list of records that we want to go through to manipulate data or calculate a result, we use a loop.

We can do this in OutSystems in two ways:

- **For Each** – For Each is an artifact that traverses a given list, so the list has to be defined before using the artifact. For that, For Each has three attributes: the list that we are going to iterate, its **Start Index**, and the **Maximum Iterations**. In cases of simple lists and without association references with other widgets (such as being used to feed a frontend table) the parameters of **Start Index** and **Maximum Iterations** can be left undefined, in which case, the entire list will be iterated. We must always consider that a list that is already being iterated by a For Each cannot be iterated inside that same loop, that is, we cannot have a For Each inside another For Each loop iterating the same list (it is only possible if the list we are going to iterate inside the inner For Each is not the same as the one we are going to iterate in the outer For Each).

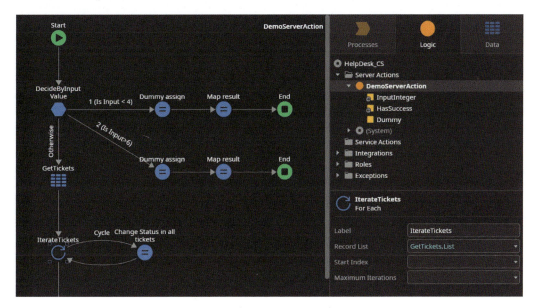

Figure 6.8 – Example use of the For Each artifact in a Server Action

- **If and support variable** – Another way to perform the loop is with **If** and a support variable, which will be the iteration counter and will be incremented cycle by cycle. Basically, in **If** we check if the support variable already has its value equal to the number of expected iterations. If yes, it follows the branch of **true**, if not, it follows the branch of **false**, executes the code to be executed, and before returning to **If** it increments that variable (a technique normally called an *ad hoc loop*).

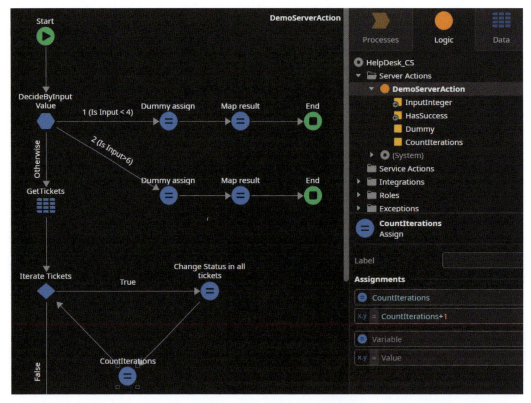

Figure 6.9 – Example of a loop created with an If artifact in a Server Action

Loops can reach different levels of complexity and can be nested (loops within loops), and you should always evaluate your algorithm to ensure the least performance impact, as the more data we are processing and the more nested loops we have, the more processing time will be needed.

Often, in cases of massive CRUD operations in databases, it is considered a good practice to eliminate the loop and do a bulk operation in the database using the SQL artifact, it being necessary to resort to the native language of the SQL engine on which our platform is running.

With loops we gain enormous mass processing capacity (although it can make sense to execute bulk operations with SQL commands, as we explained before) and manipulate the amount of information needed according to the conditions of our **Server Actions**.

But is it really that easy to create **Server Actions**? Yes, it is! And we can confirm this in the next exercise!

Exercise 2 – Creating server actions

In this second exercise, we will apply the knowledge gained in this chapter to create actions that will abstract CRUDs needed by our entities. In *Chapter 5, Modeling Data by Using Entities*, in the *Exercise 1 – creating a data model* section, we built a data model with our entities. Now, in exercise 2, we are going to learn and practice how to manipulate the data from this data model created earlier. With this, we are going to create the backend features that will support our frontend application in the future.

These actions are usually called wrappers, as they are an aggregation of manipulations that guarantee the compliance and integrity of our data and business rules.

So, starting with the exercise, let's follow these steps:

1. Create a **Server Action** called `Ticket_CreateOrUpdate`:

    I.   Select the **Logic** tab, right-click on the **Server Actions** folder, and select **Add Server Action**. Name it `Ticket_CreateOrUpdate`:

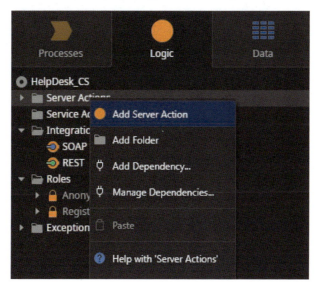

Figure 6.10 – Create a Server Action in Service Studio

II. Now let's add the input we need. We right-click on our **Server Action** and select **Add Input Parameter**. Name it `Ticket`:

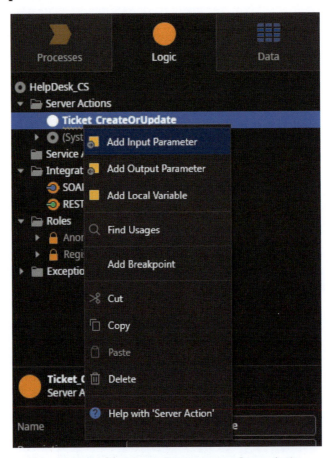

Figure 6.11 – Add an Input Parameter to a Server Action

III. Let's add the output. To do this, we right-click on our **Server Action** and select **Add Output Parameter**. Name it `TicketId`:

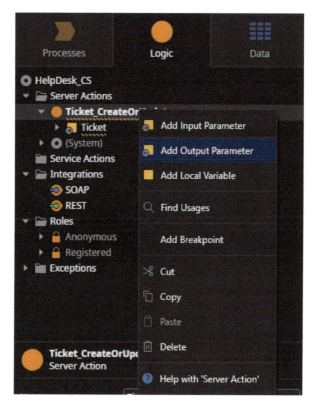

Figure 6.12 – Add an Output Parameter to a Server Action

Info

Notice that, by assigning the names according to what we need for the parameters, the platform automatically inferred the correct types for them. However, we can, whenever necessary, change the types in the parameter properties section.

2.   Create the necessary logic within our **Ticket_CreateOrUpdate** Server Action:

    I.   First let's use an **If** to check if the Ticket is new or not. We drag the **If** from the toolbox on the left and add it to the flow. In the **If** condition we check if **Ticket.Id** is null (`Ticket.Id = NullIdentifier()`). If it is null, then the record is new:

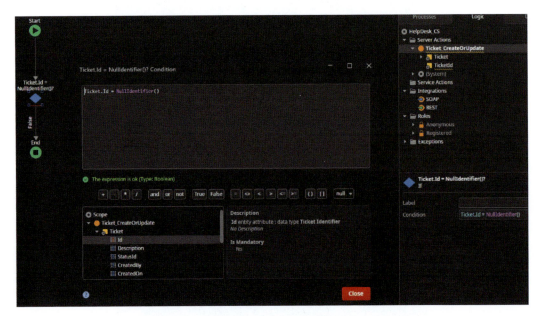

Figure 6.13 – Create decision logic in the Server Action

II. Now, let's add an **Assign** to the **True** branch of **If** and another to **false** (by dragging **Assign** from the toolbox to the canvas). The attributes to be filled in the **Assign** of the true branch are **CreatedBy** and **CreatedOn** (with the results of the GetUserId() and CurrDateTime() functions respectively):

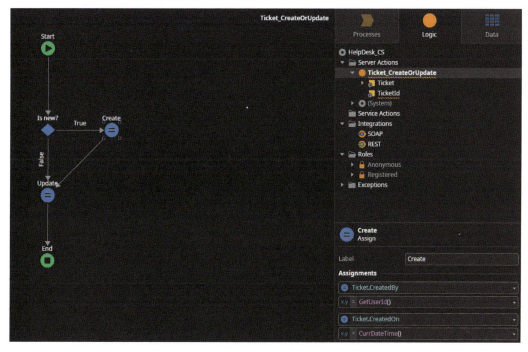

Figure 6.14 – Map values for the True branch based on the decision

III. The attributes to be filled in the **Assign** of the false branch are **UpdatedBy** and **UpdatedOn** (with the results of the `GetUserId()` and `CurrDateTime()` functions respectively):

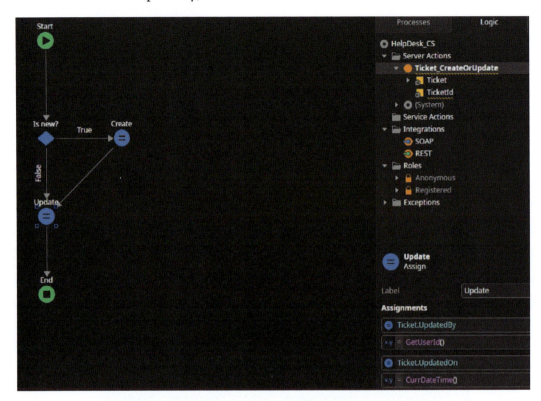

Figure 6.15 – Map values for the False branch based on the decision

IV. Now, we select the **Data** tab, expand the **Ticket** entity, and drag the **CreateOrUpdateTicket** CRUD operation to the flow. The selected source must be the **Ticket** parameter:

Figure 6.16 – Add a CRUD operation to the Server Action and map its input

V. After inserting the CRUD operation, we must map the Id returned to the
    TicketId output parameter. To do this, we drag **Assign** from the toolbox to the
    flow and place the **TicketId** with a match to the **CreateOrUpdateTicket.Id** field
    from the CRUD operation:

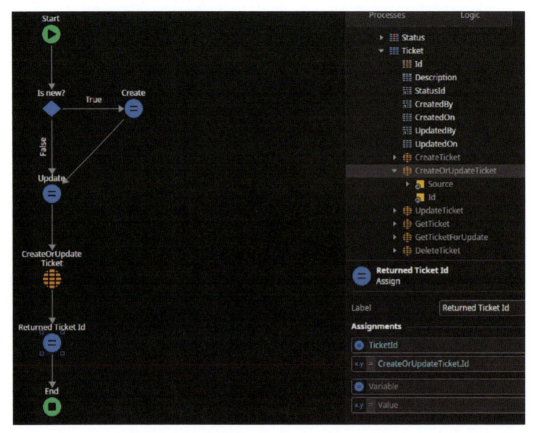

Figure 6.17 – Map the identifier returned by the CRUD operation to the Server Action output variable

VI. Now we select the **Data** tab, click on the **Ticket** entity, and in the properties, we
set the **Public** and **Expose Read Only** attributes to **Yes**:

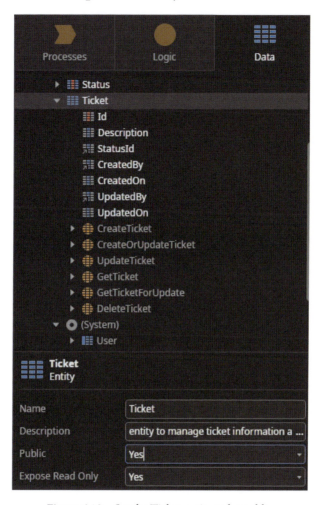

Figure 6.18 – Set the Ticket entity to be public

VII. Finally, we click on **Server Action**, set the **Public** attribute to **Yes** in the properties, and click on the **Publish** button:

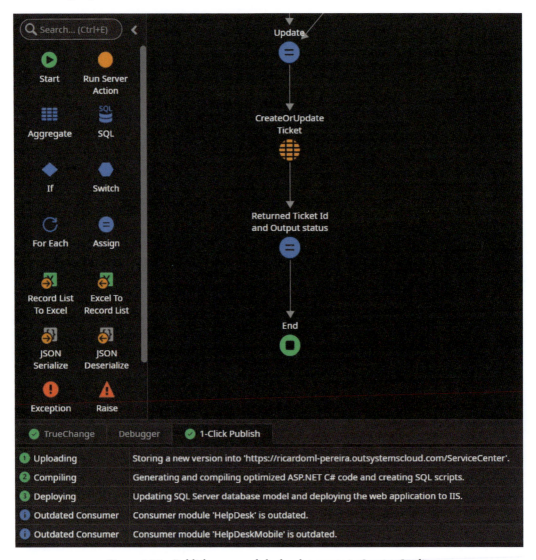

Figure 6.19 – Publish new module developments in Service Studio

3. Create a **Server Action** called `AffectedAreaByTicket_Create`:

I. Select the **Logic** tab, right-click on the **Server Actions** folder, and select **Add Server Action**. Name it `AffectedAreaByTicket_Create`. Then, right-click on our Server Action and select **Add input parameter**. Name it `AffectedAreasByTicket`:

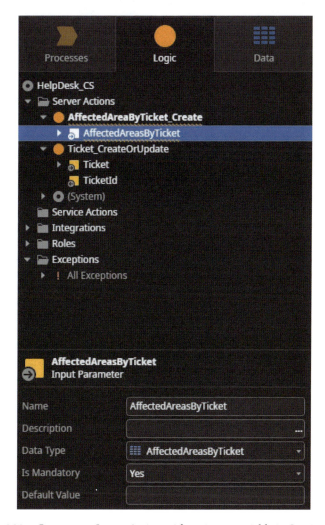

Figure 6.20 – Create new Server Action with an input variable in Service Studio

II. Let's add the output. To do this, we right-click on our Server Action and select **Add output parameter**. Name it `AffectedAreasByTicketId`:

Figure 6.21 – Add a new output variable to Server Action

III. Now, we select the **Data** tab, expand the **AffectedAreasByTicketTicket** entity, and drag the **CreateAffectedAreasByTicket** CRUD operation to the flow. The selected source must be the **AffectedAreasByTicket** parameter:

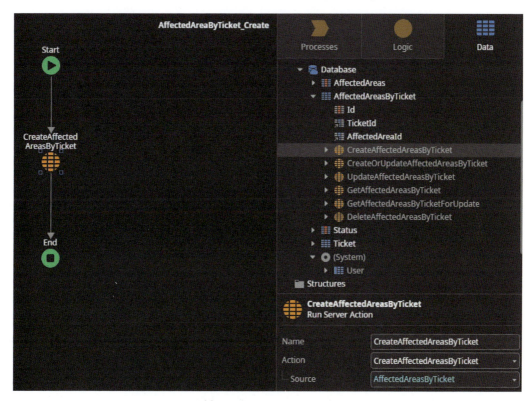

Figure 6.22 – Add a CRUD operation to the Server Action

IV. After inserting the CRUD operation, we must map the Id returned to the output parameter, **AffectedAreasbyTicketId**. To do this, we drag an **Assign** from the toolbox to the flow and place the **AffectedAreasbyTicketId** with a match to the **CreateAffectedAreasByTicket.Id** field from the CRUD operation:

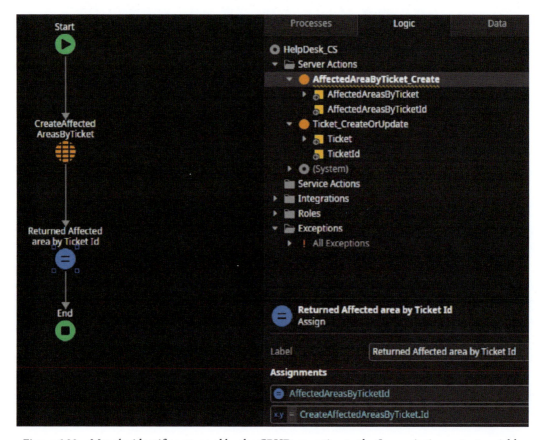

Figure 6.23 – Map the identifier returned by the CRUD operation to the Server Action output variable

V.   Now we select the **Data** tab, click on the **AffectedAreasByTicket** entity, and in
the properties, we set the **Public** and **Expose Read Only** attributes to **Yes**:

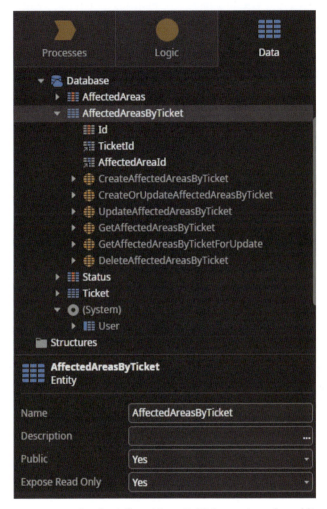

Figure 6.24 – Set the AffectedAreasByTicket entity to be public

VI. Finally, we click on **AffectedAreasByTicket_Create** Server Action, set the
Public attribute to **Yes** in the properties, and click on the **Publish** button:

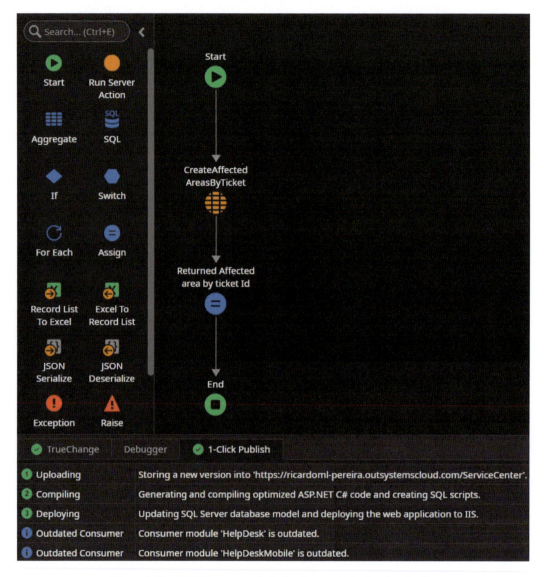

Figure 6.25 – Publish new module developments in Service Studio

As we've seen, creating a **Server Action** is simple. Furthermore, the visual way in which the code is presented to us facilitates its interpretation when complexity increases.

With this knowledge and some practice, you will realize that Server Actions can be used extremely intelligently in order to benefit from code reuse and abstraction, simplifying future developments.

Summary

In this chapter, we learned how server-side logic works, the artifacts available, and how to combine them to obtain the intended behaviors from our actions.

We learned what Server Actions are, the concept of variables in the context of **Server Actions**, how to create logic in Server Actions, and the properties of the attributes used.

Something very important to remember from this chapter is the fact that we should, whenever possible, abstract and isolate the manipulation of our data in Server Actions so that we can better control their integrity. In addition to being careful in **Server Actions**, we must always remember to set the **Expose Read Only** attribute of our entities to **Yes**. With this we guarantee that the data in our entities is only handled by our Server Actions in the consumer modules, thus guaranteeing that no user or application can write or change the data without complying with the defined rules, preventing the existence of dirty data.

As we have seen, we are able to develop code in a super intuitive way, with little margin for errors (the typical issues in textual languages that take hours to understand are solved here in less than half the time) and largely in a visual way. And we still have a lot more to see!

In the next chapter, we will learn how to handle unexpected behaviors and errors that occur while using our applications, namely with the Raise Exception and Exception Handler elements. We'll also look at a simple way to transparently expose errors to the consumer modules of our actions.

Enthusiastic? Yes, absolutely!

7
Exceptions Handling

It's great that everything was a bed of roses while our applications were running, but sometimes incidents happen or even something unexpected.

The process of Exception handling is what allows us to handle these types of events. It's something that allows us to avoid catastrophes and turn around unexpected situations. Basically, in the midst of chaos, it gives us control. Errors can be caused by various reasons, such as the following:

- **Unavailability of third-party systems**: Communication failure caused by the unavailability of both internal and external producer systems

- **Database unavailability**: Communication failure caused by the unavailability of the database server

- **Frontend server unavailability**: Communication failure caused by a crash or DNS resolution of the frontend server(s)

- **Handling of access authorizations**: Attempts to access data or functionality by users not provided with the necessary permissions

- **Errors foreseen by the developers derived from attempts to misuse the applications**: Use of preventive code to protect applications from malicious attempts of corrupting data or the application itself

To better understand these concepts, the material in this chapter is divided as follows:

- Raising Exceptions
- Exception handler flows
- Global Exception handler
- Exercise 3 – raising and handling of an Exception

By the end of this chapter, we should be able to understand the usefulness of Exceptions, in what context we should use them, and how to throw and handle them.

Technical requirements

Check out the following video to see the code in action: `https://bit.ly/3FFpQBu`.

Raising Exceptions

The OutSystems platform, out of the box, already provides a system to handle Exceptions. However, we can raise them in our code wherever we see fit. With this, we can gain greater control over unexpected events and process them in a more user-friendly and understandable way. Once again, it all comes down to being able to take a neat leap.

Something to bear in mind whenever we raise an Exception is that it will be logged and visible on the Service Center console, which allows us to subsequently have a more careful and in-depth analysis of anomalies and a more precise intervention.

We can perform raise Exceptions on our Server Actions, Service Actions, and Client Actions (these last two will be seen in *Chapter 10, Client-Side Logic*).

Whenever we foresee a possibility of unexpected behavior, through the decision elements seen in *Chapter 6, Server-Side Logic* (If and Switch), we can trigger an Exception of the following types:

- **User Exceptions**: Exceptions created by us (that is, customized) as needed:

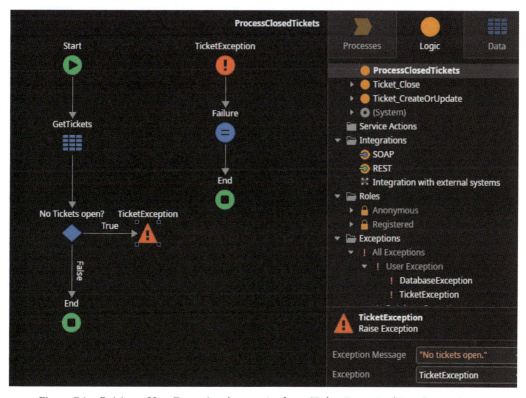

Figure 7.1 – Raising a User Exception (customized as a Ticket Exception) in a Server Action

- **Database Exceptions**: Exceptions used for unexpected behavior related to databases:

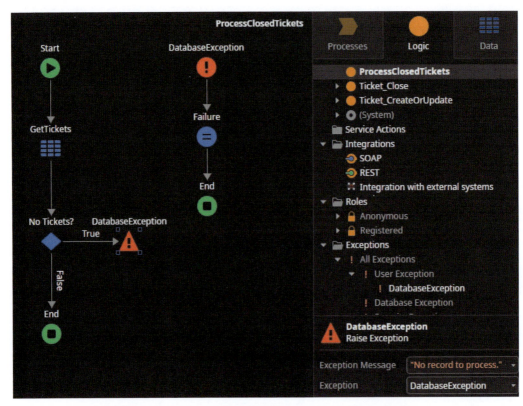

Figure 7.2 – Raising a Database Exception in a Server Action

- **Security Exceptions**: Exceptions related to user authentication and authorization:

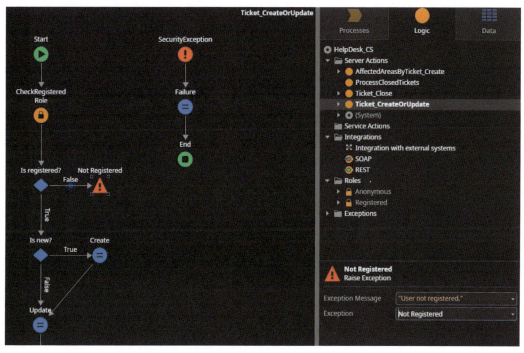

Figure 7.3 – Raising a Security Exception in a Server Action

- **Abort activity change Exceptions**: Exceptions related to anomalies in BPT processes that allow their control at the level of retries or aborts

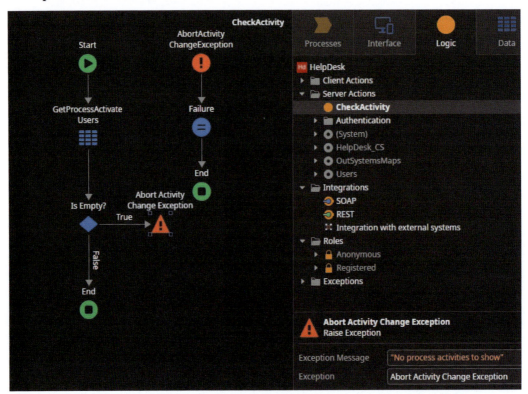

Figure 7.4 – Raising a Abort Activity Change Exception in a Server Action Exception

As a rule, if we want the log of this event to be scaled to the module level in which it occurs, we must add the respective handler in parallel to the "happy path" flow of the respective Server Action (as we can see in *Figure 7.1*).

We can also create Exceptions as needed by our applications, since many times, the ones that already exist by default do not cover all the scenarios we intend. Our custom Exceptions are called **user Exceptions** and we can raise them in our flows whenever necessary. These Exceptions are considered child nodes of general user Exceptions and we can create them in the **Exceptions** section in the Service Studio **Logic** tab. Just right-click on **User Exceptions** and select the **Add User Exception** option. The only property we have to define is its name (we must be careful to choose a self-explanatory name). From that moment on, that Exception can be invoked in our flow and we have the handler available to use in our Actions.

What can we do to treat our Exceptions? How do we process the flow of our handlers? That's what we'll see in the next section!

Exception handler flows

Whenever an unexpected event of an Action occurs and it is redirected to a handler, it can be customized and have its own logic in order to give us flexibility in handling errors and allow a reduction of impact on the end user.

In Exception handlers, we can choose between aborting the transaction or not (rollback of all inserts, updates, or deletes made to the database during the flow that has not been committed) and whether we want to log the error or not, as shown in *Figure 7.2*:

Figure 7.5 – Parameterization of an abort transaction and log error of an Exception handler

Sometimes, in scenarios where we want to scale the error to module or consumer Actions, we define an output variable for this purpose, being of the type of a structure with two attributes:

- `HasSucess`: A Boolean that returns `True` if everything goes as expected or `False` if unexpected behavior occurs.

- `Message`: A text field used to return a specific message. If `HasSuccess` is `False`, it usually returns either the error message returned by the Exception handler or a more user-friendly message that can be easily interpreted by consumers (should be used as a best practice when implementing our own Exceptions).

In the flows of Exception handlers, we can manipulate these variables and any others within the scope of the Action. There are cases of high complexity where the logic used in Exceptions handlers allows us to carry out sets of operations that keep all types of information related to the error, thus facilitating its tracking and allowing faster analysis, as shown in *Figure 7.3*:

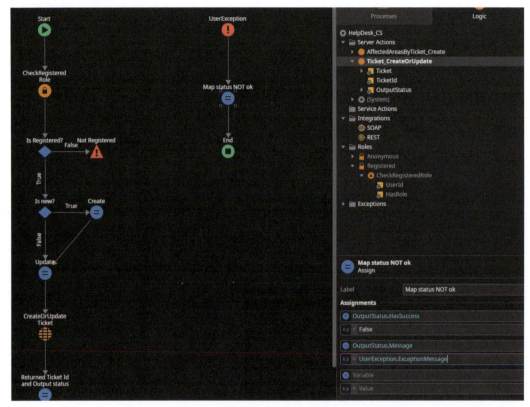

Figure 7.6 – Handling variables in the Exception handler's flow

We can make raise Exceptions without having the Exception handler defined in our Server Action, so that the same Exception bubbles up to the next modular level until it finds its handler. In cases where you reach the highest level without finding the Exception handler, it is processed by the **global Exception**.

Tip

If you are curious, you can see the official documentation on handle Exceptions at `https://success.outsystems.com/Documentation/11/ Developing_an_Application/Implement_Application_ Logic/Handle_Exceptions` and `https://success. outsystems.com/Documentation/11/Developing_an_ Application/Implement_Application_Logic/Handle_ Exceptions/Exception_Handling_Mechanism`.

What is a global Exception and how does it work? What is it for? As we'll see in the next section, it can be seen as our lifeline.

Global Exception handler

A global Exception is intended to log all events arising from Exceptions not handled during the operation of applications.

In cases where there is no specific Exception handler to handle something that occurs at a certain level, it will bubble up through the functionality's call stack until it finds the handler it needs. If you don't find it until you reach the last level (usually the frontend module of the application), the global Exception of that module does the job.

These handlers are defined in a frontend flow and are then associated with the module in the **Global Exception Handler** attribute, as shown in *Figure 7.4*:

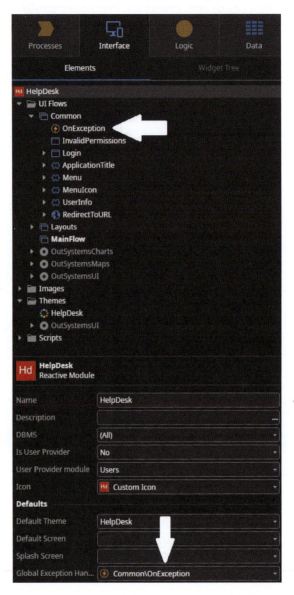

Figure 7.7 – Use and definition of a global Exception in the frontend module

With this, we realize that the global Exception handler is our *last resort* as it allows us to handle errors and unexpected events, and it prevents our application from being in limbo in case of a crash or accident. This way, we can understand what is wrong or what happened with the application.

Now, in the next section, in order to consolidate these topics, we will do an exercise (following the previous exercises related to the **Help Desk** application) where we will raise and handle an Exception.

Exercise 3 – raising and handling an Exception

In this exercise, we will implement a raise Exception and its handler to handle calls made to the `Ticket_CreateOrUpdate` Server Action by users who are not registered (who did not authenticate themselves through a set of credentials on a login page):

1. Put the **Check Registered roles** in our flow, use **If** to validate the result, and, in case of failure, set the raise Exception:

     I.   Click on the **Logic** tab, expand the **Roles** folder, expand the **Registered** role, and drag the **CheckRegisteredRole** Action to our flow, right after the start, as shown in *Figure 7.5*:

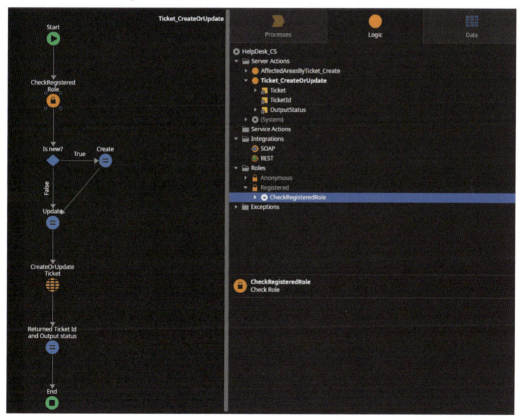

Figure 7.8 – Adding the CheckRegisteredRole Action to the flow

II. Drag and drop an **If** from the toolbox to the flow, right after the
CheckRegisteredRole Action, and in the condition, validate whether
the return of that same Action is **True**, as shown in *Figure 7.6*:

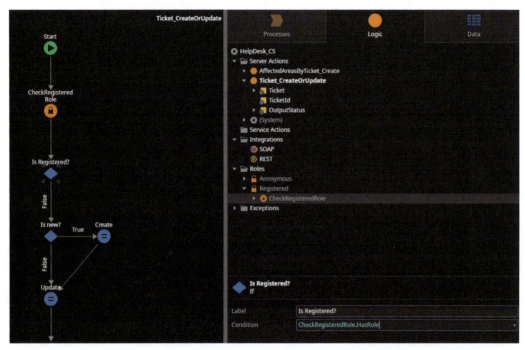

Figure 7.9 – Adding an If artifact to verify the result of the CheckRegisteredRole Action

III. Drag and drop a **Raise Exception** from the toolbox to the right side of the **If**, set it as **Not Registered** from the **Security Exceptions** group, link its **False** branch to **Raise Exception**, and set its message to **User not registered**:

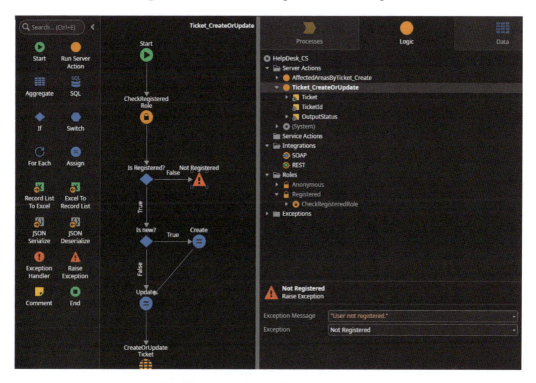

Figure 7.10 – Defining the raise Exception in the Action flow

2. Create the Exception handler and its structure and output variable to expose the error to consumers:

    I.   Drag and drop the **Exception Handler** artifact from the toolbox and place it next to our flow in the Action, setting it to **Security Exception Handler**:

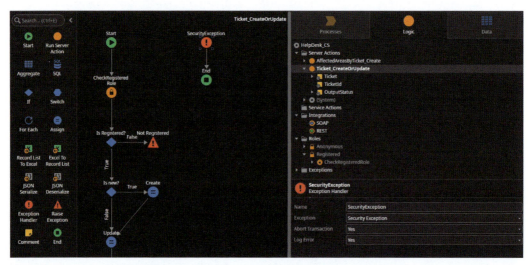

Figure 7.11 – Adding Exception Handler to the Action

II. Click on the **Data** tab, right-click on the **Structures** folder, and select **Add structure**. We call it OutputStatus. Then, we right-click on the structure and select **Add structure attribute**. We call it HasSuccess (the default value is **False**). We've repeated this last process again, but now the name is Message. We define the structure as public, as shown in *Figure 7.9*:

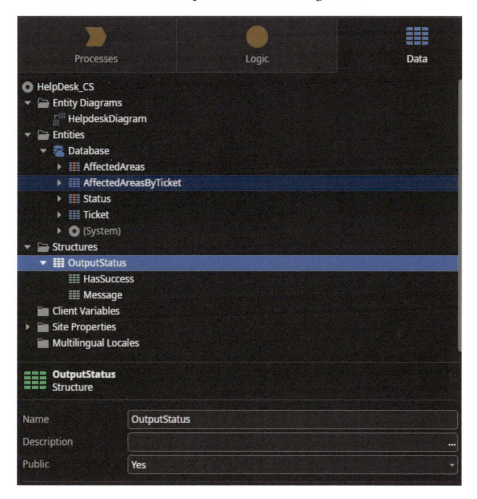

Figure 7.12 – Structure with handling attributes to be used as the type in Actions output variables

III. Click on the **Logic** tab, click with the right mouse button on the **Ticket_CreateOrUpdate** Action, and select **Add output variable**. Give it the name OutputStatus:

Figure 7.13 – Output variable in the Server Action to return success conditions

IV. Map the success values at the end of the normal flow of the Action. The **HasSuccess** attribute of the **OutputStatus** output variable is mapped with the value **True** and the **Message** field is empty (" "), as shown in *Figure 7.11*:

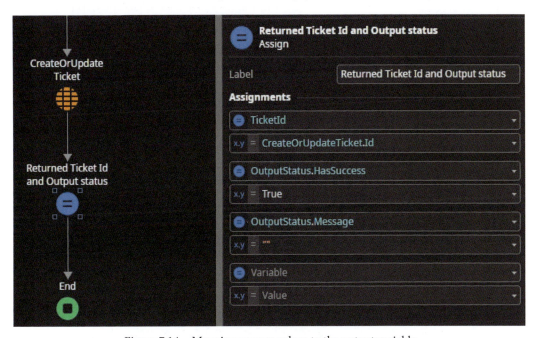

Figure 7.14 – Mapping success values to the output variable

V.   Map the failure values into the Action's Exception handler stream. The
     HasSuccess attribute of the **OutputStatus** output variable is mapped with the
     value **False** and the **Message** field has the value of the message returned by the
     Exception handler. To carry out this mapping, drag an **Assign** artifact from the
     toolbox to the Exception handler's flow and map the referred values. Click on
     the **Publish** button to save the new developments:

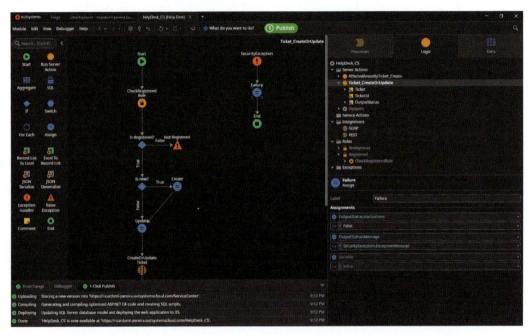

Figure 7.15 – Mapping failure values to the output variable in the Exception handler flow

With these steps, we guarantee that if someone unregistered uses the functionality, we log
the event associated with the module in question, and, in addition, we expose the error
in a user-friendly manner to consumers so that they can better understand the behaviors
obtained in the situation that triggered the exception handler.

Summary

In this chapter, we understood that the platform provides artifacts that make it easier for us to process unexpected events in our applications. Furthermore, the way they relate and can be applied provides us with much greater control over what happens to these events, thus ensuring a much more understandable behavior for users (that is, better management of expectations).

With this, we realize that we can trigger our own Exceptions, we can use the Exception handlers in the most convenient way, the platform automatically bubbling up the events that do not find a handler to the Exception that was thrown, and, as a last resort, we have our safeguard: a global Exception handler.

All these features help a lot in two extremely important points of our applications: tracking errors and trends and making our applications more robust in case of errors.

All of this is an incredibly simple and fast way, without having to lose focus on business concepts, to write countless lines of code.

Do you know where we will be able to enjoy the results of applying these features? What we'll see in the next chapter: the frontend!

Let's start by looking at premade patterns, widgets, and templates that save us a lot of development time!

We will also learn how to scaffold screens (another superb accelerator in Service Studio) and how we can easily customize our CSS and insert our JavaScript! Incredible! Come on!

Section 3: Create Value and Innovate with the Frontend

In this section, we will learn how to develop web screens for reactive web and mobile, client-side logic, how to use widgets and patterns, and how to take advantage of local storage in mobile. In this part, you will also learn the secrets of style guide implementation and how to use one of the most powerful tools provided: the debugger.

This section comprises the following chapters:

- *Chapter 8, Reactive UI Development*

- *Chapter 9, Using Mobile Patterns for Fast Mobile UI Development*

- *Chapter 10, Client-Side Logic*

- *Chapter 11, Local Storage and Data Synchronization*

- *Chapter 12, Debugging and Troubleshooting Mobile and Reactive Web Apps*

8
Reactive UI Development

All we've learned so far is about the bones and muscles of our applications. Now we need to put the skin on, preferably obtaining a beautiful, simple, and effective result.

For this, the OutSystems platform offers, through Service Studio, a set of pre-made components, screen templates, and accelerators for construction under the OutSystems UI framework. It should be noted that, in order to make all these features available, OutSystems carried out market analysis in order to understand the needs of customers and businesses. That is, if we need it, it almost certainly already exists. If it doesn't exist, it's quick and easy to develop.

To better understand how all this works, the chapter is divided into the following sections:

- Reactive patterns and templates
- Reactive widgets
- Scaffolding screens
- CSS themes and styles
- JavaScript in OutSystems
- Screen and block lifecycle events
- Events to propagate changes from a block to the parent
- Exercise 4 – Creating application screens

By the end of this chapter, we should be able to identify the widgets and patterns needed for our screens, how to use them, and how to automatically create them through scaffolding (dragging database entities from the module tree on the right and dropping them on a web flow).

Furthermore, we will understand how we can customize our frontend with CSS and JavaScript and how we can take advantage of screen and block events.

Ready to start this new challenge? Let's start by discovering widgets and patterns!

Technical requirements

Check out the following video to see the code in action: `https://bit.ly/3nNd0el`.

Reactive patterns and templates

OutSystems provides for a framework to accelerate the development of our frontend: OutSystems UI. OutSystems UI is a unified library of UI patterns, actions, and pre-built themes that respect the best trends and practices in the market.

> **Tip**
> If you are curious to explore the OutSystems UI framework in detail, you can see it here: `https://outsystemsui.outsystems.com/`.

Every time we create a frontend module, whenever we have a block or a screen on the canvas, the Service Studio toolbox immediately makes available a huge set of pre-designed and ready-to-use patterns – just drag and drop them to the site that we want from our screen or block.

Figure 8.1 – Service Studio toolbox with reusable patterns

In this way, development is abstracted, avoiding having to worry about what is inside.

The only thing we have to do is fill in the property attributes so the pattern behaves as expected and with the correct data.

Tip

We can add more patterns if we want to. Just click on the **Manage Dependencies** button, select the **producer** module and choose the desired patterns from the list presented. Finally, click on the **Apply** button.

All patterns respect the current best development practices in terms of HTML and CSS, being fully responsive. Also, if we want to customize them, we can always extend their CSS classes in properties through the **ExtendedClass** attribute. To take advantage of the **ExtendedClass** attribute, we can create the CSS class in the theme's stylesheet and, in this attribute, just put the name of this class, applying it to the component in question.

> **Tip**
> If you are curious, you can see the official documentation on patterns here:
> `https://success.outsystems.com/Documentation/11/`
> `Developing_an_Application/Design_UI/Patterns/`
> `Using_Mobile_and_Reactive_Patterns.`

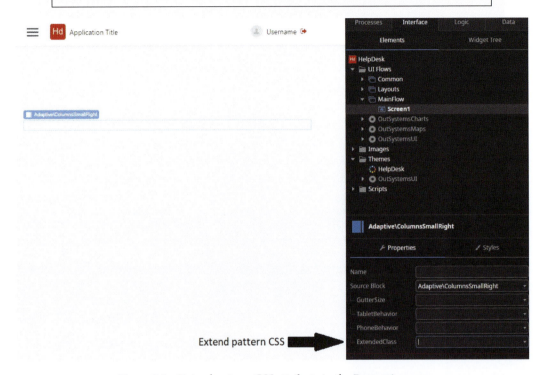

Figure 8.2 – Extend pattern CSS attribute in the Properties area

In the case of templates, we have something even more complete. A list of screens built end to end within the following categories is provided:

- **Banking**
- **Dashboards**
- **Details**
- **Forms**
- **Galleries**
- **Insurance**
- **Lists**
- **Onboardings**

The good thing about all this is that, from time to time, OutSystems updates this list, providing new templates or removing those that no longer make sense to the market and current trends.

Figure 8.3 – Popup for screen template selection in Service Studio

For the creation of the screen, OutSystems also provides sample data. How can we put real data on our screen? Simple. Just drag the desired entities to the top of the screen until the indication **Replace data with ticket** as in screenshot appears and make the drop. Done!

After replacing the sample data with real data, we should remove the dependencies from the OutSystems Sample DB module so that we don't have unnecessary dependencies.

Figure 8.4 – Drag and drop entity to replace sample data with real data

These accelerators ensure that the development complies with the best security and performance practices, being easily inspected and with an extremely low margin of bugs (and normally they only happen due to some specificity of our business rules or data).

Both patterns and templates are the available macro elements. If we develop something more custom, we can continue to take advantage of pre-built components, in this case, widgets.

Reactive widgets

Reusable widgets are small components that we use in creating our screens for viewing and using them uniformly across all screens.

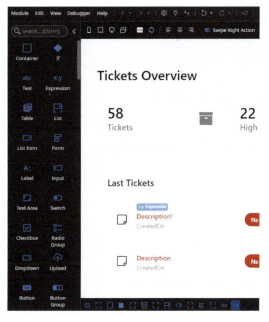

Figure 8.5 – Service Studio toolbox with reusable widgets

These already come precomposed with their HTML/CSS, without us needing to worry about their construction from scratch, thus allowing developers with a lack of experience in these languages to create intuitive and attractive applications.

But what is the difference between patterns and widgets then? This is one of the most frequently asked questions!

Well, it's all about approach. The widget is an element that we use on our screens, while the pattern is more related to the user experience. Some even argue that all patterns are widgets, but not all widgets are patterns. At the moment, there is no formalization on the topic (a good topic for discussion these days).

Right now, through a module provided by OutSystems natively, we find widgets in the following categories:

- **Adaptive** – widgets that react and adapt to the resolution and device they are displayed on
- **AppFeedBack** – widgets used to get feedback on the application the user is using
- **Content** – widgets used to aggregate data and other widgets in an organized and understandable way
- **Interaction** – widgets used to allow user interaction and animations, making viewing more dynamic

- **Licenses** – platform licensing related widgets

- **Navigation** – widgets related to in-app navigation, such as paging and breadcrumbs

- **Numbers** – widgets related to displaying numbers and counters in an intuitive way

- **Private** – widgets that allow functionality to occur in the background

- **Utilities** – widgets with extended CSS capabilities to simplify the implementation of UX/UI behaviors, such as align at center, button loading, and touch/mouse events

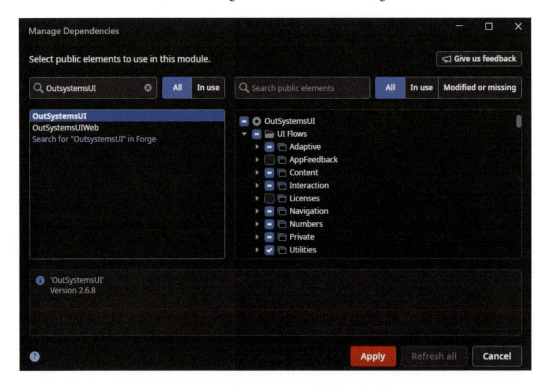

Figure 8.6 – Widget categories available in OutSystems UI

However, we can create our own widgets, either from scratch based on the pre-existing ones or by overriding or manipulating them through a clone (since the OutSystems UI module is not editable).

We must bear in mind that, from the moment we clone something and stop using OutSystems UI widgets, we no longer benefit from its updates. Furthermore, we must always ensure security at least to the same level as the system components.

Note that OutSystems accelerators, when creating screens, whether using templates or scaffolding, use these same widgets in order to standardize development and ensure that everything becomes simpler to maintain and change by the developer.

Hey, one minute! Scaffolding? What is that?

Scaffolding screens

Screen scaffolding is based on the platform's ability to infer the two types of base screens normally needed by an entity: listing and detailing.

Basically, the system is so well designed that we just drag and drop the intended entity onto the canvas of a flow and it automatically creates the list and detail pages related to the respective entity and predictable fields. We may of course have to make some adjustments to the rules and visible fields.

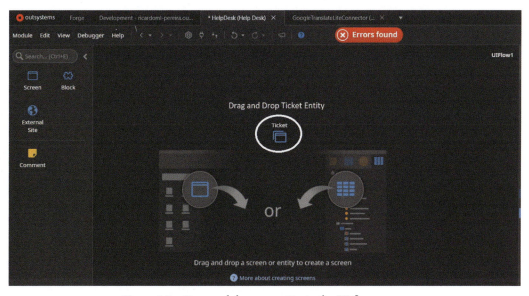

Figure 8.7 – Drag and drop an entity to the UI flow canvas

All widgets and base functionality are created automatically, such as listing ordering, pagination, direct links to details, back functionality, mandatory fields – all that!

Info

In cases of simplistic scenarios, where entities are exposed without being just read-only or if the entities belong to the same frontend module (by default, this is not good architecture, but everything depends on the use case), scaffolding automatically creates the save action and the widgets necessary for the user to enjoy this functionality (such as the **Save** button).

Through the scaffolding technique, the screens are created based on the base Flow Theme to which the screen belongs, automatically creating all the necessary functionalities. In the case of a listing screen, a table is created with the first four attributes of the Entity that provides the data, a link to create a new record, links to access the detail pages of each record in the table, search field, and the paging functionality of the table.

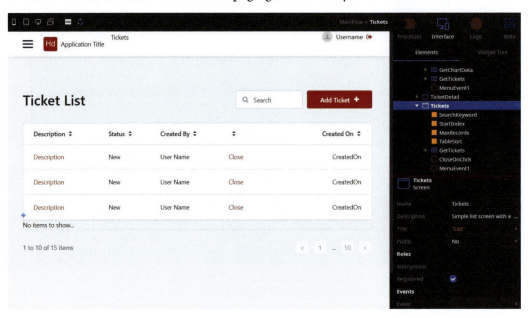

Figure 8.8 – List screen created with scaffolding technique

One of the interesting parts of scaffolding is the automatic generation of the link in the application menu to the concept to which we applied the technique. For example, if we drag and drop the **Ticket** entity to the **MainFlow** canvas, the menu link to the **Tickets** list page is generated. Cool, isn't it?

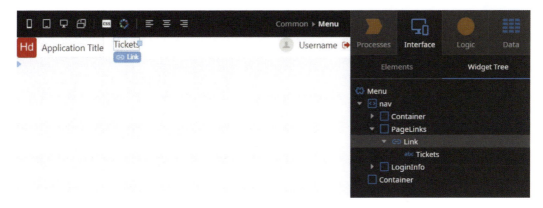

Figure 8.9 – Menu link autogenerated by scaffolding for list screen

With this in mind, we can also scaffold inside existing screens. In other words, if we have relationships between entities, when dragging the associated entity onto the detail screen, it creates a table to visualize the data.

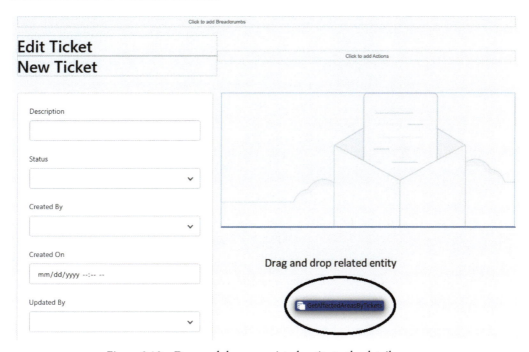

Figure 8.10 – Drag and drop associated entity to the detail screen

After dragging and dropping, we just make the necessary adjustments quickly so that everything is as intended (we can add a label at the top of the table, delete, reorder, or add the necessary columns).

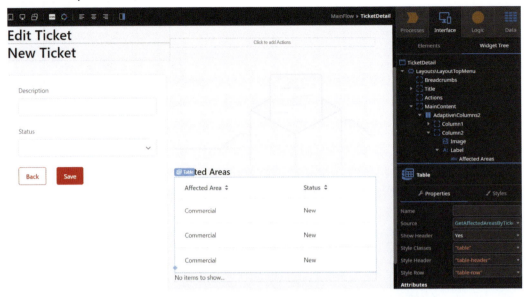

Figure 8.11 – Table created with drag and drop in the detail screen

In a way, scaffolding allows you to create the frontend of an application in minutes, always ensuring a very attractive UI and an excellent UX.

The details to customize, in most cases, are minimal and, considering the visual paradigm and the way that Service Studio provides us with information and tools, everything is done extremely quickly and in a way that allows developers to shift their focus more to business concepts.

Note that at any time, we can customize our screens, such as changing the location of widgets/patterns, changing their characteristics in properties, changing the CSS classes that support them, and even adding or removing them in order to obtain the expected result. Everything that is automatically generated remains customizable.

In addition, we can always assemble our screens or blocks manually, dragging and dropping the desired widgets and patterns into them and assigning the desired fields.

Although many of the scenarios provided at the UX/UI level are already covered by all these techniques, all of this, like any application, is based on CSS themes and styles. OutSystems has also focused a lot on this, offering a great acceleration capacity in this regard. For a better understanding, we will analyze in the next section how CSS themes and styles work on the platform.

CSS themes and styles

Layout and styling components are another focus of OutSystems accelerators, thus also reducing the need for knowledge of native technologies in order to create an application with an excellent UX/UI. With this, we are able to deliver an application to users capable of making them very satisfied with their experience.

When creating our frontend modules, Service Studio automatically adds HTML layout patterns, making them immediately available for consumption.

The practical meaning of all this is that we do not need to waste time developing this component.

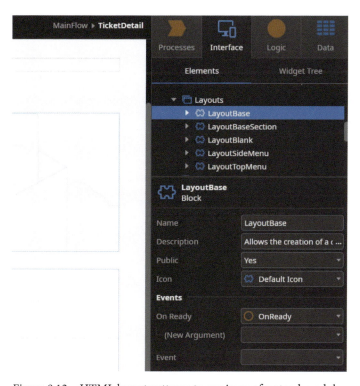

Figure 8.12 – HTML layout patterns to use in our frontend modules

Regarding styles, also when creating frontend modules, Service Studio generates the CSS file with all the necessary classes to satisfy the latest visual trends at the application level. All widgets and patterns available out of the box feed from these same classes to get the desired look.

The great particularity of CSS is that OutSystems allows its customization with native code, by using a CSS editor.

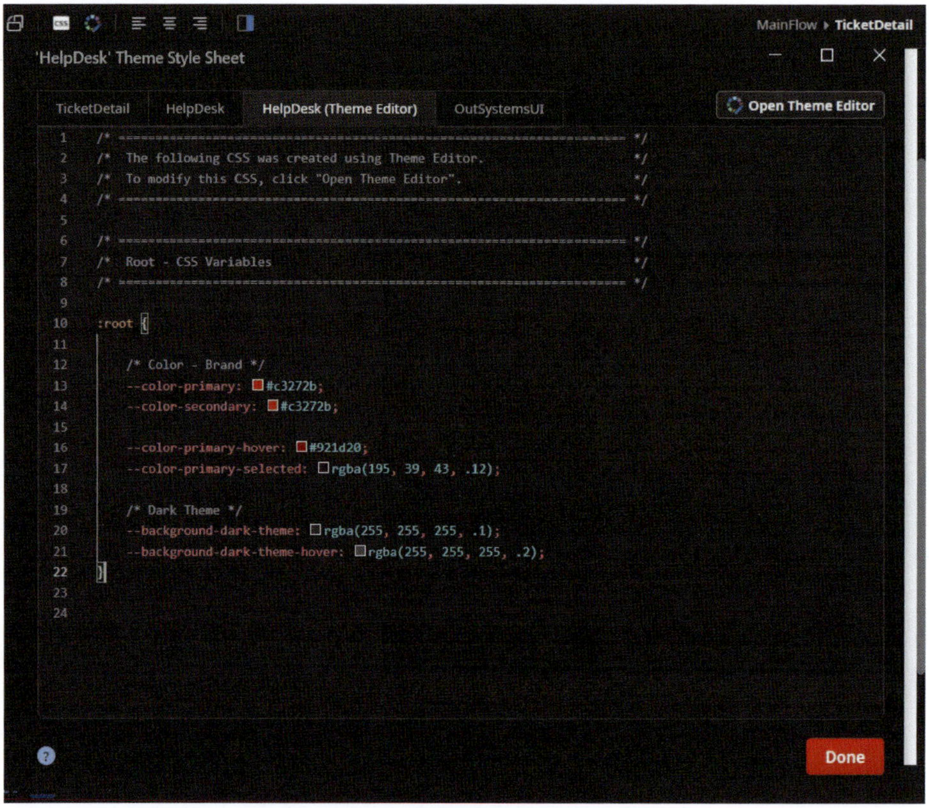

Figure 8.13 – CSS editor in Service Studio

In this editor, we can create our classes on different theme sheets and perform overrides. The CSS classes we created can then be used in our widgets and patterns, either in the **Style Classes** property (in the case of widgets) or in the **Extended Class** property (in the patterns).

With this, we were able to achieve a wide spectrum customization, and at no time were we limited by the automatic generation of our screens (or blocks) or by the use of pre-built widgets/patterns.

> **Tip**
>
> If you are curious, you can see the official documentation on CSS here:
> `https://success.outsystems.com/Documentation/11/`
> `Developing_an_Application/Design_UI/Look_and_Feel/`
> `Cascading_Style_Sheets_(CSS).`

Note that the HTML/CSS system generated by Service Studio complies with the best practices of the respective languages. It is based on the Grid model, with pre-conceived media queries, thus ensuring one of the most important features nowadays in web applications: responsiveness.

Although all these accelerators make our work easier, we often have custom cases that need some manipulation of elements and behavior changes, and JavaScript is perfect for these situations. In the next section, we will learn how JavaScript fits into our applications and its role in our development.

JavaScript in OutSystems

As is often said in web programming circles, the frontend is made up of three strands: HTML, which is the bones, CSS is the skin, and…muscles are missing!

The muscles, or the application's ability to respond and have dynamic behaviors, such as adopting certain behaviors according to the user's orders, are given by another language: JavaScript!

As in the previous cases, Service Studio automatically generates the JavaScript necessary for the correct functioning of the application, either inserted as a resource or indirectly in function calls of certain components.

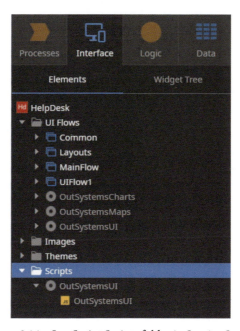

Figure 8.14 – JavaScript Scripts folder in Service Studio

The autogenerated scripts are saved in the `Scripts` folder in the **Interface** tab, and if we want to extend or customize something in our application that needs more scripts, we can add our files to that same folder. Note that the OutSystems platform accepts minified or formatted code, as JavaScript is a browser-interpreted language and not compiled.

However, we can go even further in JavaScript. We can create our own custom code for a given event exactly in the flow that we need in our client actions (which we'll study in *Chapter 10, Client-Side Logic*). With this, we get much greater power in handling the behaviors expected by the application, improving and adjusting the UX of our applications in order to match users' needs.

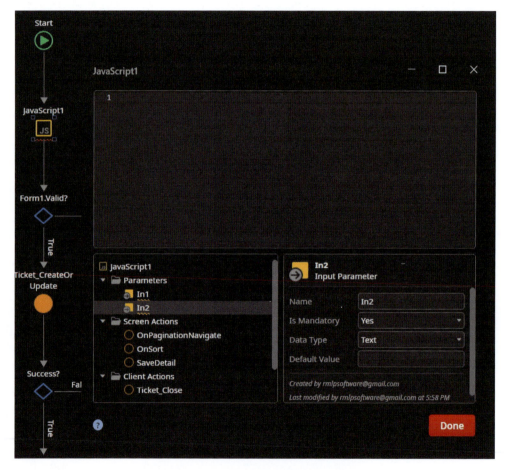

Figure 8.15 – JavaScript node and editor

In these JavaScript nodes, an editor is made available that allows you to insert your own customized JavaScript code, and it has characteristics normally used by editors in the market, such as an error identifier, suggestions, and a color scheme.

> **Tip**
>
> If you are curious, you can see the official documentation on JavaScript here:
> `https://success.outsystems.com/Documentation/11/`
> `Extensibility_and_Integration/JavaScript/Extend_`
> `Your_Mobile_and_Reactive_Apps_Using_JavaScript`.

As we can see, despite OutSystems pre-conceiving much of the code needed for our UX/UI, it has immense flexibility when it comes to customizations, tweaks, and extensibility. We can leverage all our knowledge of HTML, CSS, and JavaScript to expand our ideas and improve whatever is necessary to fit our needs.

With OutSystems, a baby is born as an adult, and we don't need to take it to the gym to make it big and strong!

But, how is this all managed on the screens, and how can we take full advantage of all those capabilities? For that, we need to understand the screens and blocks lifecycle.

Screen and block lifecycle events

Pages and blocks in OutSystems follow a set of steps in their rendering and responding to changes. These steps are called event handlers. These events occur when we open the application, when we change screens, or when the application reacts to a change in data. These events can be defined in the screen properties or in the properties of data fetch actions (aggregates or fetching data from other sources) in order to cover the full scope of occurrences that may exist.

In the application launch scenario, the normal lifecycle is as follows:

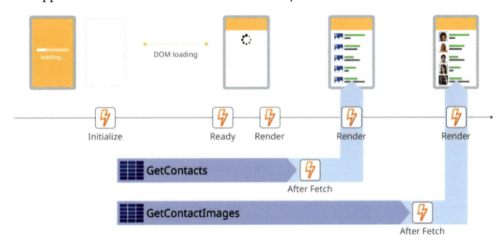

Figure 8.16 – On opening the application lifecycle

In this case (opening an application), the app shows the splash screen and then navigates to the default screen.

The other case where a screen is loaded is when we navigate from a regular screen to another regular screen, the behavior being slightly different:

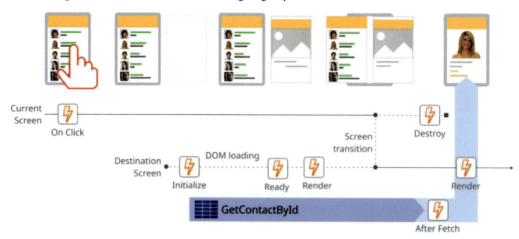

Figure 8.17 – On navigating between screens

Navigating from one screen to another is one of the most common scenarios in our applications.

This can happen with the use of links or buttons that directly call other screens or when the screen actions associated with them end on another screen (instead of the **End** node).

This capacity is usually associated with blocks that are consumed on screens. Furthermore, the block runs events whenever the data changes so that the information presented to us is correct. Basically, there are events that check if the input data has changed, and we, developers, can program the necessary data updates or other types of manipulations. These events work as follows:

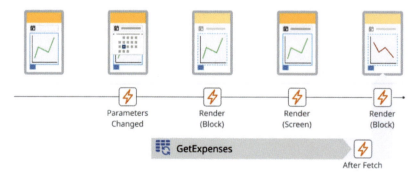

Figure 8.18 – On changing parameters screen lifecycle

In summary, the events that occur are as follows:

Event	Description
On Initialize	Occurs after checking the permission of the user to access the screen, but before navigating to the screen and fetching data. In blocks, it occurs after the navigation. You can use it to initialize the screen or block by setting its default data.
On Ready	Occurs after the screen or block DOM is ready, before the transition starts.
On Render	Occurs right after the screen or block On Ready event handler and every time the data of a screen or block changes. You can use it to update some third-party components.
On After Fetch	Occurs after an aggregate or data action has finished fetching data but before this data is rendered on the screen or block. You can use it to act upon the retrieved data.
On Parameters Changed	Occurs in a block anytime the parent screen or block changes one of its input parameters. Changes to the input value inside the block do not trigger this event handler. You can use it to react to changes in the block parameters, such as to update variables.
On Destroy	Occurs before destroying a screen or block and removing it from the DOM. You can use it to implement logic when the component is disposed of, such as to remove event listeners.

Figure 8.19 – Lifecycle event handlers

Through all these events, we can control the expected behavior of our pages and blocks in order to meet users' expectations and to avoid bad information, excessive processing in certain phases, or more iterations than necessary by those who use the applications.

> **Tip**
>
> If you are curious, you can see the official documentation on screen and block lifecycle events here: `https://success.outsystems.com/Documentation/11/Developing_an_Application/Implement_Application_Logic/Screen_and_Block_Lifecycle_Events.`

Note that these events must be handled and used with great care. We can often go wrong in choosing the right event and cause unwanted behavior.

This topic is equal in both reactive web and mobile applications. In other words, mobile uses the same events and its screens and blocks have the same lifecycle as we saw here.

There are other types of events in reactive web (and mobile) applications, these being to allow you to react to changes in interactions and data. In the next section, we will understand how these events work and in what context.

Events to propagate changes from a block to the parent

We can develop our frontend in pages or blocks. The latter are considered groupings of certain features and samples that live in their own lifecycle and with their own scope and can be reused within other blocks and/or screens. Direct or indirect recursion using blocks is not possible, that is, a block has an instance of itself in its content.

Since a block has its own scope, in order to communicate with its parent, be it another block or a screen, you need to trigger events to do so. These same events can carry data, defined as input variables.

When we define an event in a certain block, if it has its **Is Mandatory** property set to **Yes**, the parents of that block must define a handler, which can be a screen action or another event, to respond to the change made to the child block.

> **Tip**
> If you want to see a brief explanation and example of how to set up an event and its handler between a block and a parent, you can see one here:
> `https://success.outsystems.com/Documentation/11_x_`
> `platform/Developing_an_Application/Design_UI/`
> `Reuse_UI/Use_Events_to_Propagate_Changes_From_a_`
> `Block_to_the_Parent.`

In summary, to propagate changes from a block to a parent, there are two main points: event triggering on the child block side and handler development on the parent side.

Now, to better understand the content of this chapter, how about doing an exercise?

Exercise 4 – Creating application screens

Now let's apply what we've seen in this chapter in this exercise. To do this, we will create the necessary screens, using templates and scaffolding to create our screens for the My Help Desk application. Let's better understand how fast and easy it is to build the frontend of an application using the accelerators provided by OutSystems.

So, to start the exercise, we must follow these steps:

1. Create a **Reactive Web App** module with the name **HelpDesk**:

    I. To do this, we open our **My Help Desk** application, click on the **Add module** button, name it HelpDesk and select a module type of **Reactive Web App**. Then click on the **Create Module** button:

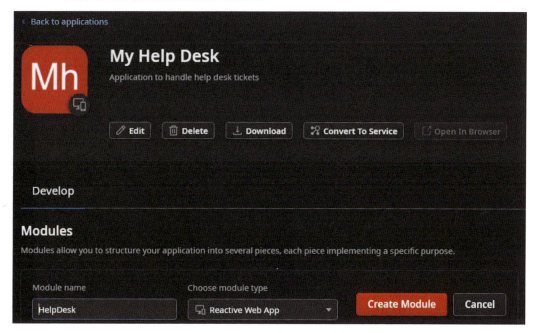

Figure 8.20 – Create a Reactive Web App module for the frontend

II. Next, we click on the green **Publish** button so that the module is generated in our environment:

Figure 8.21 – Published frontend module

2. Create our home page from a template:

I. First, we have to get the necessary dependencies on entities and actions. We click on the **Manage Dependencies** button, select the **HelpDesk_CS** module, and choose all entities and actions related to tickets. Finally, we click on the **Apply** button:

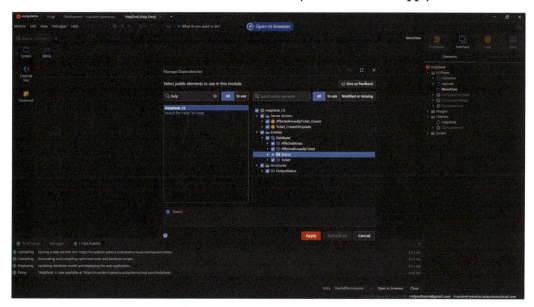

Figure 8.22 – Manage Dependencies popup with all dependencies selected from HelpDesk_CS

II. Next, click on the **Interface** tab and right-click on **MainFlow**, selecting the **Add screen** option. We click on **Dashboards** in the left column and select the template **Dashboard**:

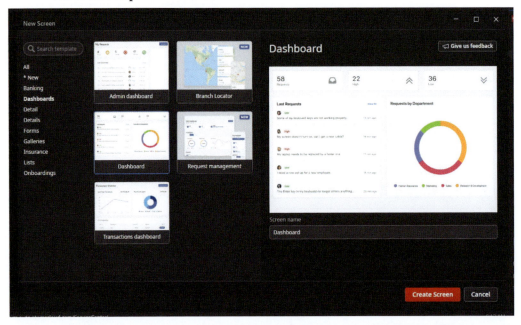

Figure 8.23 – Template selection popup with the Dashboard template selected

III. Finally, we click on the **Create Screen** button. The screen now exists inside our **MainFlow**:

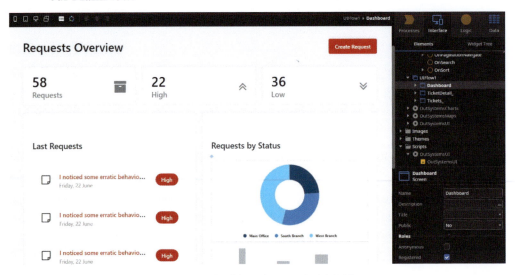

Figure 8.24 – Dashboard screen in MainFlow

IV. Now we have to replace the sample data with the real data. To do this, click on the **Data** tab and drag and drop the **Ticket** entity to the top of the list on the left until the option **Replace data** appears, and we do the same for the graph on the right. It should look something like what is shown in *Figure 8.25*:

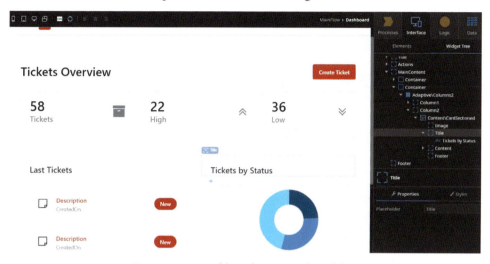

Figure 8.25 – Dashboard screen with real data

V. Now we can click on the green **Publish** button. After publication, the button changes to blue, informing us that we can open it in the browser. Let's do that to see the result:

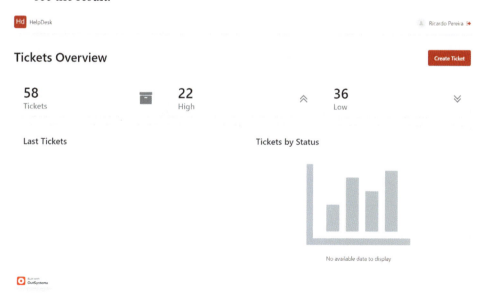

Figure 8.26 – Dashboard screen in the browser

> **Challenge**
> As a challenge, adjust the card at the top of the dashboard page to show real data!

This page has a different feature from the others we are going to create. If you notice, it shows the symbol of a house in Service Studio. That means it's our home page.

> **Tip**
> If we want to define another page as the home page, we just right-click on it and select **Mark as default screen**.

There are other accelerators to create our screens besides templates. We can do it with drag and drop, immediately creating oriented screens for the final data. So, let's create list and detail screens for tickets using the drag and drop technique:

1. For this purpose, we select the **Interface** tab and double-click on **MainFlow** in order to open the canvas. We drag and drop the **Ticket** entity in the **Data** tab to the canvas:

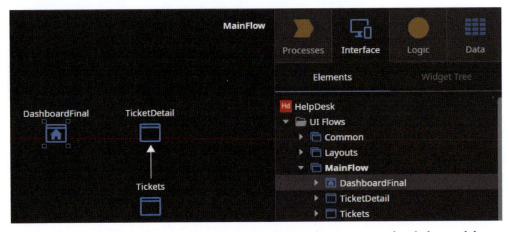

Figure 8.27 – MainFlow canvas with Tickets and TicketDetail screens created with drag and drop

2. Now, we open the **TicketDetail** screen by double-clicking on it in the **Interface** tab and click on the **Widget Tree** subtab so that we have the HTML component tree view visible:

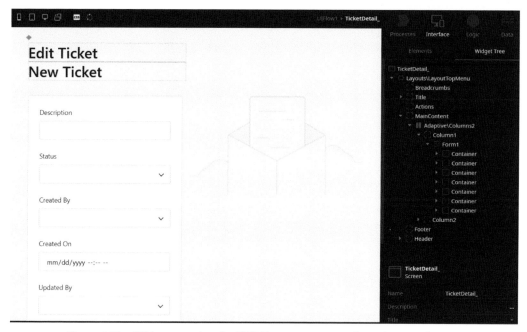

Figure 8.28 – Widget tree view for HTML components in the TicketDetail screen

3. We select the containers that group the attributes **Created By**, **Created On**, **Updated By**, and **Updated On**, right-click on them, and select the **Delete** option:

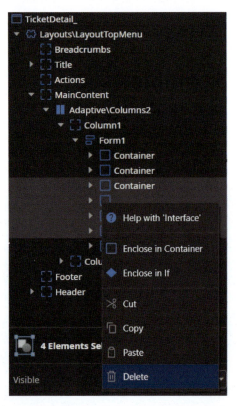

Figure 8.29 – Delete attribute frontend components from the TicketDetail screen

> **Note**
>
> These fields that we eliminated are automatically filled by the action that we created in the **HelpDesk_CS** module and that we are going to use in the action related to the functionality of creating or updating a ticket.

4.   Associate the **Ticket_CreateOrUpdate** action to the **Save** button functionality:

I.   To have functionality on the **Save** button on the **TicketDetail** screen, let's open the client action **SaveDetail** on the screen, expand the **HelpDesk_CS** module, and drag the **Ticket_CreateOrUpdate** server action to after the **If** in the branch of **True**:

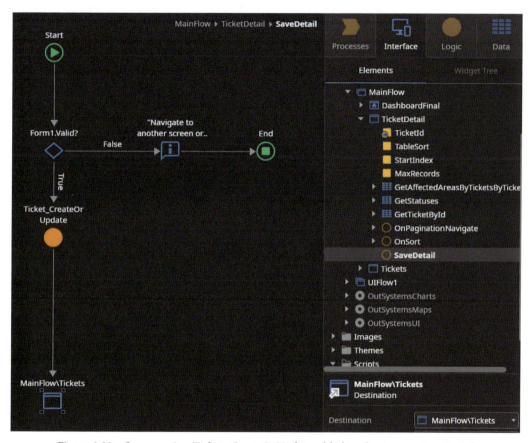

Figure 8.30 – Server action Ticket_CreateOrUpdate added to client action SaveDetail

II. Let's add the existing record on the screen to the action server input. The input value must be **GetTicketById.List.Current.Ticket** (it is the record that is mapped on the screen through the aggregate that was called):

Figure 8.31 – Mapped input record to the server action

III. Now we add an **If** after the server action to check if it returned successfully. For this, the condition of this **If** must be the verification of the **OutputStatusHasSuccess** output of the action:

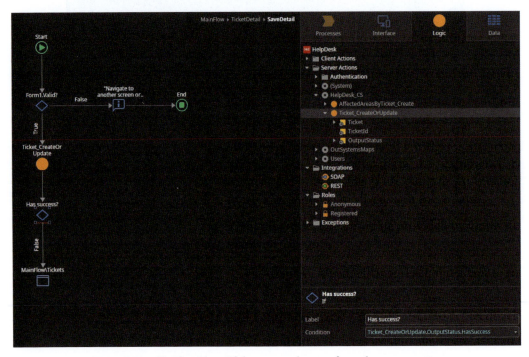

Figure 8.32 – Verify with an If the returned status from the server action

IV. On the **True** branch, we put a success message followed by a redirect to the listing page. In the **False** branch, we put an error message, map the server action error (**OutputStatus.Message**) and end up in an **End** node:

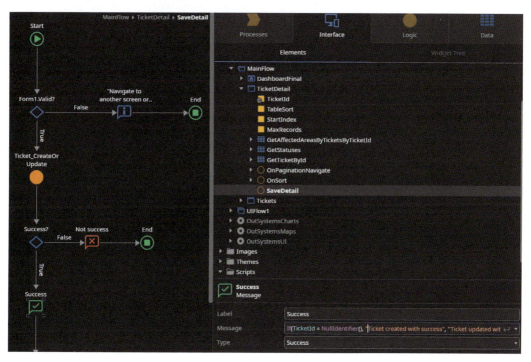

Figure 8.33 – Definition of If branches in the verification of server action success

5. Finalize the last details:

I. Eliminate the fetch data aggregate **GetUsers** (since we eliminate the dropdowns on the screen for **CreatedBy** and **UpdatedBy**, we no longer need the popular ones, so this aggregate is no longer accurate). Expand the **TicketDetail** screen, right-click on **GetUsers**, and select the **Delete** option:

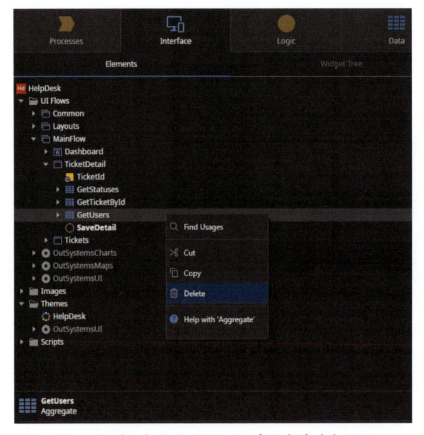

Figure 8.34 – Delete the GetUsers aggregate from the fetch data screen

II. Link the **Create Ticket** button from the **Dashboard** page to the **TicketDetail** page. Open the **Dashboard** page, select the **Create Ticket** button, and in the **Properties** section, set the **On Click** event as the redirect to the **TicketDetail** page. Set **TicketId** to **NullIdentifier()**. We can delete the **Not Implemented** action from the **Dashboard** screen:

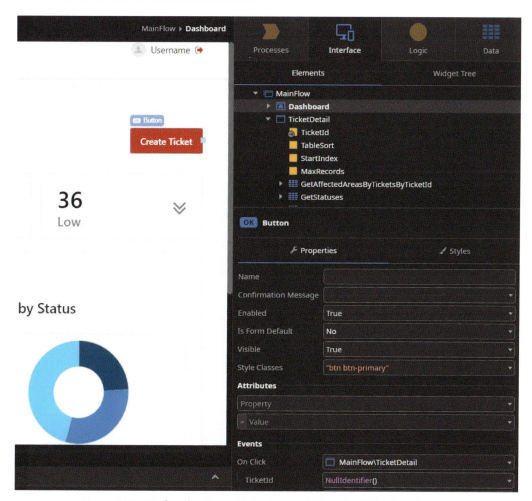

Figure 8.35 – Define the Create Ticket button link to the TicketDetail screen

III. Now we can publish the application. We click on the green **Publish** button and it becomes available to browse:

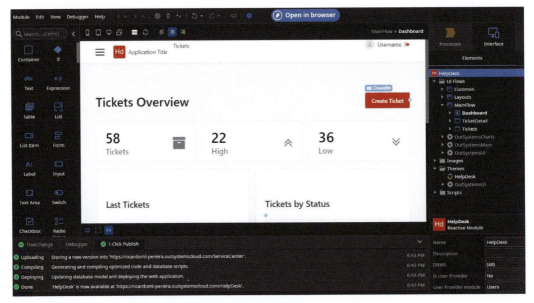

Figure 8.36 – Published app ready to use

At this moment, our application already meets the minimum standards of a ticket support web application, using the pre-conceived standards of UX/UI, security (authentication and authorization), and performance.

From here, we can evolve the application simply and quickly in order to adjust it to business needs.

Summary

In this chapter, we understood that the OutSystems platform provides a huge number of accelerators, such as pre-designed patterns and templates, automatic screen creation features such as scaffolding, and the ability to easily and quickly customize our UX styles and functionality through the CSS and JavaScript editors.

We also saw that all automatic developments respect the best performance and security rules, ensuring an excellent UX/UI, something that is one of the most important metrics nowadays for the end user.

Even without mastering native frontend technologies (HTML, CSS, and JavaScript), we were able to create fantastic applications that meet the expectations of our customers.

In the next chapter, we will see that, for developing mobile applications, things are not that different. By the way, one of the great quick wins is that the development paradigm is the same as the reactive web! The platform is so well thought out that, in order to focus on the difference in expectations between the two types of applications, the programming method is the same!

In the next chapter, we will see how easy it is to develop a mobile application!

9
Using Mobile Patterns for Fast Mobile UI Development

The OutSystems platform was so well thought out that the development paradigm is shared between reactive web and mobile.

By this, we mean that the implementation follows the same principles and forms in the development of web and mobile applications. For this reason, OutSystems changed its standard of certifications so that mobile has become a reactive specialization.

In this chapter, we will learn how to develop our screens based on pre-built patterns, templates, and widgets, and what considerations we should have for the mobile concept. This knowledge is useful for us to be able to adapt our applications to devices such as mobile phones and tablets, where the resolution and screen size are smaller compared to computers.

The main differences between web and mobile applications relate to the types of applications and their uses, as they fulfill different goals.

In this chapter, we will highlight the particular features of mobile and why it exists, including the following:

- Patterns, templates, and widgets
- Mobile design considerations
- Mobile plugins
- Native app generation
- Exercise 5 – Creating mobile app screens

By the end, we should be able to build our screens for mobile applications in a simple and understandable way, considering the type of device on which they will run.

Technical requirements

Check out the following video to see the code in action: `https://bit.ly/3xirZQR`.

Patterns, templates, and widgets

Patterns, templates, and widgets work in the same way both on mobile and reactive web (the code generation is a little bit different, but that's abstracted by the platform). The differences are based more on the type of each patterns or widget that we should use after consideration of the devices on which the applications will run.

The OutSystems platform knows that, when we create a phone or tablet-type module, it must adapt the patterns and templates to the selected type, thereby facilitating the developer's selection of which ones should be used, as we can see in *Figure 9.1*:

Figure 9.1 – Screen templates for a phone or tablet

Basically, smartphones and tablets usually have smaller screens, lower resolutions, and, in terms of usability, the fingers are usually used to navigate the applications.

In light of this, we must pay attention to how the pages are presented in order to have a coherent appearance and the components that provide functionalities (buttons, and links, among others) must be easily manipulated by our fingers (a mouse pointer is significantly smaller, so the way the features are made available must be thought of differently).

In short, it all comes down to the considerations that we must take into account when developing mobile applications, which is what we will see now!

Mobile design considerations

What are mobile design considerations? Basically, these are points to be considered when we develop applications that will run on smaller devices, with different architecture and operating systems than our computers. Furthermore, we must understand that they are applications that are installed on devices and that do not run on browsers.

Process and concept

The first considerations to bear in mind in the development of mobile applications are related to the process and the concept. There is a set of guidelines and principles that we must consider, as follows:

- *A mobile app should focus only on a business concept*: The app must have important functionality, save time or money, entertain, or clarify. In other words, the success of mobile apps lies in delivering useful benefits to the user. The general rule of thumb is that not everything on the web needs to be available on a mobile app. So, don't build an app until you have a solid idea.

- *Focus on something and do it well*: This is the most important recommendation. Brainstorming is very good. But when you're through the process, limit the best ideas to one or two.

- *Test*: Developing applications is not just about writing code, but also testing it, which is essential for internal and **business-to-business** (**B2B**) use. Assess whether you have enough time and staff to test and bug the software, especially when developing for multiple platforms.

We must always remember that this step is extremely relevant to the future success of our applications, therefore, we must never accelerate or neglect this phase.

Target audience

Another very important consideration is the target audience. We should always assess whether it will pay to develop a mobile application. Often, we are faced with a scenario in which we only satisfy a small portion of the public, thereby justifying the studying of other approaches or types of application that may correspond to the expectations of the highest possible percentage of the audience.

Design

Something we should always keep in mind is that mobile devices don't have the same features as computers. Usually, the screens are smaller, with lower resolution, and we use our fingers to navigate the applications.

For these reasons, we always have to be careful of the way we design the components we show on the screen. We have to think carefully about how to meet the expectations of end users to avoid frustration. We must always bear in mind that everything must be clearly visible, understandable, and usable.

Security

Mobile devices are generally unsafe.

They store a lot of personal information, are often used on public networks, are hackable, and can easily be lost or stolen.

For these reasons, we must be very careful when developing applications of this type. We must always follow security standards at the highest level, store as little sensitive data as possible (and encrypt what we have to always maintain a calculated trade-off with performance), use development practices that guarantee non-violation, and, above all else, always bear in mind that tomorrow, someone could find a way to break through all our barriers.

From the Forge, we can obtain and install very useful components in terms of security improvement, including the following:

- CryptoAPI: Cryptographic tools to protect your data (formerly known as ardoCrypto).

- AppShield: A component that automatically adds additional layers of security during deployment to make applications more resistant to intrusion, tampering, and reverse engineering. (You'll need a license to activate AppShield. If you don't have one yet, contact OutSystems to get more information on pricing and obtain a valid license.)

We must never forget that a small security breach can become catastrophic at any time, so we must always consider any security-related issue.

Performance

The technology that supports mobile devices, the norm, is not as powerful as that of laptops or personal computers (where we usually run our web applications). This means that processing and response times are often longer than end users expect.

For these reasons, when developing mobile applications, we must consider all aspects that can impact performance, such as the volume of data to be transferred and the components (page complexity) to be rendered on screen.

Often, in order to reduce the time taken to obtain data, we can use a feature that OutSystems makes available, **Local Storage** (this topic will be discussed in more detail in *Chapter 11, Local Storage and Data Synchronization*). This feature allows you to have data stored on the device itself, making the process of obtaining data faster, as there is no longer the need to make a web connection to a server to obtain it (we must always pay attention to security, as we talked about in the *Security* sub-section).

If we follow these considerations, we can sometimes change the approach of developing a reactive web responsive application to developing a mobile application, to be followed as this ensures that we are making our decision to develop a mobile application much more precise, since mobile applications manage to have a much more pleasant and objective behavior when it comes to mobile devices such as tablets or smartphones.

However, we must never forget that mobile devices have a considerable amount of hardware that allows us to power our applications. But for that, we have to be able to communicate with that hardware. How? By using mobile plugins!

Mobile plugins

Plugins allow us to take advantage of our mobile devices' features, such as cameras, geolocation, or notifications.

We always have to check the compatibility of plugins with the distribution modes, and the types of distribution vary between Android, iOS, and **Progressive Web Apps** (**PWAs**).

To get the plugins, we must install them from the Forge (the OutSystems repository).

The plugins supported by OutSystems are shown in *Figure 9.2*:

Plugin	Description	Supported in PWA
AppShield	Protect your mobile apps from tampering. OutSystems AppShield hardens the native mobile build, enabling the app to detect attempts of modification and misuse.	
Calendar	Access the calendar of your device.	
Camera	Enable your application to access the camera capabilities of the device.	✓
Ciphered Local Storage	Keep your mobile application's sensitive data safe using a ciphered local storage database.	
Contacts	Access the contacts of your device.	
Card IO	Automatically get the details of a credit card by taking a picture.	
File	Let you manage files and folders on a mobile device within the app sandbox.	
File Transfer	Let users upload and download files in the background.	
File Viewer	Let users view remote or app resource files.	
InApp Browser	Open external URLs directly in your application.	

Key Store	Store small amounts of sensitive information on your device. Key Store secures data by encrypting the data before storing it, and the platform itself carefully controls access to stored items.	
Location	Access the GPS capabilities of the user's device to show, for example, the present latitude, longitude, and altitude.	✓
Local Notifications	Send app notifications to the device when the application isn't running in the foreground.	
OneSignal Notifications	Push notifications using OneSignal, with deep-linking and actions.	
QR/Barcode scanner	Scan barcodes and QR codes.	
SSL Pinning	Provide an extra layer of security to HTTPS communications by adding verification of the server certificate against hashes of public keys.	
Touch ID	Use authentication with Touch ID in your application.	

Figure 9.2 – Table of the supported mobile plugins

When using plugins, we must pay attention to the following:

- Which platform the plugins will run on, since between iOS and Android, there are certain differences and there may not be compatibility for both or there might be configuration differences between them.

- Every time we change, add, or remove a plugin from our applications, we must regenerate a new build and distribute it so that users can install it.

This extensibility of our applications allows us to get much more out of mobile devices than reactive web applications. When evaluating what kind of application we want to develop, the theme of plugins and their capabilities must be taken into account.

Adding plugins to our applications

Plugins are available in the Forge. To use them, we download them, install them in the environment, and then add their functionalities to our applications.

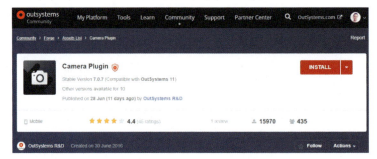

Figure 9.3 – Forge screen to install or download a camera plugin

Now we need to reference the plugin features in the mobile modules where we want to use them.

For this, we open the mobile module, open the **Manage Dependencies** window, select the producer module (in this example, **CameraPlugin**), and, in the left window, we select the desired functionalities. At the end, we click on **Apply**.

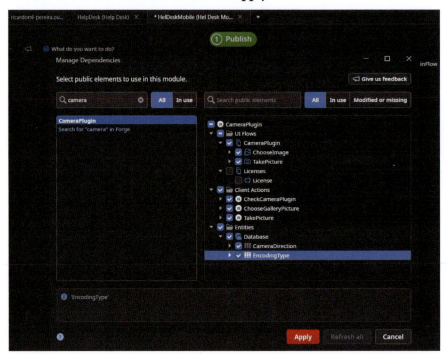

Figure 9.4 – Adding dependencies from CameraPlugin to our mobile module

However, the OutSystems platform, when generating a mobile application, uses the following built-in plugins for housekeeping and infrastructure tasks:

Plugin	Description
OS Cache	Allows your application to run offline or in bad network conditions
OS Cordova Loader	Loads the Cordova engine on your app
OS Deeplinks	Opens hyperlinks to specific screens of your app
OS DB Upgrader	Manages the local storage of your app
OS Manifest	Provides a parser for the app manifest
OS Pre-Bundle	Handles the content of the app's pre-bundled resources
OS Security	Provides the APIs for the security layer
Mobile AppFeedback	Enables the user to invoke App Feedback for submitting feedback about the app
NetworkStatus	Lets your app know when the device is online/offline and provides information on the type of network available (for example, Wi-Fi, 3G, or 4G)

Figure 9.5 – Built-in mobile plugins

Note that of all the built-in plugins, only **Mobile AppFeedback** is configurable, but is only available if we enable the App Feedback feature.

> **Tip**
> If we want, we can also create our own plugins, existing on Apache Cordova. If you are curious, you can see the official documentation on plugins here:
> `https://success.outsystems.com/Documentation/11/ Extensibility_and_Integration/Mobile_Plugins/ Using_Cordova_Plugins`.

Thanks to plugins, we can make the most of our mobile applications' potential by using the existing resources of mobile devices.

We must pay attention to the type of distribution to be used, as this can differ for certain plugins between iOS and Android.

Also, if our application is to be distributed as a PWA, we should always check whether the plugin is available for this type of app.

At this point, you might be asking how this distribution works. Let's study this now!

Native app generation

Mobile applications can be generated for different types of distribution and for different purposes.

We can generate them for iOS and Android. Furthermore, they can be generated for testing purposes, for small groups of users, or on a massive scale. This gives us an interesting set of scenarios and possible alternatives for generating our applications.

In addition, we can distribute mobile applications as PWAs without the need for them to be generated. They are distributed by a URL or QR code and opened on our devices.

PWAs also allow these 'mobile applications' to be opened in web browsers and 'installed' locally on computers as apps.

Note: On iOS devices, this is only possible via the Safari browser.

> **Tip**
> You can see the official documentation on PWA distribution here:
> ```
> https://success.outsystems.com/Documentation/11/
> Delivering_Mobile_Apps/Distribute_as_a_
> progressive_web_app.
> ```

To configure and generate mobile app packages, in Service Studio, we must navigate to the detail screen of our mobile application and click on the **Distribute** tab, as shown in *Figure 9.6*:

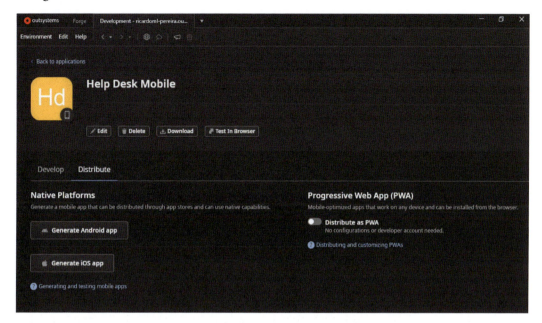

Figure 9.6 – Service Studio's Distribute tab on the mobile app detail screen

In this tab, we can generate the Android and iOS versions of our apps, and we must fill in the required fields in each of the options.

In the case of Android applications, we must fill in the **Build Type** field (**Debug**, **Release**, or **Google Play**), the **App Identifier** field (a unique identifier that identifies our application in stores and devices), and the **Keystore details (optional)** field.

We can see an overview of these configurations in *Figure 9.7*:

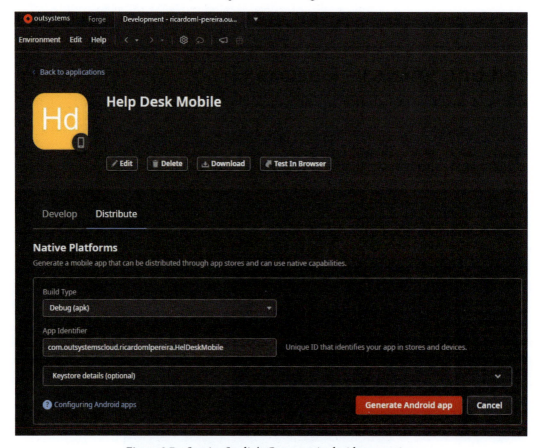

Figure 9.7 – Service Studio's Generate Android app section

Note that for Android versions, we generate an `apk` file and can install it directly on devices without going through stores (unlike iOS apps).

For iOS versions, of our apps we must also fill in a set of attributes necessary for the correct generation of our application.

First, we must fill in the **Build Type** field (**Ad-Hoc**, **Development**, **App Store**, or **In-House**), followed by the **App Identifier** field (a unique identifier used to identify the application in stores and devices), and then we must upload the certificate used in Apple's iOS developer program, the respective certificate password, and also upload the provisioning profile that matches the certificate.

We can see an overview of these configurations in *Figure 9.8*:

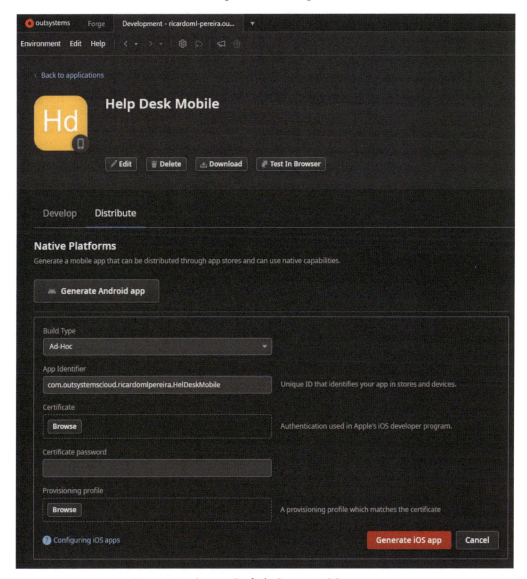

Figure 9.8 – Service Studio's Generate iOS app section

The, generation and distribution of iOS versions are more complex than for Android versions due to the rules and protocols used by Apple.

Another alternative for distributing our mobile applications is as PWAs.

We must consider the scenario and context of the application (and for which devices) in order to verify that this distribution mode meets our requirements.

However, it is a simpler and faster way to make our mobile applications available to end customers.

We can see an overview of these configurations in *Figure 9.9*:

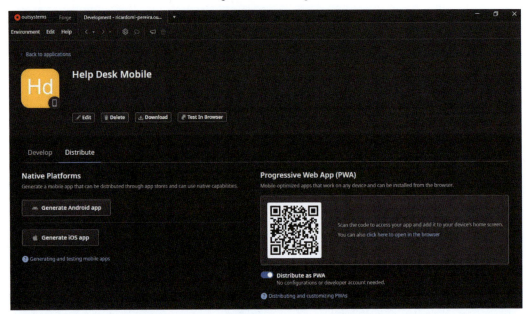

Figure 9.9 – Service Studio's Progressive Web App section

Distributing an app as a PWA is more efficient, using only a link or a QR code. The user just needs to open the link on their device and it will be suggested to add it to the main screen.

The same happens if, instead of opening the link, the user chooses to read the QR code.

> **Tip**
>
> If you are curious, you can see the official documentation on generation and distribution here: https://success.outsystems.com/
> Documentation/11/Delivering_Mobile_Apps/Generate_
> and_Distribute_Your_Mobile_App.

We can do all these operations and much more through Service Center since it provides a view and a package of features more oriented toward managing the generation of the various existing versions of our mobile applications; that is, more DevOps-friendly.

In short, the OutSystems platform enables the generation and distribution of our mobile applications for Android, iOS, and as PWAs, being fully configurable for the requirements of any platform.

Note that, in the case of PWAs, the pros and cons must be weighed, since we gain simplicity and speed in delivery but lose compatibility with several plugins. Your choice!

Joining all this to a uniform paradigm of web and mobile development, we have everything we need to triumph in solving our customers' problems in a very efficient way.

To show that the mobile development paradigm is extremely similar to reactive web, *Exercise 5 – Creating mobile app screens* will be the replication of the previous exercise from *Chapter 8, Reactive UI Development*.

Exercise 5 – Creating mobile app screens

Now, let's apply what we've seen in this chapter in this exercise. For this, we will create the necessary screens, for the Help Desk Mobile application using templates and scaffolding. By the end, we will better understand how fast and easy it is to build the frontend of an application using the accelerators provided by OutSystems.

So, let's start the exercise by following these steps:

1. Create a Phone App with the `Help Desk Mobile` name:

    ▪ To do this, open Service Studio, click on the **New Application** button, and then select **Phone App**.

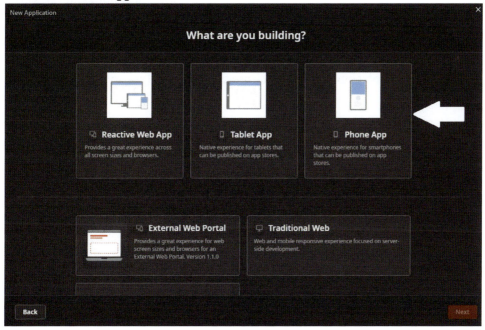

Figure 9.10 – Selecting the type of application in Service Studio

- Now, we set the name as `Help Desk Mobile`, fill in a brief description of the application's purpose, select the main color of the theme in the color picker, and click **Create App**.

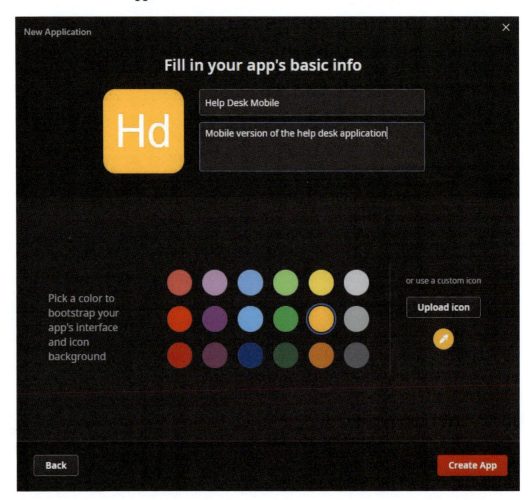

Figure 9.11 – Filling in the details for a new application in Service Studio

2. Create a Phone App module and name it `HelpDeskMobile`:

   - To do this, we open our `Help Desk` application, click on the **Add module** button, name it `HelpDeskMobile`, and select **Phone App** as the module type. Then, click on the **Create Module** button.

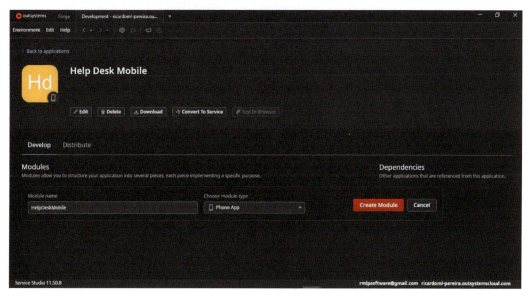

Figure 9.12 – Creating a Phone App module for the frontend

- Next, we click on the green **Publish** button so that the module is published in our environment.

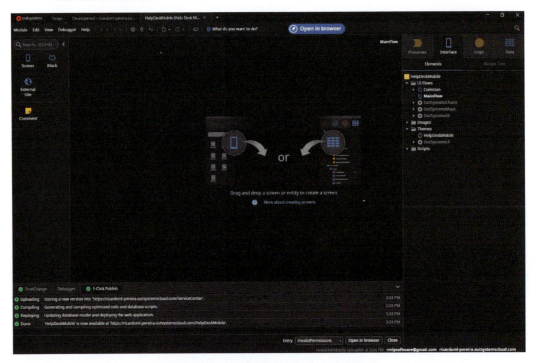

Figure 9.13 – Published frontend module

3. Create the home page from a template:

    - First, we have to get the necessary dependencies on Entities and Actions. We click on the **Manage dependencies** button, select the **HelpDesk_CS** module, and choose all Entities and Actions related to tickets. Finally, we click on the **Apply** button.

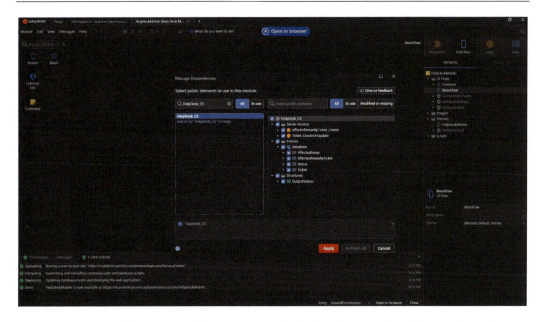

Figure 9.14 – The Manage Dependencies popup with all dependencies selected from HelpDesk_CS

- Next, click on the **Interface** tab and right-click on **MainFlow**, selecting the **Add screen** option. Then click on **Dashboards** in the left column and select the **Dashboard** template.

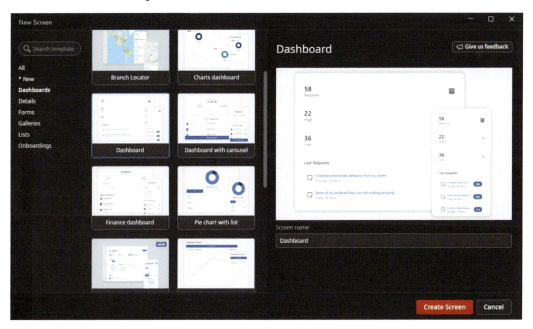

Figure 9.15 – Template selection popup with the Dashboard screen selected

- Finally, we click on the **Create Screen** button. The screen now exists inside **MainFlow**.

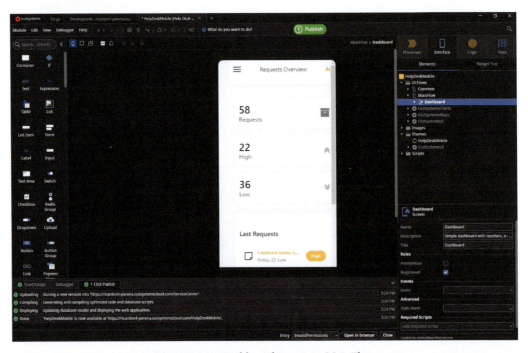

Figure 9.16 – Dashboard screen in MainFlow

- Now we have to replace the sample data with the real data. To do this, click on the **Data** tab and drag and drop the **Ticket** entity to the top of the list on the left until the **Replace data** option appears. Then we do the same for the graph on the right. It should look something like this:

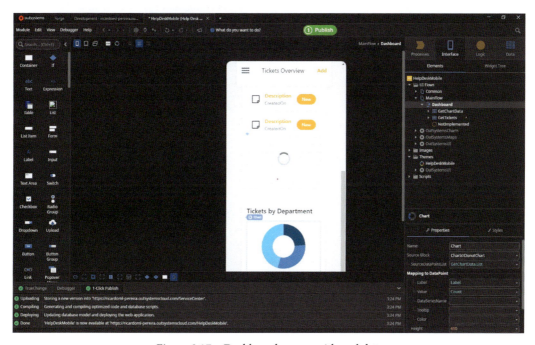

Figure 9.17 – Dashboard screen with real data

- Now we can click on the green **Publish** button. Upon publishing, the button changes to blue, informing us that we can open it in the browser, using a simulator. Let's do this to see the result.

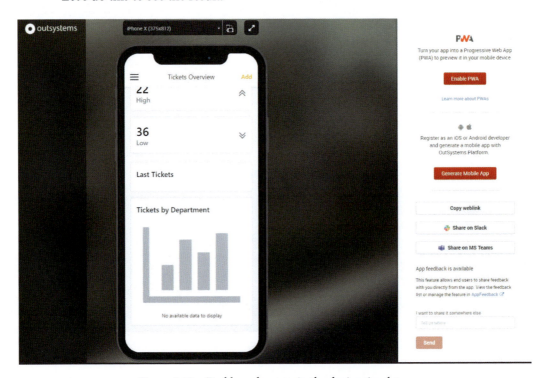

Figure 9.18 – Dashboard screen in the device simulator

> **Challenge**
>
> As a challenge, adjust the card data at the top of the dashboard page to show real data!

This page has a different feature from the others we are going to create. Notice that it shows the symbol of a house in Service Studio. That means it's our home page.

> **Tip**
>
> If we want to define another page as the home page, just right-click on it and select **Mark as default screen**.

4. Create list and detail screens for tickets:

- For this purpose, we select the **Interface** tab and double-click on **MainFlow** to open the canvas. We then drag and drop the **Ticket** entity from the **Data** tab to the canvas.

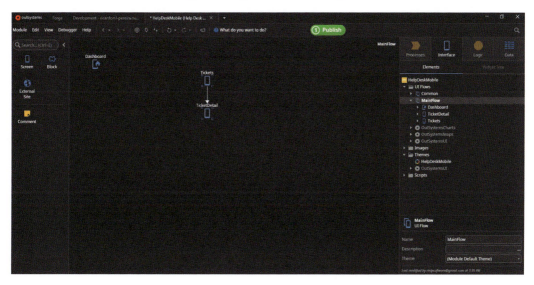

Figure 9.19 – MainFlow canvas with the Tickets and TicketDetail screens created with drag and drop

- Now, we open the **TicketDetail** screen by double-clicking on it in the **Interface** tab and clicking on the **Widget Tree** subtab so that we have the HTML component tree view visible.

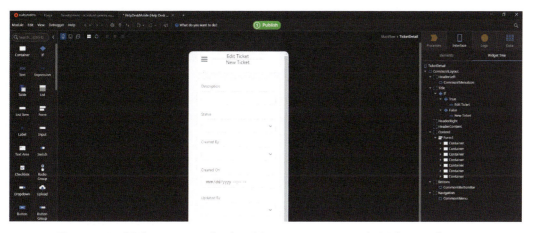

Figure 9.20 – Widget tree view for the HTML components on the TicketDetail screen

- We select the containers that group the **Created By**, **Created On**, **Updated By**, and **Updated On** attributes, right-click on them, and select the **Delete** option.

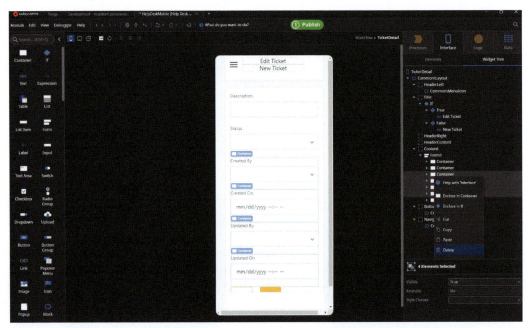

Figure 9.21 – Delete frontend attribute components from the TicketDetail screen

> **Note**
>
> These fields that we eliminated are automatically filled by the Action that we created in the **HelpDesk_CS** module and we are going to use them in the Action related to the functionality of creating or updating a ticket.

5. Associate the create ticket Action with the functionality of the **Save** button:

- To have functionality on the **Save** button on the **TicketDetail** screen, let's open the **SaveDetail** Client Action on the screen, expand the **HelpDesk_CS** module, and drag the **Ticket_CreateOrUpdate** Server Action to the **If True** branch.

Figure 9.22 – Ticket_CreateOrUpdate Server Action added to the SaveDetail Client Action

- Let's add the existing record on the screen to the **Action** server input. The input value must be **GetTicketById.List.current.Ticket** (it is the record that is mapped on the screen through the aggregate that was called).

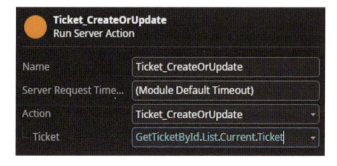

Figure 9.23 – Mapped input record to the Server Action

- Now, we add an **If** after the Server Action to check whether it returned success. For this, the verifying condition of this **If** (that will return to the **True** branch) must be the verification of the **OutputStatusHasSuccess** output of the Action.

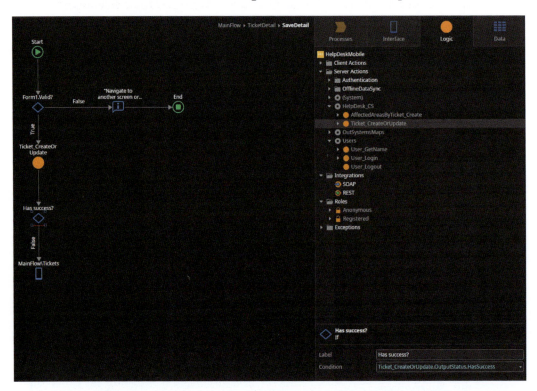

Figure 9.24 – Verifying the returned status from the Server Action with If

- On the **True** branch, we insert a success message followed by a redirect to the listing page. In the **False** branch, we put an error message, map the Server Action error (**OutputStatus.Message**), and end up in an **End** node.

Figure 9.25 – Definitions of If branches in verifying Server Action success

6. Finalize the last details:

    ▪ Eliminate the **GetUsers** fetch data aggregate (since we have eliminated the dropdowns on the screen for **CreatedBy** and **UpdatedBy**, we no longer need the data to populate those fields so this aggregate is no longer accurate). Expand the **TicketDetail** screen, right-click on **GetUsers**, and select the **Delete** option.

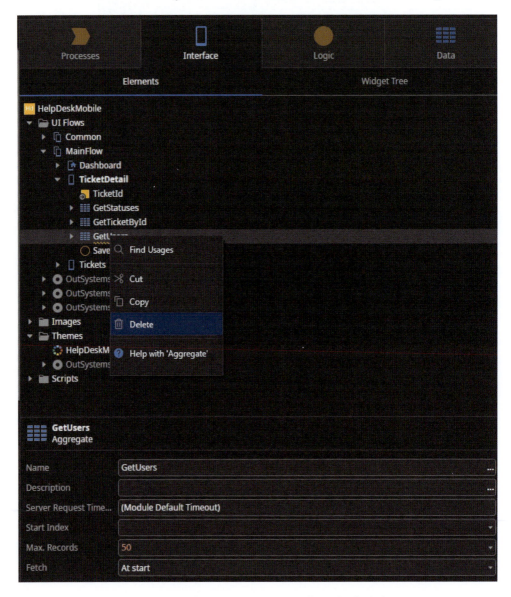

Figure 9.26 – Deleting the GetUsers aggregate from the fetch data screen

- Link the **Add** container from the **Dashboard** page to the **TicketDetail** page. Open the **Dashboard** page, select the **Add** container, and then, in the **Properties** section, set the **On Click** event as the redirect to the **TicketDetail** page. Set **TicketId** to **NullIdentifier()**. We can delete the **Not Implemented** Action from the **Dashboard** screen.

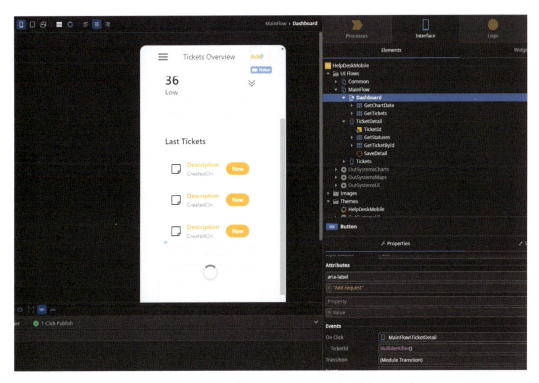

Figure 9.27 – Defining the Add container link to the TicketDetail screen

- Now we can publish the application. Click on the green **Publish** button and it becomes available to browse.

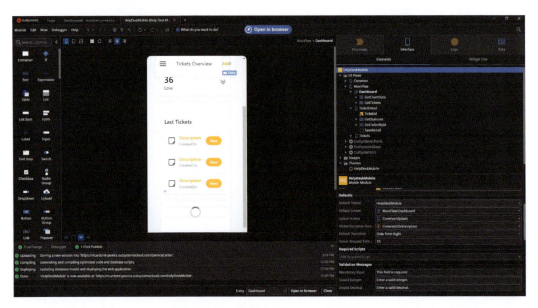

Figure 9.28 – Published app ready to use

With these developments, we have a good basis for creating an attractive solution for our customers.

In *Chapter 11*, *Local Storage and Data Synchronization*, we will learn ways to optimize our mobile applications using local storage and server data synchronization, thus improving performance.

Then it's all about choosing the most suitable distribution mode for our application in order to reach our customers quickly and easily.

Summary

In this chapter, we saw how the development paradigm for mobile applications is identical to the reactive web development paradigm, which makes the learning curve much easier. The application and use of patterns, templates, and widgets is similar on both types, and in the mobile version, they are adjusted to the devices on which they will be shown.

We also realized that in the case of mobile, we have several considerations, both in the development and in the choice of solutions, in order to deliver the best possible product to our customers.

Something we discovered is the fact that we can take advantage of the capabilities and functionality of the devices on which the applications will be used by implementing plugins.

In addition, we verified that the OutSystems platform offers a good variety of distribution solutions, facilitating our work in delivering our applications to our end customers.

Now we need to figure out how we can improve our functionality through client-side code. This code has a different responsibility than server-side code. How can we do that? Let's see in the next chapter, entitled *Client-Side Logic*!

10
Client-Side Logic

For our frontend to work smoothly, efficiently, and with all the necessary capabilities, it's just not enough for us to have a good backend and very well-designed screens.

There is a very powerful feature in frontend development that gives us the ability to work our features down to the smallest detail: Client Actions!

These actions are implemented in a very similar way to server actions but must always be developed considering that they occur on the client side—that is, in the browser. In short, they're implemented in the same way, but the approach is slightly different.

Client Actions can exist at a screen level and a module level.

In this chapter, we will focus on client-side logic and explore the following topics:

- Screen actions
- Data actions
- Client logic actions
- Exercise 6 – creating Client Actions and using them on the frontend

By the end of this chapter, we should be able to implement screen actions and understand their scope, obtain data from the server or other sources with data actions, and create Client Actions and use them on the frontend.

Technical requirements

Check out the following video to see the code in action: `https://bit.ly/3rcHLvt`.

Screen Client Actions

In this section we will learn how to develop the features on our applications screens. For that we need actions. These actions are Screen Client Actions

Screen Client Actions implement logic that can only be used in the scope of the screen itself.

> **Note**
> Screen actions can be created and used in blocks as well, as they are reusable elements of screen parts.

With this, they have access to the existing scope on the screen and can even be called to the logic of another screen action on the same screen.

You can see an example of a screen action, that is **SaveDetail** Screen Client Actions under the TicketDetail screen scope, as shown in the following screenshot:

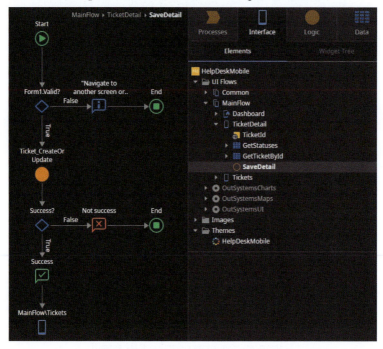

Figure 10.1 – Screen action example

The behavior, use, and implementation of these actions are identical in both reactive web and mobile applications (as mentioned, the development paradigms are very similar).

These actions have the following properties:

Property name	Description
Name	Identifies an element in the scope where it is defined, such as a screen, action, or module
Description	Text that documents the element
	Useful for documentation purposes
	The maximum size of this property is 2,000 characters.

Figure 10.2 – Screen action properties

A screen action can have input variables and local variables (it does not need output variables, as they are used in the context of the screen and have access to all data and variables used in the generalized streams of the screen). These can be of any available type—from text, entity, or structure records, lists of records or structures, or even a composition of several types.

Note that local variables used and defined within Client Actions only have a context within themselves.

A limitation found in these actions is the fact that it is not possible to obtain information from the database (server side), and for that, there is another type of action at the screen level: a data action (if it is not a request for complex data or external systems, we can do this with aggregates).

Data actions

For our applications to work, we have to get data from certain sources. This can be the OutSystems database as an external source.

To obtain data from the OutSystems database, we can use aggregates. These can trigger further actions that run in **On After Fetch** events.

We can configure its name, description, server request timeout, its start index, the maximum number of records to return, and when it happens—if at the start or only when we ask for it (only on demand)–as illustrated in the following screenshot:

> **Note**
>
> The **Fetch** property is very important because this helps us to manage the data we need at the start of the screen or when we need it, which is called on demand.

Figure 10.3 – Screen aggregate properties

Sometimes, we need to get data that the aggregates cannot supply—that is, we have high complexity. We may also have cases where our data sources are external (such as **Simple Object Access Protocol** (**SOAP**) web services or **Representational State Transfer** (**REST**) methods). For this, we have another way to obtain this data: through **data actions**.

In these data actions, we have as properties, the action's name, description, server request timeout, and when we intend to get the data: at the beginning or only when necessary (only on demand).

These data actions have an **On After Fetch** event where we can decide what to do after getting the data.

Note that these actions must have at least one output, which will be the result (assigned inside the data action) of the data retrieval, as illustrated in the following screenshot:

Figure 10.4 – Screen aggregate properties (continued)

With these two mechanisms, we are able to fetch the data that we intend to display and manipulate in our applications, providing an enormous capacity for adjustment and measurement to the different application contexts required in the market.

But after fetching the data, we often need to operationalize the smallest detail of the features of our applications, which often need to be centralized for reuse or complexity reduction. For that, we have **Client Actions** (these are not at the screen level).

Client logic actions

General Client Actions work on the client side (in the browser), just as with screen actions (which are also Client Actions as discussed earlier).

This artifact is extremely useful for manipulating data and behaviors on the browser side, allowing a **user experience** (**UX**) within expectations and without resorting to the server side for processing.

These actions can be found under the **Logic** tab in the **Client Actions** section, as illustrated in the following screenshot:

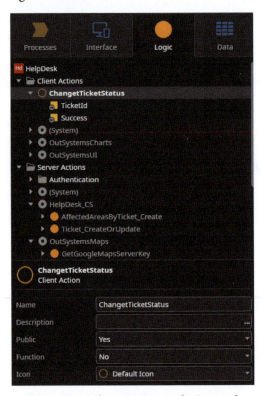

Figure 10.5 – Client Actions in the Logic tab

Regarding Client Actions, these differ from screen actions in the following aspects:

- They can be used in any other client action, general action, or screen action
- They allow you to have outputs
- They can be defined as public in order to be shared and reused by other modules
- They can be defined as functions to be used in expressions and calculation formulas (this is only possible if, on the action flow, *no* server action is used)

Furthermore, these are its main features:

Name	Description	Mandatory	Default value	Observations
Name	Identifies an element in the scope where it is defined, such as a screen, action, or module	✓		
Description	Text that documents the element			Useful for documentation purposes The maximum size of this property is 2,000 characters.
Public	Set to Yes to allow the element to be added as a dependency by other modules	✓	No	
Function	Set to Yes to define the action as a function Functions must return a value and can be used in expressions.	✓	No	This property is only available in the global scope actions. Client actions set as functions can only be used in client action expressions.
Icon	Picture to be displayed to help identify this element	✓		The recommended dimensions for the icon are 32 × 32 pixels.
Original Name	Name of the element as defined in the module that implements it (producer module). This property is read-only.	✓		This property is only visible for referenced elements.

Figure 10.6 – Client Actions properties

We must always bear in mind that Client Actions cannot be defined as public if any of their inputs or outputs are not defined as public (in case they are structures or records of entities).

> **Tip**
>
> If you are curious, you can see the official documentation on Client Actions here:
>
> ```
> https://success.outsystems.com/Documentation/11/
> Reference/OutSystems_Language/Interfaces/Adding_
> Data_and_Logic/Client_Action
> ```

Client Actions can call server actions if they need, and for code optimization, they should only call *ONE* server action in all their flow. This is because each server action corresponds to a transaction to the server, which has an impact on performance (in fact, if there is more than one server action in the flow, Service Studio's **TrueChange** will throw a warning about it).

We must always keep in mind when using Client Actions that the client side is much more vulnerable in terms of security issues, so we always have to calculate the trade-off between performance and security.

As we can see, Client Actions allow us to have much more power over what goes on in our frontend without having to resort so often to the server or JavaScript in order to get the expected behaviors.

Now, as a good way to better understand how we should use Client Actions let's do a simple exercise to see how this can help us!

Exercise 6 – creating Client Actions and using them on the frontend

In this exercise, we will continue the application that has been developed in the previous exercises. Let's create a client action that allows us to change the state of a ticket to **Closed** and use it on the ticket listing page, making it available for each of the tickets that are not yet in that state. Proceed as follows:

1. Select the **Logic** tab, right-click on the **Client Actions** folder, and select **Add client action**. Name it `Ticket_Close`, as illustrated in the following screenshot:

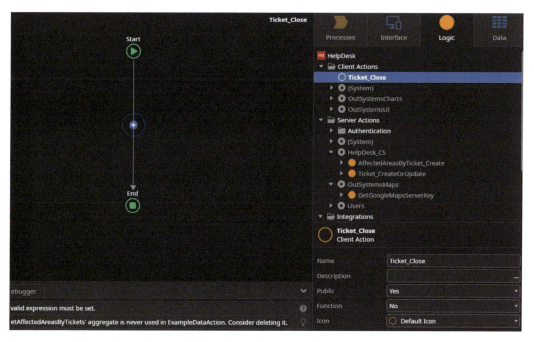

Figure 10.7 – Creating Ticket_Close client action in the Client Actions section

2. Now, let's create an input variable of type `TicketId`, as illustrated in the following screenshot:

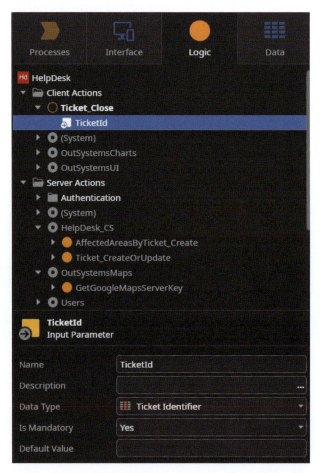

Figure 10.8 – Creating TicketId input parameter of type Ticket Identifier

3. Next, open the **Manage Dependencies** popup and select the `Ticket_Close` server action from the `HelpDesk_CS` module, as illustrated in the following screenshot:

> **Tip**
>
> First, we must create a `Ticket_Close` server action in the `HelpDesk_CS` module, as we learned in *Chapter 6, Server-Side Logic.*

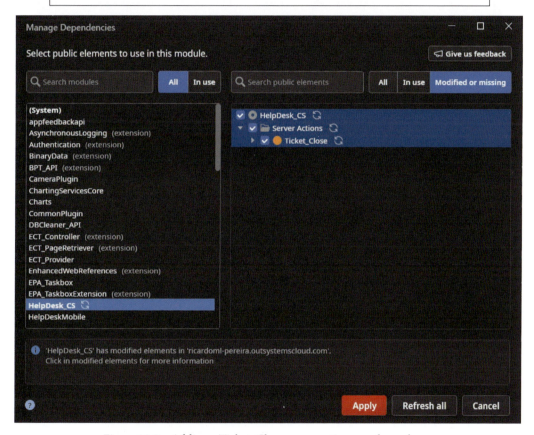

Figure 10.9 – Adding a Ticket_Close server action as a dependency

4. Navigate to the **Logic** tab and drag the `Ticket_Close` server action into the flow of the `Ticket_Close` client action and assign the `TicketId` variable to its input, as illustrated in the following screenshot:

Figure 10.10 – Dragging and dropping Ticket_Close server action into the client action flow

5. Let's add a success message to the end of the client action flow, just before the **End** node, as follows:

Figure 10.11 – Adding a success message at the end of the client action flow

6. Finally, we go to the **Interface** tab and open the **Tickets** screen. In the table, we add a column at the end and put in a link, as illustrated in the following screenshot:

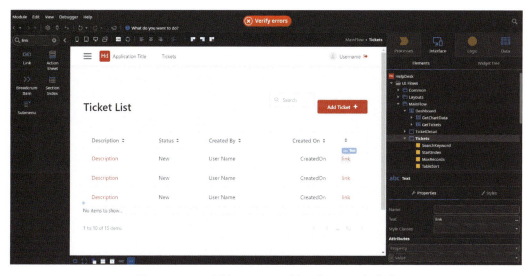

Figure 10.12 – Adding a new table column and a link

7. We then change the text inside the link to **Close**. Then, for the **Visible** attribute in the properties of the link, we put that it only must be visible if the status of the current ticket is different from **Closed**. In the **On Click** event, we select **New Client Actions** and drag to its client action flow we created earlier, and pass TicketId as the **identifier (ID)** of the current record, as illustrated in the following screenshot:

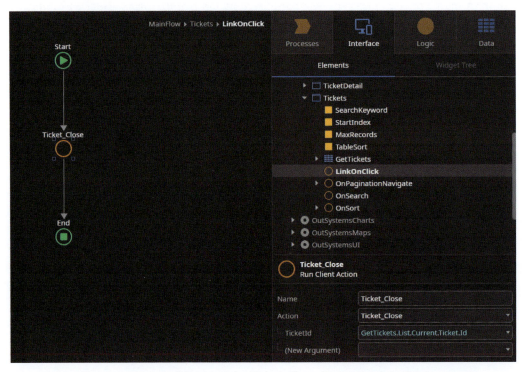

Figure 10.13 – Dragging and dropping the Ticket_Close client action into the screen action

8. We can now publish our application and try it out, as illustrated in the following screenshot:

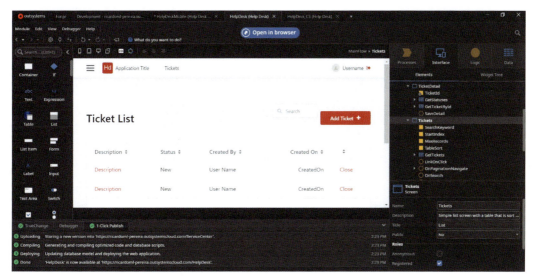

Figure 10.14 – Published HelpDesk reactive web application

> **Tip**
>
> The procedure is exactly the same for building these features in both reactive web and mobile applications.

With this type of approach, we can abstract the complexity of our logic, making the code reusable and easier to maintain.

Furthermore, in case it is something transversal to several concepts, we can have the Client Actions as public and make them available as dependencies.

Summary

In this chapter, we learned how client-side logic works, about the available artifacts, and how to combine them to obtain the behaviors intended by our actions in our frontend.

We learned what screen actions, Client Actions and data actions are and looked at the concept of variables in the context of Client Actions how to create logic in Client Actions and the properties of the action attributes.

We should never forget the following: screen actions are defined at the screen level, Client Actions are defined at the module level and run on the client side, and server actions are defined at the module level and run on the server side!

Something very important to remember is this: whenever possible, abstract and isolate the manipulation of our data in data actions or aggregates so that we can better control their integrity (since these calls are asynchronous).

As we can see, we were able to develop code in a super-intuitive way, with little scope for errors (the typical cases in textual languages that take hours to understand were solved here in less than half the time) and largely in a visual way. Another good thing is that we develop client-side logic in a very similar way to server-side logic, although we have to take some extra care and attention due to the context in which it is used (security, performance, and UX/UI).

In the next chapter, we will cover a very particular feature that exists for mobile applications and that can benefit a lot in terms of performance. However, as these are applications that run on less secure devices, we must always take security into consideration. So, right away, let's move on to local storage and data synchronization!

11
Local Storage and Data Synchronization

When we talk about the concept of "mobile," we must always consider particular aspects of the devices used – things such as processing power, passive safety, and a very common case: offline operation.

We often find ourselves without network connectivity on our devices, either because we don't have a Wi-Fi network within our reach or because the network signal does not allow us to take advantage of data packets.

For that, there is an interesting concept in mobile development, Local Storage since we can have the necessary data for our applications to run on our device without needing an internet connection to obtain it. Of course, in most cases synchronization will be necessary later to keep the data up to date, both on our device and on the database server.

In this chapter, we will learn how Local Storage works, how to use it, and how to synchronize our data from Local Storage with existing data on the server side (in cases where there is such a need).

The chapter covers the following topics:

- Creating and using Local Storage entities
- Fetching data from Local Storage
- Analyzing data synchronization patterns

By the end of the chapter, you will know how to create local entities, fetch and manipulate data from them, and synchronize the data existing in those entities with entities existing on the server side.

Let's get to it!

> **Info**
>
> For now, Local Storage is a feature that only exists in mobile, but it is expected that something similar, even with a different technology, will emerge for reactive web applications.

Creating and using Local Storage entities

It may seem like we are facing a completely new concept, but we're not. The implementation of local entities in Service Studio is extremely similar to the implementation of entities that we have already seen (existing in a database server).

To create these entities, click on the **Data** tab, open the **Entities** folder, and go to the **Local Storage** section:

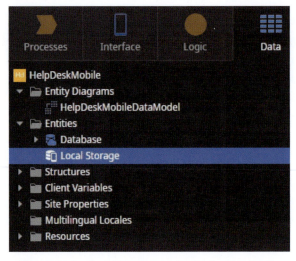

Figure. 11.1 – Local Storage section in Service Studio

> **Info**
>
> The **Local Storage** section is only available in the **Phone App** and **Tablet App** modules.

We can create our entities manually, or we can create them directly based on an existing entity on the server side (we'll look at this in more detail later):

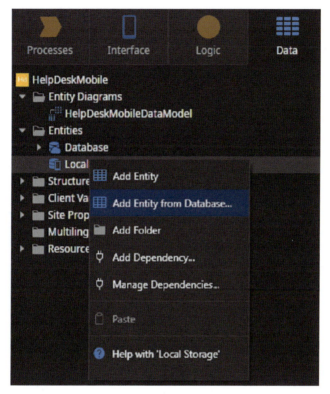

Figure 11.2 – Local Storage options

These entities, when created, have the following properties:

- **Attributes** – Attributes are the fields where we store local data. They can be of several simple types. We can define some properties, varying according to the configured type, and one of the transversal properties is mandatory configuration.

- **Primary key**– The primary key is the entity identifier. This is created automatically at entity creation time and cannot be a composite key. It is a mandatory field.

- **Foreign Keys** – Foreign keys are attributes that define the relationships between entities. A foreign key in an entity refers to a primary key of the table to be related.

A difference we found regarding database entities is the fact that there is no possibility to create indexes. However, everything else is quite similar, as we can see in the local entity's properties window:

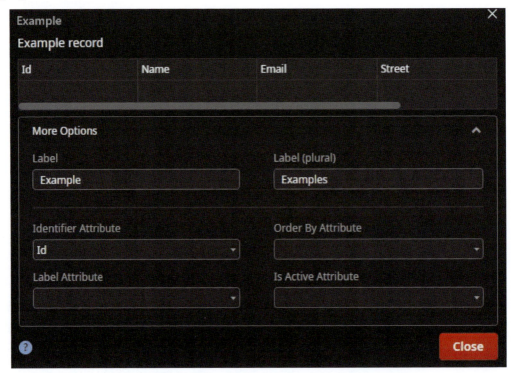

Figure 11.3 – Local Storage properties window

Also, in order to facilitate some synchronization techniques, there is one more CRUD operation, **DeleteAll**:

Figure 11.4 – Local entity representation with the DeleteAll operation

If we want to create a replica of an entity from the database as a local entity, we click the right mouse button on **Local Storage**, select the **Add entity from database option**, and, in the popup that opens, we choose the entity of the database that we want to replicate:

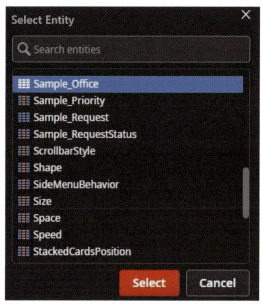

Figure 11.5 – Database replica selection popup

Then we can select the fields we want to replicate. We must always bear in mind that for mobile applications, databases should always be as light as possible, as we are dealing with devices that will probably have less capacity than usual computers:

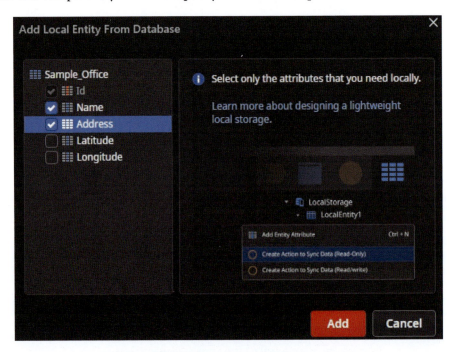

Figure 11.6 – Database replica selected attributes

> **Tip**
> You can see more details about the construction of local data models, taking into account the weight of entities, here: `https://success.outsystems.com/Documentation/Best_Practices/Development/OutSystems_Mobile_Best_Practices?utm_source=ost-outsystems+tools&utm_medium=ost-servicestudio&utm_campaign=ost-docrouter&utm_content=ost-helpid-30155&utm_term=ost-contextualhelp#Design_a_Lightweight_Local_Storage`

And it's ready! Just click on the **Add** button and the entity will exist in **Local Storage** with the selected attributes:

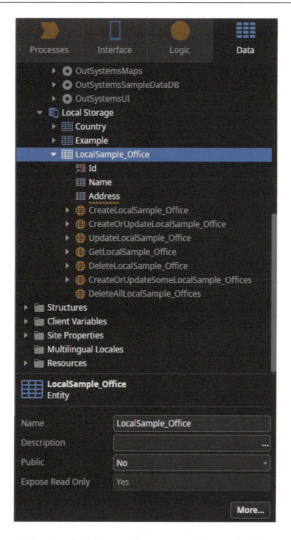

Figure 11.7 – Local Storage entity generated from a database entity

In the *Analysing data syncronization patterns* section, we will see that the entities generated based on database entities allow the execution of accelerators to perform the synchronization between data in the Local Storage and in the server.

A peculiarity regarding Local Storage entities is that, unlike database entities, there is no concept of static entities (but they can still be synchronized – they're transformed to regular entities).

Local Storage entities shouldn't completely mirror the data in a server entity. Keep them to the absolute minimum required (performance advice). Local Storage entities can be used entirely on their own too (without any kind of server replica scenario, as standalone).

Now that we understand how we can create our entities in Local Storage we have to understand how we can get the data from these entities to use them in our applications. And we'll see that it's not that different from the way we get data from the database in the next section!

Fetching data from Local Storage

Since we're going to talk about aggregates, let's start by reviewing the definition.

An aggregate is a visual element of the OutSystems language that allows querying entity data. In an aggregate, you can define source entities, filter data, or sort data as needed.

We can visually fetch data from Local Storage using aggregates, just as we do when fetching data from the database. In fact, they are pretty much defined the same way.

The three tabs at the top of the editor allow us to add different data sources, create filters, and define the sorting:

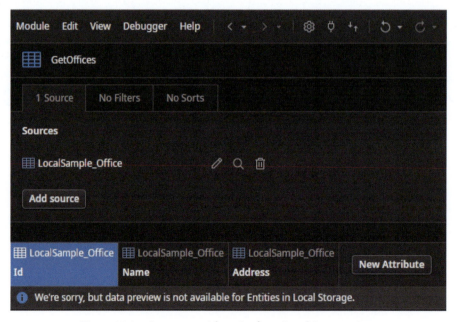

Figure 11.8 – Aggregate with entity from Local Storage view

The first major difference about database aggregates that we can see is that they don't have test values or a data visualization. Since the data is not on the server, aggregates cannot view data directly from the device or use test values, even if the aggregate uses any variables. Keep in mind that there is Local Storage on each of your mobile devices.

The **Sources** section determines the source from which data is retrieved. We can add one or more Local Storage entities as a source and joins between source entities can also be added normally (we need to take into consideration that the "cost" of doing joins in local entities is very high in terms of performance).

> **Note**
>
> An aggregate does not allow mixing Local Storage entities and database entities in its source section.

The **Filter** section allows us to define one or more conditions to filter the aggregate output. To define the filters, we can use the attributes of the Local Storage entities defined as sources, as well as the logical operators or built-in functions that the platform provides:

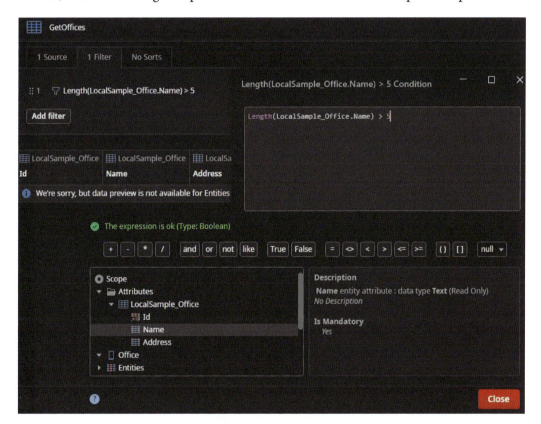

Figure 11.9 – Filter functionality in aggregates with entities from Local Storage

The **Sorting** section allows you to define one or more attributes to sort the query results, in ascending or descending order.

The order of attributes in this section influences the output, with the first being the main sorting criteria and the others being used as tiebreakers:

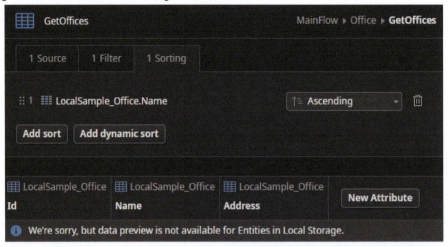

Figure 11.10 – Sorting functionality in aggregates with entities from Local Storage

Local storage aggregates also allow calculated attributes. As with any other aggregate, these calculated attributes can be created through expressions, which have access to all attributes in the source Local Storage entities, as well as OutSystems built-in functions and variables accessible through the aggregates. A calculated attribute creates a new column in the aggregate output:

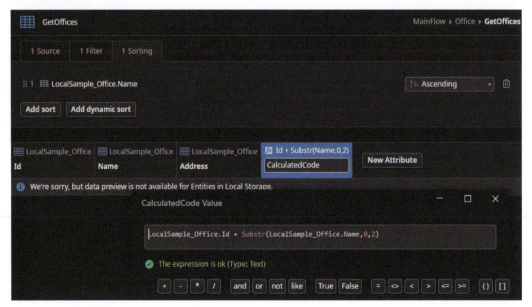

Figure 11.11 – Calculated attribute in aggregates with entities from Local Storage

There is also support for aggregating records, such as grouping multiple rows, or using aggregation functions such as sum or average. When we are aggregating records, only the aggregated columns will be part of the output.

On a mobile application screen, we can also define aggregates to fetch data from Local Storage and make the data available in the screen's scope.

> **Note**
>
> These aggregates cannot be used within data actions, since data actions are executed as server-side code.

Local Storage aggregates can also be used in client actions, either in the scope of a screen or in a global client action. They are defined in the same way as any other aggregate after being added to the action stream:

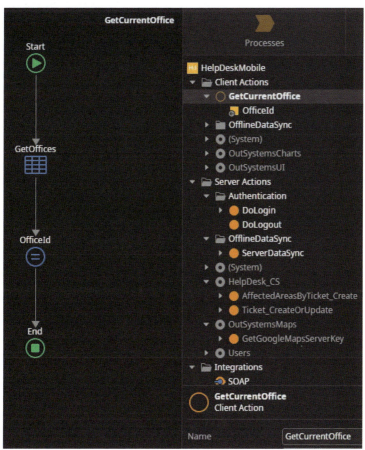

Figure 11.12 – Aggregates with entities from Local Storage used in Client Action

Widgets can be linked to data fetched from Local Storage. This can be done using the widget's source property so that when the widget is rendered, it will know what data will be displayed:

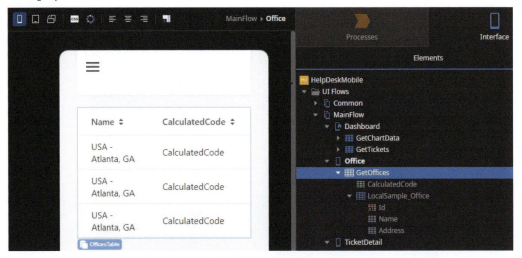

Figure 11.13 – Table widget linked with aggregate fetched from Local Storage

As we can see, fetching data from Local Storage is similar to fetching data from a database, with aggregates being defined in the same way.

In many cases, data present in Local Storage entities must conform to existing data in database entities. That is, there is a need to synchronize all this data. The platform offers a set of patterns for us to take full advantage of the data synchronization functionality, based on a set of criteria. Curious? Let's analyze this topic in the next section!

Analyzing data synchronization patterns

One of the capabilities that allow mobile applications to be quite functional is the fact that they allow data synchronization between the database and Local Storage These scenarios are very useful in contexts where applications work offline and data needs to be synchronized on both sides.

For this, OutSystems designed five synchronization patterns:

- **Read-Only data** – This pattern is useful for applications that only need to read data offline and the volume of data to transact between the database and Local Storage is low. This pattern is based on the principle of deleting all existing data on the Local Storage side, retrieving the data from the database, and creating it again on the Local Storage. An action for synchronizing Local Storage entities generated from database entities can be created automatically:

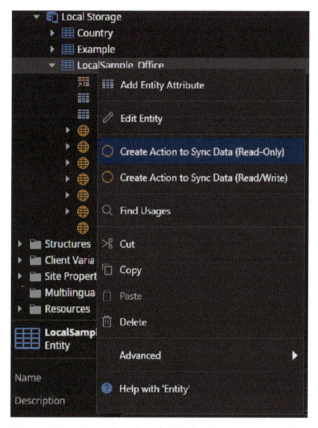

Figure 11.14 – Sync data (Read-Only) action autogeneration

- **Read-Only data optimized** – This pattern is useful when the mobile application needs to work offline and requires synchronization just to get data from the database to update Local Storage, but this time with a large volume of data. For this, the method is to save the data that was referenced when the last synchronization was done (we need to create an entity in Local Storage to manage this) and only carry out the processing of records modified, created, or deleted after the last synchronization. Here is an example:

This sample defines a database entity, **Company**, and its Local Storage counterpart, **LocalCompany**. Additionally, the **SyncProperties** Local Storage entity keeps the date and time of the last synchronization:

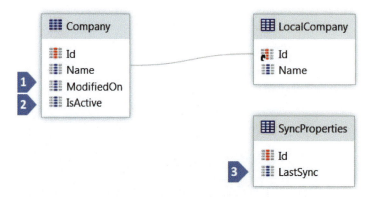

Figure 11.15 – Sync data (Read-Only) data model example

These are the steps we must follow to successfully carry out this synchronization model:

1. Track changed records by storing the timestamp of when the record was last updated or created.

2. Track deleted records.

3. Timestamp of the last synchronization. Note that this timestamp is established by the server to avoid problems due to clock differences between the client and server.

4. The application logic must keep the **ModifiedOn** and **IsActive** entity attributesupdated (marked as 1 and 2).

The following is a description of the logic of the **OfflineDataSync** client action:

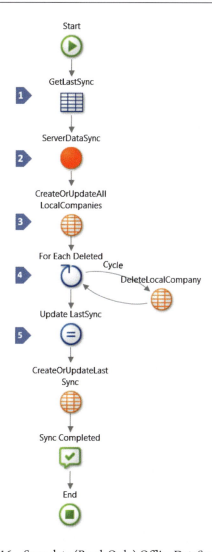

Figure 11.16 – Sync data (Read-Only) OfflineDataSync example

These are the steps we must follow to successfully carry out this synchronization model:

1. Obtain the timestamp of the last synchronization.

2. Call the **ServerDataSync** server action to retrieve data from the database that changed since the last synchronization. The server returns a list of changed or added Company records, a list of deleted (inactive) Company records, and the timestamp of this synchronization.

3. Update the Company records in the Local Storage using the list of changed or added records returned by the server.

4. Iterate the list of deleted (inactive) Company records returned by the server and delete the corresponding records in the Local Storage.

5. Update the entity attribute **SyncProperties.LastSync** with the timestamp of this synchronization returned by the server.

The following is a description of the logic of the **ServerDataSync** server action:

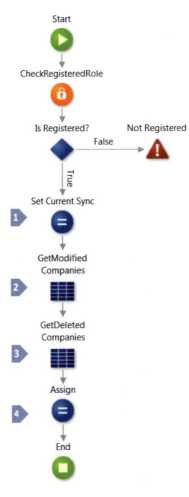

Figure 11.17 – Sync data (Read-Only) server DataSync example

These are the steps we must follow to successfully carry out this synchronization model:

6. Assign the timestamp of this synchronization to an output parameter.

7. Obtains the list of changed or added Company records since the last synchronization. The aggregate uses the following filter:

8. `Company.IsActive = True and (Company.ModifiedOn = NullDate() or Company.ModifiedOn >= LastSync)`

9. Obtain the list of all deleted (inactive) Company records since the last synchronization. The aggregate uses the following filter:

10. `Company.IsActive = False and (Company.ModifiedOn = NullDate() or Company.ModifiedOn >= LastSync)`

11. Assign the timestamp and the two lists of Company records to the output parameters of the action.

- **Read/Write Data Last Write Wins** – This pattern is typically used where it is unlikely that multiple end users will change the same data while applications are offline. The database contains the main data that can change over time and the **Local Storage** contains a subset of the main data and can be modified. Synchronization sends the modified data on **Local Storage** entities to the database and vice versa. On the server, data is updated in a "last write wins" strategy. That is, the latest data update replaces previous updates. An action for synchronizing **Local Storage** entities generated from database entities can be created automatically:

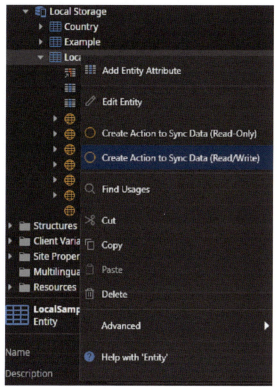

Figure 11.18 – Sync data (Read/Write) action autogeneration

Here is an example:

To automatically generate the logic needed to implement this pattern for an entity, follow these steps:

1. In Service Studio, open the **Data** tab.

2. Under **Local Storage**, select the local entity of the entity you want to synchronize with the server.

3. Right-click on the local entity and choose the **Create Action to Sync Data (Read/Write)** option (as in *Figure 11.18*).

4. This option is only available if the local entity is linked to the database entity (with the ID as a foreign key to the database entity). That happens if you create local entities with a right-click on **Local Storage** and choose **Add Entity from Database**.

This creates the actions needed to implement the Read/Write synchronization pattern:

- **SyncLocal<Entity>** – A client action that starts the synchronization between the local entity and the entity in the server database. It sends the added, changed, and deleted local records to the `Sync<Entity>` server action that handles the synchronization of the entity on the server side.

- **Sync<Entity>** – A server action called by the `SyncLocal<Entity>` action, which synchronizes the received local entity records with the server database records. It returns the current records of the entity in the database to be updated in the client's Local Storage.

Along with these actions, the new `IsFromServer`, `IsModified`, and `IsActive` attributes are added to the local entity to track changes and store meta-information needed by the synchronization process. To keep these new attributes updated and coherent for the synchronization process, the accelerator creates new client actions that must replace the use of the default local entity actions of the local entity:

- `CreateOrUpdateLocal<entity>ForSync` – Replaces the `CreateOrUpdateLocal<entity>` client action

- `DeleteLocal<entity>ForSync` – Replaces the `DeleteLocal<entity>` client action

- `UpdateLocal<entity>ForSync` – Replaces the `UpdateLocal<entity>` client action

These client actions are created in the **Logic** tab, under **Client Actions**,
`SyncActions_Local<entity>`.

To guarantee the success of the synchronization process when using this
accelerator, you must replace the use of all entity actions of the local entity with the
corresponding new actions created by the accelerator.

If you want this pattern to run in the synchronization template mechanism,
add a call to the `SyncLocal<entity>` client action in the `OfflineDataSync`
client action.

This example defines a database entity, **Company**, and its Local Storage counterpart,
LocalCompany. Additionally, the **LocalCompany** entity defines three metadata
attributes to keep track of the synchronization status of the records.

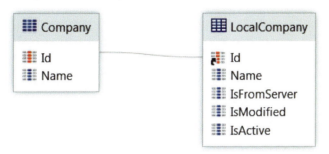

Figure 11.19 – Sync data (Read/Write) data model example

The application logic must update the `IsFromServer`, `IsModified`, and
`IsActive` metadata attributes of the local entity according to the following:

- `IsFromServer`: If `True`, the record exists on the server.

- `IsModified`: If `True`, the record has been modified locally.

- `IsActive`: If `False`, the record was deleted locally but may not yet have been
  removed from the server.

The following is a description of the logic of the `OfflineDataSync` client action:

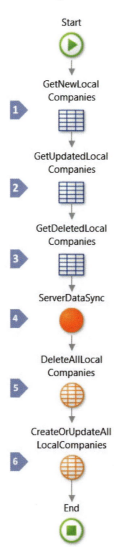

Figure 11.20 – Sync data (Read/Write) offline DataSync example

These are the steps we must follow to successfully carry out this synchronization model:

1. Obtain the list of locally added Company records. The aggregate uses the following filter:

2. `LocalCompany.IsFromServer = False and LocalCompany.IsActive = True`

3. Obtain the list of locally updated Company records. The aggregate uses the following filter:

4. `LocalCompany.IsModified = True and LocalCompany.IsFromServer = True and LocalCompany.IsActive = True`

5. Obtain the list of locally deleted (inactive) Company records. The aggregate uses the following filter:

6. `LocalCompany.IsActive = False and LocalCompany.IsFromServer = True`

7. Call the `ServerDataSync` server action with the lists of locally added, updated, and deleted Company records as inputs. The server updates the data in the database and returns the list of updated Company records.

8. Delete all Company records in the Local Storage.

9. Recreate the Company records in the Local Storage using the list of records returned by the server.

The following is a description of the logic of the `ServerDataSync` server action:

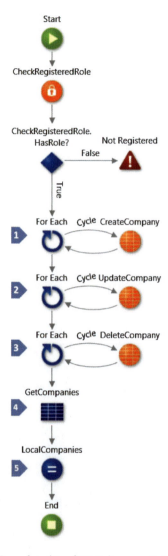

Figure 11.21 – Sync data (Read/Write) server DataSync example

- **Read/Write Data with Conflict Detection** – This pattern is typically used where there is a likelihood that multiple end users will change the same data while applications are offline. The database contains the main data that can change over time and the Local Storage contains a subset of the main data and can be modified. Synchronization sends the modified data on Local Storage entities to the database and vice versa. On the server, the data is updated and if conflicts are detected, they are marked for future resolution.

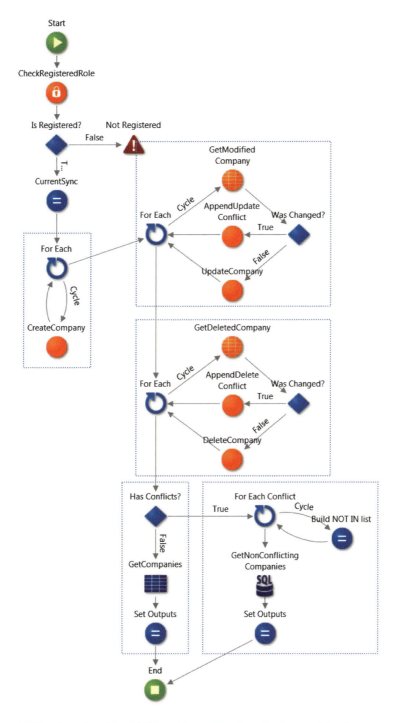

Figure 11.22 – Sync data (Read/Write with conflict detection) server DataSync example

- **Read/Write Data One-to-Many** – This pattern is typically used with data models where "one-to-many" relationships exist and where multiple end users are unlikely to change the same data while applications are offline. The database contains the core data that can change over time and the Local Storage contains a subset of the core data and can be modified. Synchronization sends the modified data in Local Storage entities to the database and vice versa. On the server, data is updated in a **last write wins** strategy. That is, the latest data update replaces previous updates:

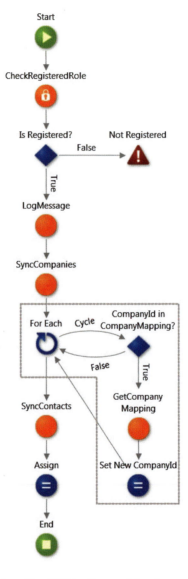

Figure 11.23 – Sync data (Read/Write One-to-Many) server DataSync example

> **Tip**
> You can see more details about data synchronization patterns at the following link: `https://success.outsystems.com/Documentation/11/Developing_an_Application/Use_Data/Offline/Offline_Data_Sync_Patterns`.

The best way to internalize these concepts is to see how they are actually used. OutSystems makes available on the Forge examples of the implementation of all patterns identified in this section. You can download the application here: `https://www.outsystems.com/forge/component-overview/1638/offline-data-sync-patterns`.

In a general context, patterns can be customized to suit business and user needs. We can see these patterns as accelerating templates and as being the best algorithms for most real cases, but at any time, we can create our own patterns if warranted. This functionality guarantees much more cohesive and satisfactory behavior in offline scenarios, which are frequent on mobile devices.

Summary

In this chapter, we understood what Local Storage entities are, and saw that the way they are created and manipulated is not that different from database entities. Furthermore, we realized that we can create them as replicas of existing ones in the database, thus also allowing us to speed up the creation of synchronization mechanisms between them.

We also learned how to obtain data from these entities for our applications and that we cannot mix Local Storage entities with database entities.

Finally, we understood the fundamentals of the most common data synchronization patterns between Local Storage and the database, and that `OfflineDataSync` ensures the functioning of offline mobile applications in a much more cohesive and satisfying way.

In the next chapter, we're going to shift our focus a bit. Let's think more about the frontend at the UX/UI level and how we can make our applications more attractive by using style guides! Curious? So, let's turn the page!

12
Debugging and Troubleshooting Mobile and Reactive Web Apps

Often, despite the OutSystems platform aiding in the reduction of errors, we get unexpected behaviors in our applications and we need to find out what is going wrong.

Applications are composed of client-side code and server-side code, and in the case of anomalous behavior or errors at runtime, we may need to troubleshoot one or both contexts.

To perform this analysis, we can analyze logs in Service Center and use the debugger in Service Studio or use browser tools.

In order to allow a solid understanding of these topics, this chapter is divided into the following sections:

- Debugging reactive web applications
- Debugging native mobile applications
- Using Service Center logs to support troubleshooting

By the end of this chapter, we should be able to analyze the behavior of our applications in real time through the debugger, as well as understanding the error logs in Service Center and how to support debugging in order to be more precise in using the debugger.

Now, to better understand how all this works, let's start with debugging reactive web applications.

Debugging reactive web applications

Debugging in our applications consists of pausing the application's execution at breakpoints that we define at specific points, allowing it to run later step by step and with data visualization in use.

But what is a **breakpoint**?

A breakpoint is a flag that is added to the stream we want to analyze that, when the debugger is running, stops the stream at that same point. We can see it as a traffic light that gives the order to stop.

These breakpoints can be added to any element of our flows.

To add or remove a breakpoint, we first right-click on that element in the module tree. Then, select the **Add Breakpoint** or **Remove Breakpoint** option from the context menu, as shown in *Figure 12.1*:

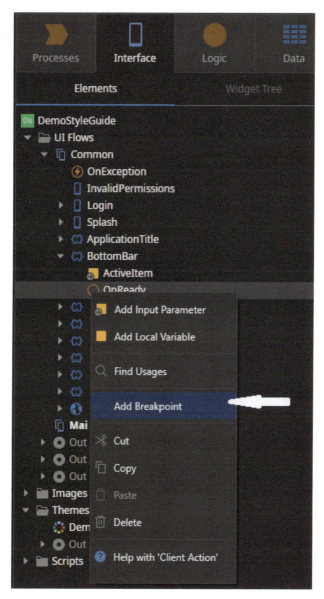

Figure 12.1 – Adding a breakpoint in the module tree

We can also add a breakpoint in the element itself; just right-click on it and select the **Add Breakpoint** option, as shown in *Figure 12.2*:

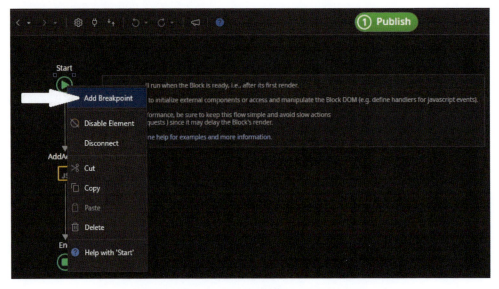

Figure 12.2 – Adding a breakpoint in the element

Or, click on the element to select it and press *F8*. This shortcut toggles between adding and removing a breakpoint.

The element where the breakpoint was set will show a small red circle:

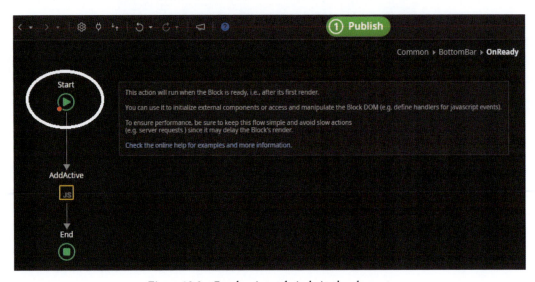

Figure 12.3 – Breakpoint red circle in the element

We can remove a breakpoint in a given element by right-clicking on it and selecting the **Remove Breakpoint** option, as shown in *Figure 12.4*:

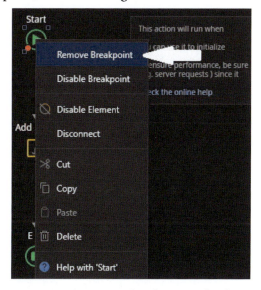

Figure 12.4 – Removing a breakpoint in the element

You can remove all breakpoints at once by selecting the **Remove All Breakpoints** option from the **Debugger** menu, as shown in *Figure 12.5*:

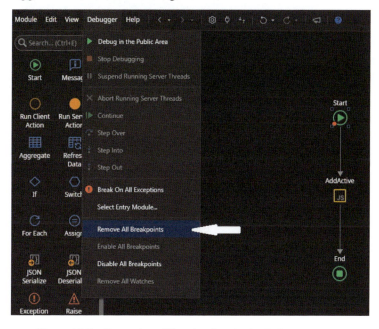

Figure 12.5 – Removing all breakpoints in the Debugger menu

More than adding or removing breakpoints, we can also disable them without removing them.

To temporarily disable a breakpoint without removing it, do the following:

- Right-click on the element (on the canvas or in the module tree) and select the **Disable Breakpoint** option from the context menu:

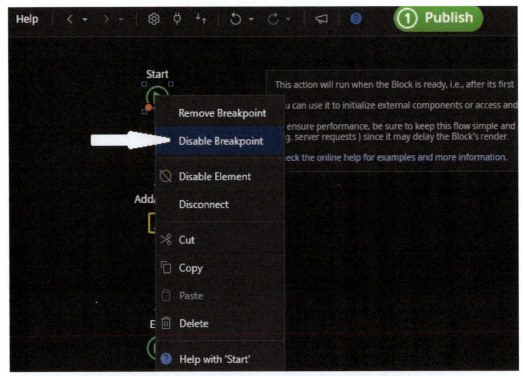

Figure 12.6 – Disabling a breakpoint in the element

- Or, click on the element to select it and press *Ctrl + F8*. This shortcut toggles between enabling and disabling the breakpoint.

The element where the breakpoint was disabled will show an empty red circle.

Follow the same procedure to reactivate a breakpoint, selecting the **Enable Breakpoint** option.

You can also disable all breakpoints at once by selecting the **Disable All Breakpoints** option from the **Debugger** menu or from the context menu displayed by right-clicking anywhere in the **Breakpoints** tab area:

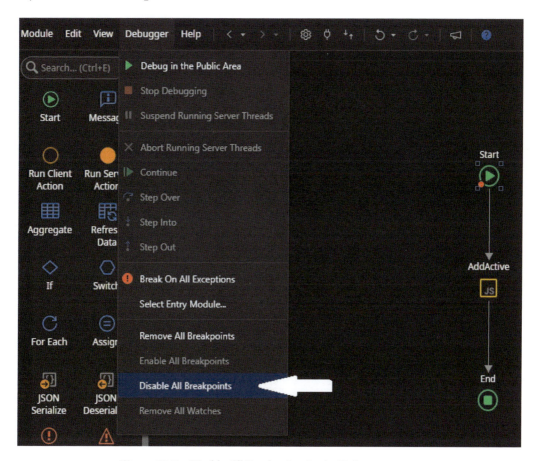

Figure 12.7 – Disable All Breakpoints in the Debugger menu

From here, we can prepare the start of our debug session.

To facilitate and enhance the tool, Service Studio provides a tab that shows us the variables and values at runtime.

In addition, it also transmits the current debug context to us, such as current thread, event name, action UI flow, and screen (the latter two when applicable. We may be debugging a Server Action, a Service Action, or a general Client Action and in this context, there is no screen or UI flow):

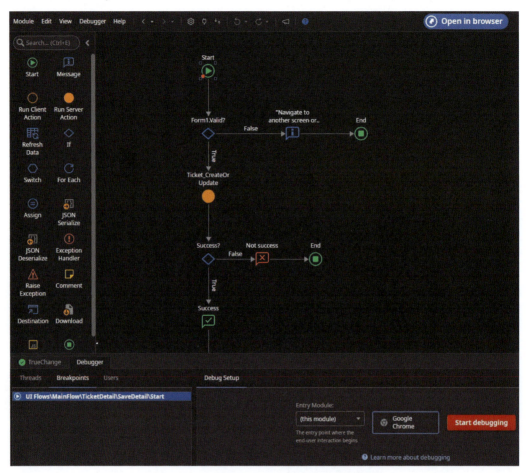

Figure 12.8 – Debug tab before starting debugging

To debug your application, click the **1-Click Publish** button to save the latest changes to the module before debugging. Then, set one or more breakpoints in the module you are debugging.

Start the debugger by clicking the **Start Debugging** button on the **Debugger** tab or by selecting **Debug** from the public area from the **Debugger** menu:

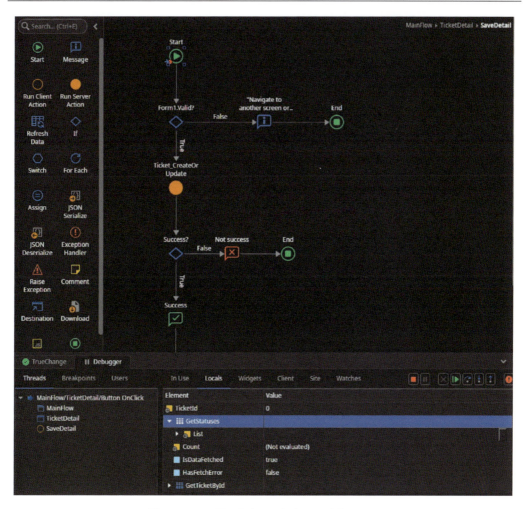

Figure 12.9 – The Debug tab during debugging

Service Studio will open a new browser window with your instance.

Access your application's functionality up to the point where the execution hits a breakpoint and is suspended.

When switching to the Service Studio window, the stream or canvas containing the element with the breakpoint is displayed on the canvas. Service Studio selects the element with the breakpoint and marks it with the debug icon.

The execution context is shown in the **Threads** tab of the **Debugger** tab, marked with the current thread icon of the current thread, showing the current execution stack of the module's elements. The **Debugger** tab also shows additional information that you can explore.

After analyzing the runtime values at this runtime point, you can continue running the application.

Select one of the available commands to advance the execution of the application logic:

- **Continue**: Resumes the execution and leaves the debugger for the current iteration
- **Step Over**: Goes to the next element in the same flow
- **Step Into**: Goes to the next element inside the current element, such as entering each assign inside an Assign node
- **Step Out**: Goes to the execution trace in the next element in the main level (as shown in *Figure 12.10*)

The execution point advances according to the executed command.

Right-click on an element on the screen (or in the module tree) and select the **Continue To Here** option from the context menu. Execution continues until it reaches that element on the screen.

Figure 12.10 – Debugging commands in the Debug tab

In some scenarios, you need to debug some functionality exposed by another module (called a producer module). In these cases, we must select the input module for the respective Action as the final module where the user has contact with the application (frontend module):

Figure 12.11 – Entry module selection in the Debug tab

This is true for consumers who run the same transactions as producers.

If the producers run in independent transactions, such as Service Actions and REST APIs, we must activate the debugger in both modules, and in the producer module, the entry module must be itself (**this module**).

This is because they are transactions that take place in their own context (as explained in *Chapter 6, Server-Side Logic*).

> **Tip**
>
> Also, there is another interesting scenario. Sometimes we need to debug deeper, going beyond the two layers. If the producer module is not being referenced in some way by the final consumer module, we can, through Manage Dependencies, add any reference (it will be something dummy) for the producer module in the consumer module and publish it. From there, in the dropdown for selecting the entry module in the producer module, the intended consumer module will appear.
>
> ATTENTION: When it is no longer necessary, we must remove the dependency of the producer module on the consumer module! You can see more details about debugging producer modules here: `https://success.outsystems.com/Documentation/11/Developing_an_Application/Troubleshooting_Applications/Debugging_Applications/Debugging_Producer_Modules`.

Through this powerful feature, we can detect unwanted behaviors or harmful trends in our code, allowing us to visualize everything that happens in real time.

As expected (and you probably already understand), the OutSystems platform has great standardization between the reactive web and mobile paradigms, and debugging is no different.

So, how do you debug a mobile application? It's not very different and we'll see it in the next section!

Debugging native mobile applications

As we mentioned before, the debug method in the mobile paradigm is not very different from the reactive web paradigm.

Thus, and in order to simplify the transfer of knowledge, in this section, we will focus on the differences compared to what we saw in the previous section.

Basically, we can debug mobile applications in two ways:

- **Emulate the mobile app using the Google Chrome browser on your PC**: Use the Chrome browser on your PC to debug your mobile app if you don't need to execute native plugins, as the native plugins can't run on PC. This option is very good to test the logic of the app. However, to check the performance or experience of the mobile app, test your app on a mobile device.

  NOTE: Don't forget that if your application depends on native Cordova plugins, you won't be able to test in the web context.

- **Install the mobile app on a device**: We can test the mobile app directly on a device as our users would run it. It's the best place to test the performance and experience of your app. You can do it on iOS or Android. Generate the native app package for your app in Service Studio using the **Debug** (for Android) or **Development** (for iOS) build type, install it on the device, and follow the next steps:

These are the steps to allow your **iOS** device to debug your application:

I.   Install iTunes on your PC (needs to be iMac).

II.   On your device, turn **Web Inspector** on.

III.   Connect your device through a USB cable to your PC.

IV.   On your iOS device, allow the PC to debug.

These are the steps to allow your **Android** device to debug your application:

I.   Turn USB debugging on your Android device.

II.   Use a USB cable to connect your device to the PC.

III.   Allow the PC to debug the device.

To debug, the tab will present three different options: **Emulate using Chrome**, **Android device**, and **iOS device**. Just choose what you want and click on the **Start debugging** button:

Figure 12.12 – Debug tab for mobile modules

With this knowledge, it becomes much simpler and faster to get the best behavior from our applications, improve the user experience, and fix bugs.

But how do we find the right place to debug and create our breakpoints? Is there any way to get this information in order to speed up the discovery process?

Yes, we can check the error logs in Service Center, which often gives us an indication of where we got the errors and their characteristics. We'll find out how to do this in the next section.

Using Service Center logs to support troubleshooting

We can often get errors and we don't quite know where they occur or where to start investigating.

A very interesting way to have something to start with and be more effective and quicker to find out where the errors are is through the logs generated automatically by the platform.

Remember in *Chapter 7, Exceptions Handling*, we talked about exception handlers? Well, it is at this point that we thank them for their existence, as if they have the option of **Log Error** as `Yes` it will allow us to obtain the error information.

> **Tip**
> These errors are caught in the debugger when the flow enters the exception handler and exits the predicted flow. By default, these errors enter the most appropriate exception handler with their context. For example, an error caused by writing to the database is caught in the exception handler dedicated to database exceptions. If it does not exist explicitly, the error is handled by all exceptions.

In order to access the error log, access Service Center via the `*yourenvironment*/`
`ServiceCenter` URL and click on the **Monitoring** menu and then the **Errors** tab:

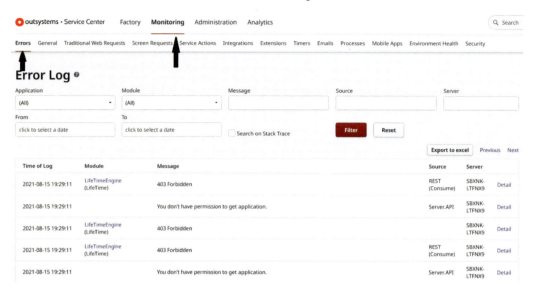

Figure 12.13 – Errors screen in Service Center

In the list of errors that is presented to us, we have already managed to obtain some
context for each of the errors logged. However, if we click on the **Detail** link for the error
we intend to inspect, we are redirected to a page with much more detail about it:

Time of Log	Module	Message	Source	Server	
2021-08-15 19:29:11	LifeTimeEngine (LifeTime)	403 Forbidden	REST (Consume)	SBXNK-LTFNX9	Detail
2021-08-15 19:29:11		You don't have permission to get application.	Server.API	SBXNK-LTFNX9	Detail

Figure 12.14 – Link to error log details

On the details page, we can get very relevant information about the error:

- **Id**: Log identifier
- **Time of Log**: Date and time of log registration (in the time zone of the database server)
- **Request Key**: Key used to make the log request
- **Module**: The name of the module that requested writing the error (that is, where the error was handled)
- **Tenant**: The tenant of the module that generated the error

- **User**: Registered user in session (if any)

- **Session Id**: ID of the session in effect when writing the error

- **Server**: Server where the error occurred

- **Source**: Source of the error

- **Message**: Message generated by the exception when the error occurred

- **Environment Information**: Data obtained from the environment at the time of the error

- **Stack**: Shows the entire code that ran at the time the error was triggered, always in hierarchical order from the highest point of the call (for example, the Action triggered on a screen) to the lowest (for example, a failed attempt to perform a update of a record in the database).

Through this data, it becomes much easier to see where the error occurred.

In fact, an useful tip is to understand well the information that appears in the **Stack** field, since there you can often understand or infer the path followed to the very place where the error was generated.

Also, the **Message** field often conveys a lot of valuable information about the problem.

Error detail

Back to Log

Id	0417afc1-6221-4dc5-9348-034a9acecceb
Time of Log	2021-10-01 02:27:32
Request Key	90059f2d-cf99-439f-8171-b0d2a0c89500
Module	LifeTimeEngine
Tenant	ServiceCenter
User	PlatformServices (3)
Session Id	JCMfqr6CBUKEUiabxDGWwQ==
Server	SCPI1-LTGS8R
Source	REST (Consume)
Message	**403 Forbidden**
Environment Information	eSpaceVer: Id=154, PubId=0, CompiledWith=11.13.0.31107 RequestUrl: http://cipfsm022.outsystemscloud.com/LifeTimeEngine/_ActivityHandler.asmx (Method: POST) AppDomain: /LM/W3SVC/25/ROOT/LifeTimeEngine-20-132739736610800930 FilePath: C:\OutSystems\Sandboxes\CIPFSM022\Platform Server\running\LifeTimeEngine\ ClientIp: 127.0.0.1 Locale: DateFormat: yyyy-MM-dd PID: 27724 ('w3wp', Started='8/20/2021 9:52:32 PM', Priv=1042Mb, Virt=2116176Mb) TID: 168 Thread Name: .NET: 4.0.30319.42000
Stack	403 Forbidden at ssLifeTimeCore.CcServer_API.ActionGetApplicationConfig(HeContext heContext, ICcServer_APICallbacks ConfigurationStructure& outParamResponse)

Figure 12.15 – Error log detail example

In addition to the error log, we can rely on other types of logs to inspect unwanted application behavior.

For this, we can access any of the other tabs in the **Monitoring** section of Service Center, namely the following:

- **Errors**: What we've seen so far.

- **General**: In this section, the logs that are created by the **LogMessage** action, or those of a more general character, such as slow queries, are presented.

- **Screen requests**: Here, logs regarding the response times to requests from reactive web and mobile applications are presented. With this, we can understand that screens or sections of our applications are taking longer to be processed, allowing us to come up with improvements.

- **Service actions**: This screen provides information about the execution of Service Actions, such as the time taken to run. The amount of information depends on the logging level of the module where the respective Service Action exists.

- **Integrations**: Here, we can see information regarding the runtimes and payloads of our integrations, such as SAP, REST, or SOAP integrations.

- **Extensions**: In this section, all extension actions that run during a request, the caller module, and how long the extension action took to reply are presented.

- **Timers**: This screen shows information regarding the execution of the existing timers in our applications. Here we can see when they ran, when they were planned to run, how long it took them to run, and when they are expected to run again.

- **Emails**: In this section, we can see the emails that were sent, their status (successful, error, or pending), and, if they are configured to log content, we can also access the email itself.

- **Processes**: This screen displays the number of currently active, suspended, and closed instances for each business process. It also shows the number of instances with errors.

- **Mobile Apps**: This screen displays the list of mobile app packages requested per application, including the native platform for which the package was generated and the status.

> **Tip**
>
> You can see more details about the module logging level here: `https://success.outsystems.com/Documentation/11/Developing_an_Application/Troubleshooting_Applications/Troubleshoot_Service_Actions_Using_Logs#how-to-change-the-logging-detail-level-for-service-action`.

As we can see, Service Center provides a lot of information that allows us to be more effective and accurate when it comes to correcting errors and anomalous behavior of our applications. With this, we were able to save a lot of time when choosing the correct place to add breakpoints for debugging, and it is often even possible to correct the error without having to resort to this tool (if the log is very specific and we have a lot of context about the code where the failure occurs).

Furthermore, we can use the **LogMessage** System Action (just add it as a dependency in the **Manage Dependencies** window) and place it wherever we want in our flow (we can also place it in the exception handling flow) and customize the message that we want to appear, as well as textually defining the module where it occurs.

Summary

In this chapter, we saw that the OutSystems platform provides us with a very powerful feature to handle errors and unwanted behavior in our applications: the debugger. We learned how to use it and got to know its artifacts.

In addition, we learned about its context in reactive web applications and what the small differences in mobile are.

Finally, we realized how we can rely on existing logs in Service Center to better interpret and understand the errors and behaviors of applications in order to be more effective and faster when debugging.

The development of applications may not be, many times, a paradise, but with this knowledge, our work is much easier and going through difficult times is more comfortable.

At this point, we can already look ahead and think about how we can take all this knowledge further and try to figure out how we can extend our platform and how we can design our application architectures to make the most of what we've learned.

Well, we'll cover that in the next chapter, where we'll talk about how to design a well-performing, secure, and scalable architecture for our applications.

Let's talk about the importance of good architecture, in the Architecture Canvas (3 Layer Canvas), the design process, and the types of elements that exist in each of the types of modules. For this, we will rely on information already mentioned in *Chapter 4, Using Your Modules to Simplify and Encapsulate Your Code*, since the following chapter (*Chapter 13, Designing the Architecture of Your OutSystems Applications*) is a complement to it.

You're certainly excited, so let's turn the page to the next chapter!

Section 4: Extensibility and Complexity of the OutSystems Platform

In this section, we will explain how we can extend the platform in order to connect with other systems, how to implement native C#/. NET code, and how we can solve high complexity cases using OutSystems tools out of the box, proving that it is a complete tool and adaptable for the future.

This section comprises the following chapters:

- *Chapter 13, Designing the Architecture of Your OutSystems Applications*
- *Chapter 14, Integrating OutSystems with Your Ecosystem*
- *Chapter 15, BPT Processes and Timers – Asynchronous Tools in OutSystems*

13
Designing the Architecture of Your OutSystems Applications

In this chapter, we will understand how we should segment and lay out our modules and applications at the architecture level in order to allow for scalability, robustness, and security.

We will focus on the best practices and standards advised by OutSystems in order to understand the standard and regularly used model. This does not mean that in our professional careers there are no variant cases, but we must always consider the trade-off and the context scenario.

In this chapter, we will complement the information already explained in *Chapter 4, Using Your Modules to Simplify and Encapsulate Your Code*, and we can see this chapter as an extension of that one.

In order to better understand this topic, the chapter is divided into the following sections:

- The importance of architecture
- The 3 Layer Canvas (Architecture Canvas)
- The architecture design process

By the end of this chapter, we should be able to understand why we should design a good architecture before starting to develop code and that architecture is not immutable during its life cycle. We'll also learn how to distribute our modules across Architecture Canvas layers and sub-layers and what each layer is used for.

Above all, this is an ongoing process, always in constant change. Applications change, new applications appear, others disappear and all this means that we have to constantly adjust the architecture of our software factory.

Excited? Let's get this trip started!

The importance of architecture

First of all, we need to understand why the existence of good architecture is important.

As applications are developed, their size and complexity grow, increasing the design problem and exceeding data structures and algorithms. Therefore, designing an architecture that facilitates the understanding of these components becomes a more-than-necessary path. Bad architecture can also impact performance, lead to life cycle issues, and cause dependency problems, increasing technical debt uncontrollably and potentially leading to more catastrophic scenarios. As with everything in life, no matter how good it is, we have to be smart when using it.

Among the aspects that need to be observed in this process, issues such as communication protocols, feature assignment to certain parts, and the control structure are included.

A clear example can be found in reactive web and mobile OutSystems applications, where a solution needs to rely on several layers to distinguish client-side and server-side components, as well as possible intermediate structures that may exist as needed.

This structuring, despite seeming laborious for professionals not used to it, aims to facilitate the organization of components and improve the flexibility and portability of the system, making maintenance much easier.

Based on these principles, OutSystems created a very solid, robust, and viable architectural model for application development: the Architecture Canvas (often called 3 Layer Canvas or just 3LC).

Furthermore, the method in which strong and weak references are managed between modules and consumed elements allows for very controlled flexibility and helps to reduce technical debt.

> **Tip**
>
> You can see more details about technical debt here: `https://www.outsystems.com/blog/posts/technical-debt/`.

So, what is the Architecture Canvas model all about? How is it divided? What are layers and sub-layers used for? Let's analyze this topic in the next section!

The 3 Layer Canvas (Architecture Canvas)

The Architecture Canvas is the tool that allows us to streamline and easily create a scalable, robust, and well-performing architecture.

This model is prepared and designed for the most critical scenarios with multiple applications and modules existing in an OutSystems factory.

The Architecture Canvas has layers and sub-layers in its base into which the application context is divided. Each layer and its respective sub-layers will contain applications and modules with different characteristics and types of functionality.

As such, the layers are organized as shown in *Figure 13.1*:

End user Modules	**Services**	**UI and processes** That provide functionality to the end users
Core Modules	**Reusable**	**Business services** Services around business concepts
Foundation Modules	**Services**	**Non-functional requirements** Services to connect to external systems or to extend your framework

Figure 13.1 – Architecture Canvas (3 Layer Canvas) layers

In addition, and in order to make the interpretation and segmentation of the code simpler and more correct, the same layers are divided into sub-layers, allowing a quicker inference of the nature of each module and application. The layers are organized as shown in *Figure 13.2*:

End User	external	Frontend User Interface modules
Core	external	Reusable services around business concepts, exporting Entities, business rules, and web blocks
API	external	Provides APIs to expose Core Services
Core Widgets	external	Core Widgets
Composite Logic	external	Reusable Business Logic or Logic to Synchronize Data
Core Service	external	Reusable Core Service
Foundation	external	Non-Functional requirements or integration modules, reusable in any business context
Style Guide	external	Reusable UI Patterns, themes, and theme templates
Foundation Service	external	Integration services to wrap up external services and services to suport NFRs (e.g. Audit trailing)
Library	external	Reusable libraries and plug-ins

Figure 13.2 – Architecture Canvas (3 Layer Canvas) sub-layers

As we saw in *Chapter 4, Using Your Modules to Simplify and Encapsulate Your Code*, there are certain types of modules that best fit each of the Architecture Canvas layers. As such, for the Foundation Layer, we have the following:

- Library modules
- Extension modules
- Blank modules

For the Core Layer, we have the following:

- Service modules
- Blank modules

For the End User Layer, we have the following:

- Reactive web modules
- Phone app modules

- Tablet app modules
- Blank modules

For more details on each of these types of modules, we can consult the *Applying modules to the correct layers* section in *Chapter 4, Using Your Modules to Simplify and Encapsulate Your Code*.

Taking these layers and their properties into account, we can start thinking about how to design the architecture of our applications.

In the next section, let's see the architecture design process recommended by OutSystems.

The architecture design process

Designing an architecture is a process that must include the following three important steps:

1. **Disclose**: Find out the business concepts of the project and what kind of integrations they need. We must consider the functional and non-functional requirements of the business concepts.

2. **Organize**: Organize and distribute the concepts across the Architecture Canvas layers.

3. **Assemble**: Organize and match these concepts with recommended patterns. We must bear in mind that we must join concepts if they are conceptually related and we must separate them if they have different life cycles and/or are too complex.

At the end of these three steps comes one of the most important phases: iteration. We must iterate this cycle of steps as many times as necessary until we have a solid, understandable, and scalable architecture. Furthermore, we must bear in mind that an architecture is not immutable and we may have to repeat this process even during other phases of the project than the design phase.

One of the processes that we should consider in addition to the creation of modules is how we can organize them at the application level, in other words, in addition to the layer and sub-layer with which each module is concerned, we also have to consider in which applications they should be placed. This is because in a software factory with some complexity, we must consider the issue of reuse and development concepts with which business subjects is concerned.

For this, we must always consider that an application is inserted in the layer of its topmost-level module, as we can see in *Figure 13.3*:

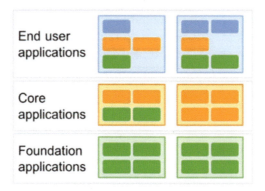

Figure 13.3 – Applications distributed in the Architecture Canvas

The distribution of modules by applications and their insertion in layers must respect three fundamental principles, as we can see in *Figure 13.4*:

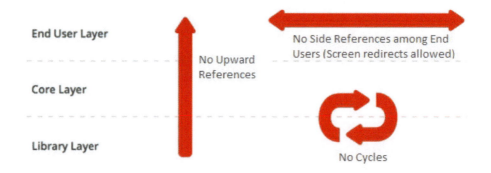

Figure 13.4 – Architecture violations to avoid

These three principles must be taken seriously to ensure that our developments allow us to scale in the future, always with high robustness. They are explained in detail as follows:

- **No upward references**: A module from a lower layer should never reference a module from a higher layer (for example, a module from the Core Layer should not reference an end user module). The same for applications: a lower-layer application must not reference an upper-layer application.

- **No side references among end user modules**: An End User Layer module must not reference another end user module. The only exception is when only screens are referenced. Screens are considered a weak reference, as the only thing referenced in the consumer module is the screen URL of the producer module. The same principle holds true for applications. Applications from the End User Layer must not reference applications from that same layer, even if the module they are consuming is from a lower layer.

- **No cycles**: A consumer module must not simultaneously be a producer module of the module it is consuming. This leads to problems with refreshing dependencies, since whenever you update one of the modules the other will always get outdated and vice versa. The only way to solve this problem is by publishing a solution. If this scenario happens, the concepts shared in the same module should be considered, either in an existing one or in a new module, which may belong to a different sub-layer (it could be a business logic module, `_BL`, an engineering module, `_ENG`, or in the case of synchronization, a `_SYNC` module).

> **Tip**
> You can see more details about these three rules of validating application architecture here: `https://success.outsystems.com/Support/Enterprise_Customers/Maintenance_and_Operations/Designing_the_Architecture_of_Your_OutSystems_Applications/Validating_your_application_architecture`.

Another issue that we should pay attention to is application composition. By this, we mean that it is often not easy to understand when we should divide our applications into smaller ones to ensure the correct reuse of features.

For this, there are four rules that help us obtain the desired results:

- **Correctly layer your modules**: We must place our modules in the correct layer and sub-layer according to the purpose of the code they contain. This helps to ensure the absence of breaches, allowing you to maintain a sustainable architecture.

- **Correctly layer your applications**: We should use the same Architecture Canvas rules and principles that we use in application modules.

- **Don't mix different owners**: If we have applications or modules in which developers of multiple projects work, it becomes difficult to manage the complexity of the requirements, since the life cycles of different projects will probably be different. In this case, developments should be separated into separate modules/applications in order to promote ownership and avoid bottlenecks:

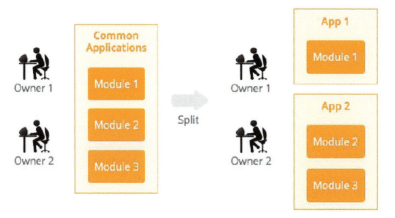

Figure 13.5 – Split application ownership

- **Don't mix different sponsors**: We shouldn't mix different sponsors in the same applications, as the difference in line of business, budget, and requirements can impact everyone else. Applications should be separated by sponsor whenever necessary to avoid collisions or points of indecision, thus ensuring autonomy in the life cycle:

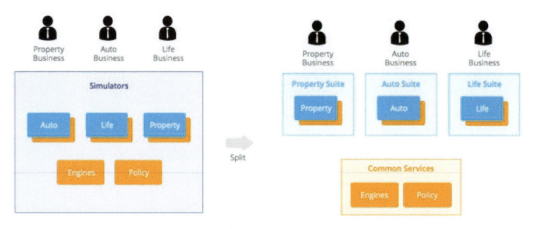

Figure 13.6 – Splitting applications by sponsors

These rules must be applied with care, as misinterpretations of contexts can lead to wrong and painful separations for our developments. We must always keep in mind that the goal is for the architecture to be as sustainable as possible, with great scalability, while maintaining the highest level of performance and security. We must always remember that architecture is an ever-changing concept and we must design it in such a way as to have a heightened capacity to respond to this change.

Sometimes, to meet all these rules, we need to change the application modules; that is, the application to which these modules belong has to be another one. This is normal to ensure the correct applicational and functional layer since, as we mentioned earlier, applications assume the module layer contained in itself with the highest layer.

In order to change the module in Service Studio, we must access the application where the module is and click on the move button, as we can see in *Figure 13.7*:

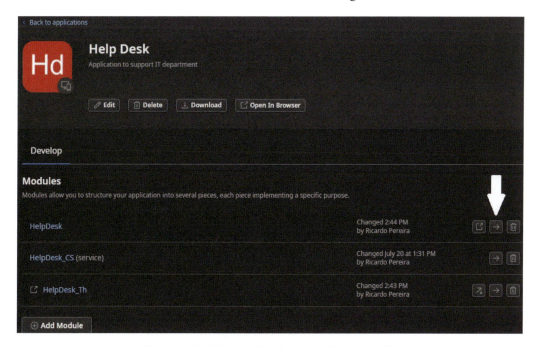

Figure 13.7 – Move module button in Service Studio

We can find more complex cases, such as having to put logic that we have inside a module in a new module of another layer and sub-layer. This happens when the logic does not match the purpose of the module into which it is inserted.

To solve this, we must do the following:

1. Identify the logic to be moved to another module:

Figure 13.8 – Identified logic to move to another module

Basically, we select the logic we want to change modules for and copy it.

2. Create a new module inserted in the desired layer and sub-layer:

Figure 13.9 – Creating a new module in the correct layer

We create a module of the desired type. In this example, as we are talking about service core logic, we create a module of the **Service** type in an application of the Core Layer.

3. Move the identified logic from the current module to the new one:

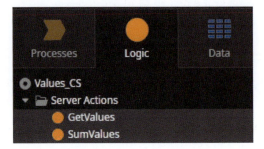

Figure 13.10 – Moving identified logic to the new module

Here, we paste the actions (the logic) that we copied from the original module.

4. Reference the logic required in the original module to the new module:

Figure 13.11 – Reference the logic through the Manage Dependencies window

In the original module, or in any module that needs to consume the actions that migrated to the new module, just open the **Manage Dependencies** window, select the new module, and select the actions in question.

This way, the logic is isolated in a module in the correct layer and sub-layers.

> **Tip**
> You can see more details about designing the architecture of your OutSystems applications here: `https://success.outsystems.com/Support/Enterprise_Customers/Maintenance_and_Operations/Designing_the_Architecture_of_Your_OutSystems_Applications/Validating_your_application_architecture.`

Given the information we've covered throughout this chapter, we can now better understand the effectiveness of applying modules to their correct layer (as we mentioned earlier, you can find more information in *Chapter 4, Using Your Modules to Simplify and Encapsulate Your Code*).

To support us in these journeys, we have three tools that can help us:

- **Electronic Canvas (not officially supported by OutSystems)**: Allows us to build our architecture based on the OutSystems Architecture Canvas in a digital way

> **Tip**
> You can see more details about Electronic Canvas here: `https://www.outsystems.com/forge/component-overview/706/electronic-canvas.`

- **Architecture Dashboard**: Manages OutSystems infrastructure technical debt during every stage of development

> **Tip**
>
> You can see more details about Architecture Dashboard here: `https://success.outsystems.com/Documentation/11/Managing_the_Applications_Lifecycle/Manage_technical_debt`.

- **Discovery**: Visual tool to help analyze, measure, and understand how to improve factory architecture

> **Tip**
>
> You can see more details about Discovery here: `https://www.outsystems.com/forge/component-overview/409/discovery`.

These tools can help us support various tasks in the design, development, and refactoring process of our architectures. In addition to making everything more visual (if it weren't for low code), it allows us to access information that we would otherwise hardly be able to access.

Let's think of developing application solutions as building a house: if the foundations are well made, the house will be more robust and it will be easier to extend it. These principles and rules are the foundations that will guarantee a promising future for our solutions.

Summary

In this chapter, we learned that it is important to design a robust, scalable, performant, and secure application, in order to support the growth of solutions, both in volume and in complexity.

We learned that we can do this by applying an architectural model called the Architecture Canvas (or 3 Layer Canvas), and we examined its layers and sub-layers and what types of modules fit into each of them.

In addition, we analyzed the process of designing an architecture, including its steps (disclose, organize, assemble, and iterate through them as often as necessary) and which rules and principles serve as a foundation for this process. We saw some refactoring techniques to align the architecture with the expected model and mentioned some useful tools for OutSystems architecture support.

But how much further can we go? Now that we have figured out how to build our "home," how far can we go? Can we "stretch" the OutSystems universe beyond what already exists?

Of course! We can use other tools and techniques to do this, and without further ado, we'll see how in the next chapter: *Chapter 14, Integrating OutSystems with Your Ecosystem*!

14
Integrating OutSystems with Your Ecosystem

When we reach an enterprise level, we need to integrate the OutSystems platform with the existing systems in the enterprise ecosystem. For this, we have to resort to different ways of doing it, from connections to web services (REST/SOAP or SAP), connections to external databases, or even, in the case of older legacy systems, through customized C#/.NET extensions. Using the last one, we can also extend features that are not found in OutSystems through native code.

To understand all this, the chapter is divided into the following sections:

- Creating your own C#/.NET code and using it inside the OutSystems platform
- Connecting with external databases
- Connecting with other systems through web services (REST/SOAP)

By the end of this chapter, we should understand how to set up the necessary connections to external systems and how to assess the best way to do this. We should understand the importance of Integration Studio when it comes to connecting to external databases and creating C#/.NET native code.

Furthermore, we must master the basic and simple principles of web services integration directly in Service Studio.

From a description alone, we are already excited! So, let's start by creating our own C#/ .NET code!

Creating your own C#/.NET code and using it inside the OutSystems platform

> **Tip**
> To get the most out of this section, you should have some knowledge of C#/ .NET development, as the intention is to adapt our custom code to be available in OutSystems.

Sometimes, we can come across situations where the external systems we want to connect with only have services that cannot be integrated in OutSystems natively, or we need to integrate a feature of our custom code.

In order for us to create our custom code in C#/.NET, Integration Studio integrates with Visual Studio (Microsoft's IDE). With this, we define our Actions, inputs, and outputs in Integration Studio, before moving on to editing it (developing its content) in Visual Studio.

With this, we can abstract our code into Actions that can be used according to the Service Studio visual model.

This feature allows us to do the following:

- Write our own C# code.
- Reuse all .NET frameworks.
- Reuse all existing libraries.

There is an example of an extension that wraps **AddTimetoDatetime**, which is available in the Forge.

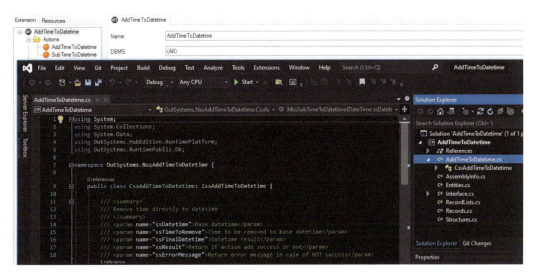

Figure 14.1 – Extension example made with Visual Studio integrated with Integration Studio

The Actions defined in Integration Studio are available for use in Service Studio within the visual paradigm (one of the great definitions of low code), while also acquiring the following capabilities:

- **Exception logging**: Exceptions generated by Actions abstracted in the extension are generated and logged automatically, and can be consulted in the Service Center.

- **Monitoring**: The code is automatically monitored by the platform, and its performance can be analyzed and reports generated for this (Service Center features).

Since we've already done the Integration Studio walk-through in *Chapter 2*, *Components, Tools, and Capabilities*, we'll go on to show you how the **AddTimeToDatetime** extension was created by taking advantage of existing libraries.

First, an extension was created in Service Studio.

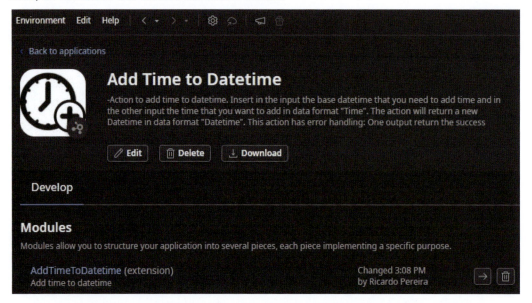

Figure 14.2 – Creating a new extension – AddTimeToDatetime

Then, and after authenticating in Integration Studio, the necessary Actions were created (in the case shown, there are two: adding time and removing time from a **Datetime** variable):

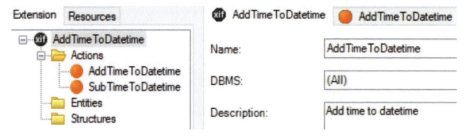

Figure 14.3 – Actions created in the new extension

In the next step, the necessary input and output variables were created (in this case, there are two error-handling variables, `Result` and `ErrorMessage`). In both Actions, the output is a **Datetime** variable resulting from the calculation made in the Action:

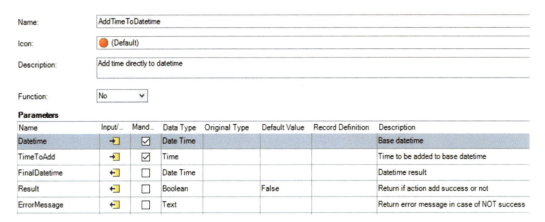

Name:	AddTimeToDatetime						
Icon:	● (Default)						
Description:	Add time directly to datetime						
Function:	No ▾						

Parameters

Name	Input/...	Mand...	Data Type	Original Type	Default Value	Record Definition	Description
Datetime	⊡	☑	Date Time				Base datetime
TimeToAdd	⊡	☑	Time				Time to be added to base datetime
FinalDatetime	⊡	☐	Date Time				Datetime result
Result	⊡	☐	Boolean		False		Return if action add success or not
ErrorMessage	⊡	☐	Text				Return error message in case of NOT success

Figure 14.4 – Variables created in the action

After this parameterization in the two Actions, the button in the upper area of **Edit Source Code .NET** (we can see that button in Figure 14.1, in top right) was pressed to open Visual Studio.

After opening Visual Studio, open the corresponding `.cs` document:

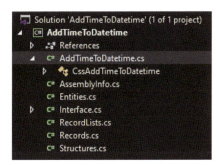

Figure 14.5 – Solution Explorer in Visual Studio

The custom code for the Actions looks like this:

```
public class CssAddTimeToDatetime: IssAddTimeToDatetime {

    /// <summary>
    /// Remove time directly to datetime
    /// </summary>
    /// <param name="ssDatetime">Base datetime</param>
    /// <param name="ssTimeToRemove">Time to be removed to base datetime</param>
    /// <param name="ssFinalDatetime">Datetime result</param>
    /// <param name="ssResult">Return if action add success or not</param>
    /// <param name="ssErrorMessage">Return error message in case of NOT success</param>
    1 reference
    public void MssSubTimeToDatetime(DateTime ssDatetime, DateTime ssTimeToRemove, out DateTime ssFinalDatetime, out bool ssResult, out string ssErrorMessage) {
        ssFinalDatetime = new DateTime(1900, 1, 1, 0, 0, 0);
        ssResult = false;
        ssErrorMessage = "";

        try
        {
            TimeSpan buffer = new TimeSpan(ssTimeToRemove.Hour, ssTimeToRemove.Minute, ssTimeToRemove.Second);
            ssFinalDatetime = ssDatetime.Subtract(buffer);
            ssResult = true;

        }

        catch (Exception ex)
        {
            ssResult = false;
            ssErrorMessage = ex.Message;
        }
    } // MssSubTimeToDatetime
```

Figure 14.6 – Customized code in action

Note the use of `Result` and `ErrorMessage` variables in line with **Try/Catch** so as to allow better tracking and debugging of the functions themselves.

The next step was to build the solution, through the **Build** menu, by selecting the **Build Solution** item.

Finally, in Integration Studio, **Publish** was performed.

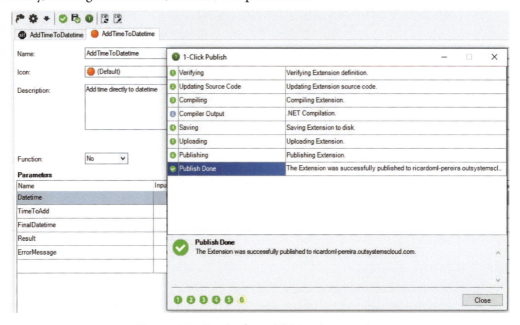

Figure 14.7 – Result after publishing the extension

From this moment on, the Actions are ready to be used in the modules that need their functionalities. Just add the dependency via the **Manage Dependencies** dialog, selecting the extension and the Actions you want.

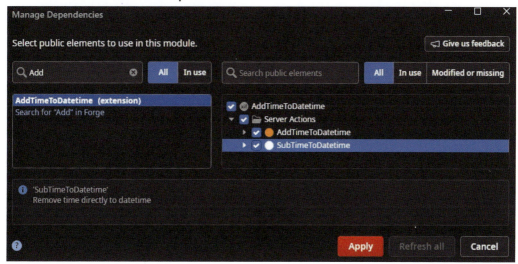

Figure 14.8 – Adding extension Actions as a dependency

> **Tip**
> You can see more details about using C# code here: https://www.
> outsystems.com/training/courses/117/using-c-code/.

As we can see, in addition to the need to have some knowledge of C#/.NET to take full advantage of this ability, the process for taking advantage of it is relatively simple and can be achieved with practice.

Another of the uses that Integration Studio has, in partnership with the Service Center, is the creation of links to external databases.

Curious? Well, let's read about it in the next section!

Connecting with external databases

The scenario of connecting to external databases is somewhat common in the enterprise context. We often need to fetch, create, or edit data on other systems, and they may not have another standardized way of doing it.

With that in mind, OutSystems allows you to make these connections simply.

These connections are made in two steps: the creation of the database connection, and the mapping of tables to entities in an extension. Note that we can also map to existing views in these databases.

At this time, out-of-the-box connections with databases from the following systems are natively possible:

- Microsoft SQL Server
- Microsoft Azure SQL
- Oracle
- MySQL
- IBM DB2

> **Tip**
> You can see more system requirements for external database connections here:
> `https://success.outsystems.com/Documentation/11/`
> `Setting_Up_OutSystems/OutSystems_system_`
> `requirements#integration-with-external-systems.`

Creating an integration with an external database follows a sequential set of steps to ensure everything runs smoothly:

1. Define an external database connection in Service Center.
2. Create an extension-type module in Integration Studio to map the necessary tables and views to OutSystems entities.
3. Configure the extension created in Integration Studio on Service Center to use the connection created in *step 1*.
4. Finally, reference the entities we need in our applications by calling them in the **Manage Dependencies** functionality.

So, let's look at these items in more detail.

To start, open Service Center in the **Administration** tab and select the **Database Connections** option.

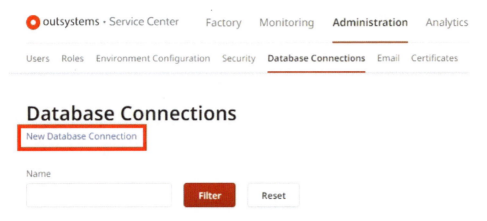

Figure 14.9 – Database Connections screen in Service Center

Then, click on the **New Database Connection** link and fill in the necessary fields for the configuration of the connection (don't forget to choose the correct DBMS so that the correct fields to fill in appear).

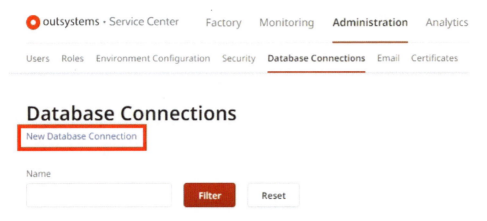

Figure 14.10 – Database Connection form screen in Service Center

After filling in all the necessary fields, click on the **Test Connection** button to validate that the connection is working. If successful, we can click on **Create**.

The next step is to map the tables and views we want from this database into OutSystems entities. For this, an extension is created with Integration Studio.

In this case, we open the application where we want to create the extension in Service Studio, select the **New Module** option, and create a new one of the **Extension** type.

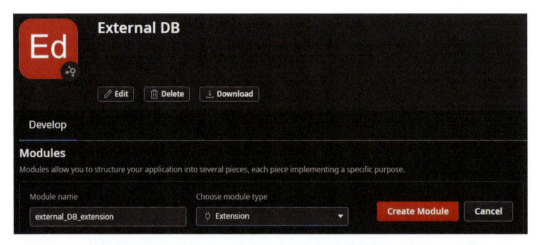

Figure 14.11 – Creating an extension to map external tables into entities

When we click on **Create Module**, Integration Studio opens automatically. We must authenticate ourselves in the environment where we created the connection in Service Center.

The next step is to right-click on the **Entities** folder and select the **Connect to External Table or View…** option.

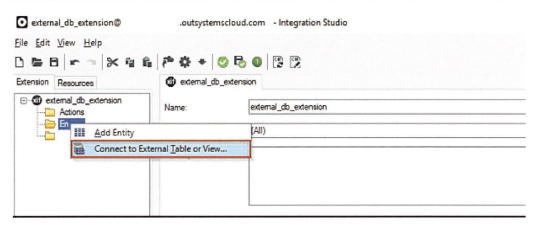

Figure 14.12 – Selecting the Connect to External Table or View... option in Integration Studio

Then, follow the wizard presented, making sure you select the connection created previously and to select the tables and views we need.

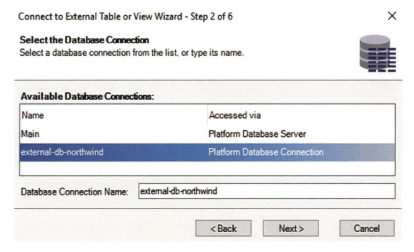

Figure 14.13 – Connect to External Table or View Wizard in Integration Studio

Upon completion of the wizard, we should review the imported content, such as Entity names, attribute names, and their types. Following confirmation, click on **1-Click Publish**.

During the publishing phase, Integration Studio will ask us to configure the connection to the database that the extension will use. For this, in the **Publish** window, we select the **Missing Configuration** warning and then click on the **Configure** button.

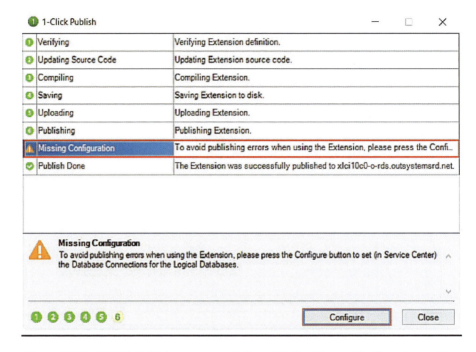

Figure 14.14 – 1-Click Publish summary window with the Missing Configuration option

This action redirects us to Service Center, to the **Operation** tab of the extension we are creating. In this section, we must select the connection that was created at the beginning of the procedures associated with the extension and then click **Apply**.

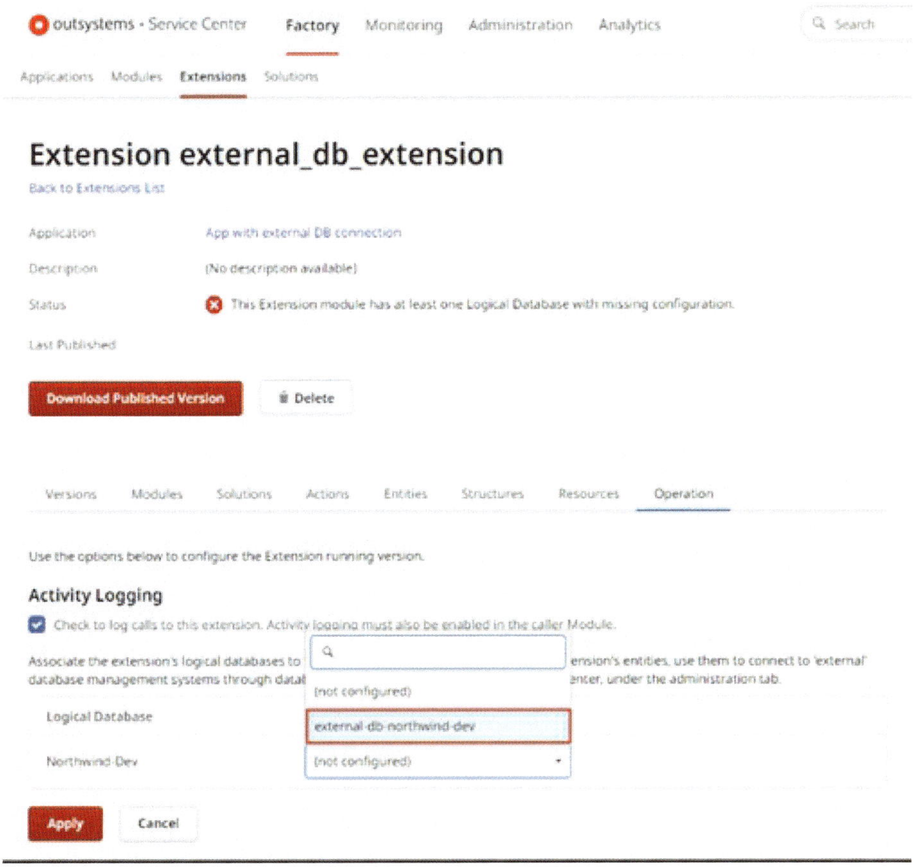

Figure 14.15 – Mapping a database connection to the extension created in Service Center

From this moment on, the entities are ready to be used by our applications. Just use **Manage Dependencies** and, from there, select the extension created and the respective entities.

We should always keep in mind that, in OutSystems, values that are returned as NULL in the attributes of external entities will never be NULL. A NULL integer will be 0, a NULL string will be an empty string (""), an empty Boolean will be False, and so on.

In terms of performance, we must bear in mind that queries made to external entities have a degrading performance the bigger they are. The fact that they have to be executed and then loaded leads us to think of alternatives, such as mapping the data to OutSystems entities and using them as a cache.

With regard to making joins (`Left`, `Right`, `Full`, or `Inner`), we cannot make joins between OutSystems entities and external database tables. This is one more reason to consider whether it makes sense to map data to OutSystems entities and use them as a cache.

This type of solution for connecting with external systems has some functional limitations since business rules or extra validations to databases are not provided for in order to generate information.

If external systems have an API interface, it is preferable to use these interfaces, since, as a rule, they have these necessary validations and rules to avoid obtaining data that should not arise and creating data without complying with the rules planned.

In other words, in the case of external systems having an interface for REST, SOAP, or SAP web services, we can make the integration through these protocols quickly and simply. This is the subject of the next section.

Connecting with other systems through web services (REST/SOAP)

The concepts of SOAP and REST APIs in OutSystems are very simple.

The way we can consume and expose these services is done very simply and always within the visual concept used in everything else in OutSystems development.

In addition, the platform has built-in debug, monitoring, and troubleshooting features for these services.

To better understand how it works, let's separate REST from SOAP and each of them into consuming and exposing.

Consuming SOAP

To ensure that we comply with the ideal architecture model, we should make this type of implementation in layered foundation application modules and of the integration type (`*_IS`).

Starting with the consumption of SOAP services, in Service Studio, open the **Logic** tab, right-click on the **SOAP** icon in the **Integrations** folder, and select the **Consume SOAP Web Service SOAP** option.

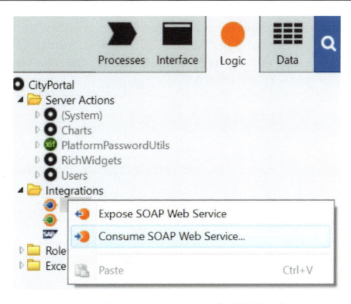

Figure 14.16 – Preparing to consume the SOAP web service

Next, we must insert the URL for the web service's WSDL in the window to do this.

Figure 14.17 – WSDL input in the Service Studio window

> **Tip**
> We can directly insert a WSD file that is on our machine by clicking the
> **Upload file** button and uploading the file.

Automatically, the OutSystems platform will create the web service with the respective available methods and their inputs and outputs. Furthermore, if the input and/or output are complex types, the platform also creates the structures in the **Structure** section of the **Data** tab in order to support those types.

Figure 14.18 – Consumed SOAP web service integrated in OutSystems

From now on, we can use the methods of this service directly in our code in the same way we use any other type of action. Just drag the methods to the location of the flow you want.

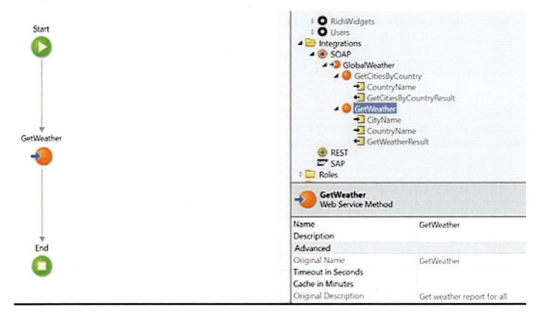

Figure 14.19 – Using the SOAP method in the OutSystems Server Action

If we so wish, to improve our understanding of the code, we can change the name of the SOAP services, their methods, parameters, and structures, and they will continue to work.

Exposing SOAP

Sometimes, instead of consuming data from other external systems, we have to provide it ourselves. We can do this by exposing SOAP web services.

To ensure that we comply with the ideal architecture model, we must make this type of implementation in application modules of the Core Layer and interface type (*_API).

To expose a SOAP web service, on the **Logic** tab, we click on the **SOAP** icon in the **Integrations** folder and select the **Expose SOAP Web Service** option.

Figure 14.20 – Preparing to expose the SOAP web service

Then, set the name of the SOAP web service and the remaining properties.

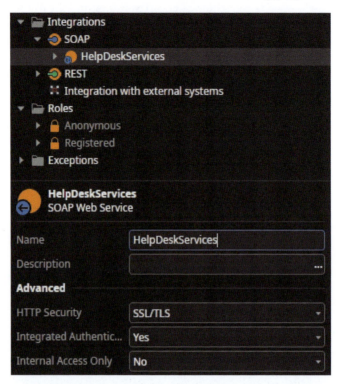

Figure 14.21 – New exposed SOAP web service and the property section

Right-click the new SOAP web service and select **Add Web Service method**.

Then, set the method name and create some logic for it.

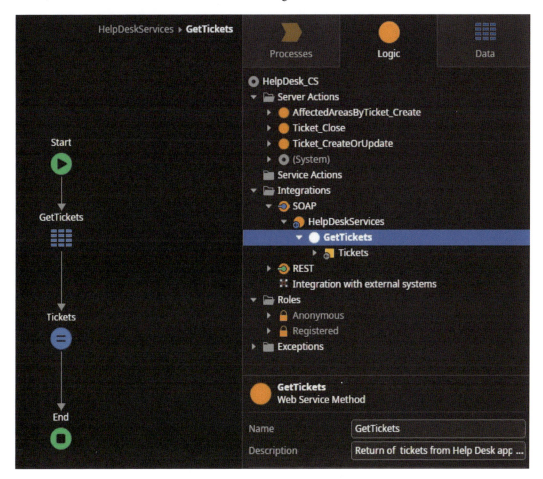

Figure 14.22 – SOAP method and its logic

When it's done, just publish the module. The service's WSDL is available at `http(s)://<hostname>/<ModuleName>/<WebServiceName>.asmx?WSDL`.

The SOAP web service will be exposed using a WSDL document/literal with SOAP 1.1 and SOAP 1.2 bindings.

If you want, and if it is necessary to provide to those who will integrate the services created, we can open the documentation by right-clicking on the SOAP web service created and selecting the **Open Documentation** option.

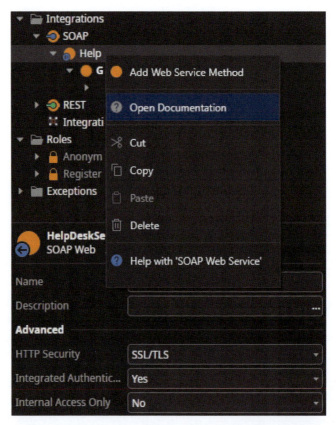

Figure 14.23 – Opening SOAP web service documentation

So far, we have understood how to work with SOAP web services. But what about REST web services? They are not very different. In fact, these integration mechanisms were so well thought out that we can easily adapt them to one another. So, let's start by looking at how to consume REST services.

Consuming REST services

The first thing to do in order to consume a REST API is to read its documentation and get a good feel for how it works. We must keep in mind that we must know its base URL, authentication requirements, and definitions of its methods.

To ensure that we comply with the ideal architecture model, we should make this type of implementation in layered foundation application modules and of the integration type (*_IS).

In order to integrate the REST service, click on the **Logic** tab and then right-click on the **REST** icon in the **Integrations** folder, selecting the **Consume REST API**... option.

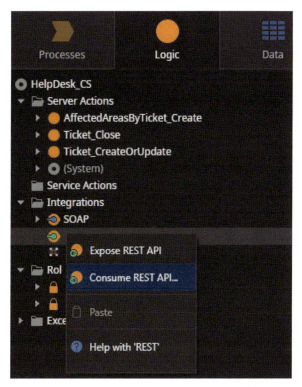

Figure 14.24 – Preparing to consume a REST API

Next, in the **Consume REST API** window, we must select whether we want to integrate only one method or all methods. Note that to add all the methods of a REST API, it must be compliant with the Swagger specification, otherwise, you must integrate it method by method.

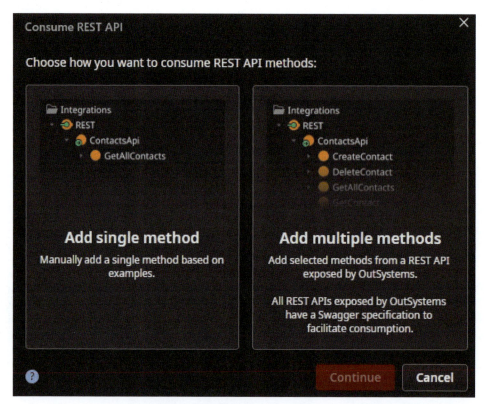

Figure 14.25 – Consume REST API window for selecting the integration approach

Since, if we select the **Add multiple methods** option, the integration is done automatically, we will demonstrate the case of single-method integration.

In this case, we must fill in the information of the method itself, from the URL, the verb (GET, POST, PUT, DELETE, or PATCH), and parameters. Input parameters can be inserted with { } in the URL, following the ?.

If, in the documentation, we identify that the API has an authentication mechanism and specific headers, we can open the **Headers and Authentication** tab and insert the necessary information there.

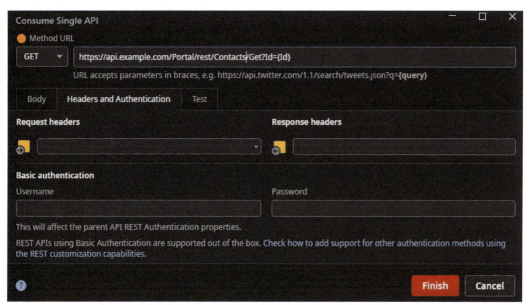

Figure 14.26 – Configuring the REST API method

The next step is to fill in the **Request** and **Response** information. The simplest way to do this is to run a test in the API and use the test result – alternatively, you can add the JSON structure or plaintext example directly to the **Request** and **Response** fields on the **Body** tab. Open the **Test** tab. If you have parameters in the method URL, you will need to enter the parameter values to run the test.

The most complex cases are the methods of the **PUT** and **POST** verbs, in which we must complete the **Request** field with the intended structure as shown in *Figure 14.27*:

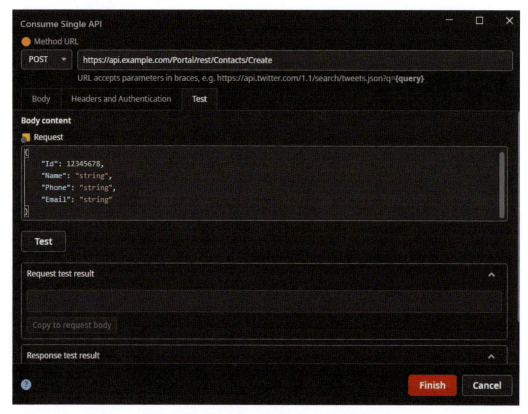

Figure 14.27 – Configuring the REST API method

To confirm that the structure defined in the **Request** field is correct, we click on the **Test** button and check the result on the **Response** tab.

If everything is OK, we click on **COPY TO RESPONSE BODY** in the **Response** tab. If the method is from **POST** or **PUT** verbs (manipulation methods), we do the same in the **Request** tab, clicking **COPY TO REQUEST BODY**.

After confirming on the **Body** tab that all the parameters comply, we click on the **Finish** button.

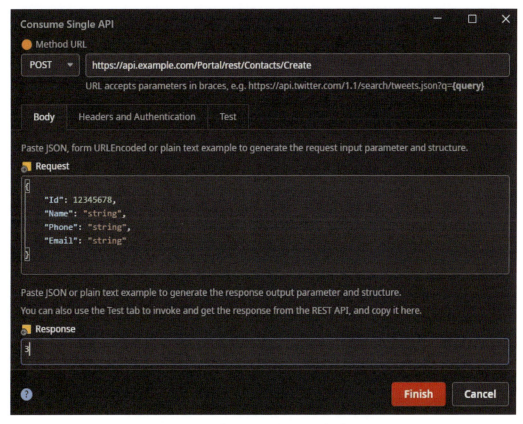

Figure 14.28 – Finalizing REST API method integration

From that moment on, the platform automatically creates the integration with the REST API, the respective methods (in the case of selecting all methods when choosing the type of integration process, integrates all those defined in Swagger), and structures necessary for the correct functioning of the API.

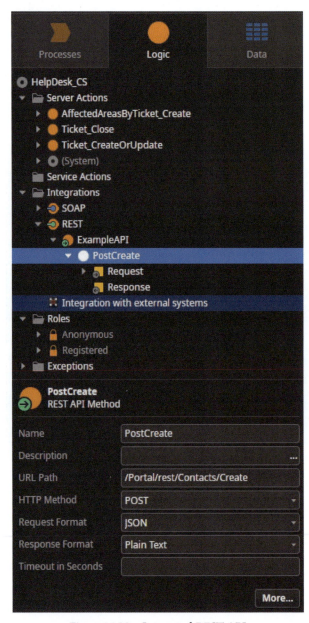

Figure 14.29 – Integrated REST API

As with the SOAP services consumed, from this moment on, we can use the REST API methods directly in our code in the same way we use another type of action.

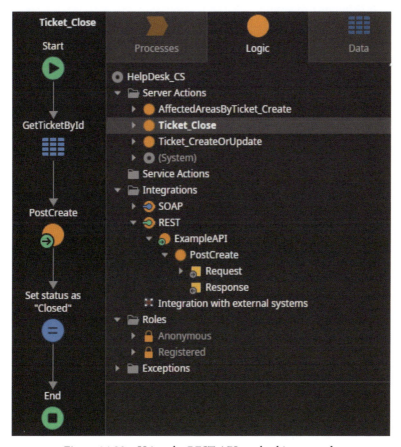

Figure 14.30 – Using the REST API method in our code

If we so wish, to improve our understanding of the code, we can change the name of the REST API and its methods, parameters, and structures, and they will continue to work.

Exposing REST

Just like with SOAP web services, we can provide data or functionalities to external systems by exposing the REST API.

To ensure that we comply with the ideal architecture model, we must make this type of implementation in application modules of the Core Layer and interface type (*_API).

In order to expose a REST API, on the **Logic** tab, we click on the **REST** icon in the **Integrations** folder and select the **Expose REST API** option.

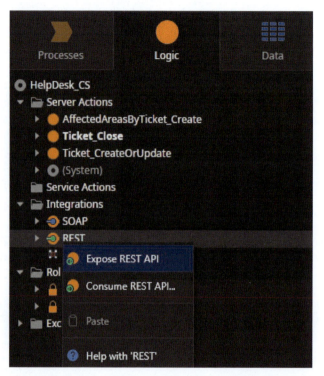

Figure 14.31 – Preparing to expose the REST API

Then, set the name of the REST API and the remaining properties.

Figure 14.32 – Configuring the REST API name and properties

In the **Properties** window, we can configure some strategic points of the REST API.

We can configure the authentication type. This can be as follows:

- **None** – Without any authentication type
- **Basic** – Uses the default authentication of the user provider defined in the module
- **Custom** – For advanced cases that we want to handle in a customized way

We can also define whether we want the application to be for internal use only, which is an added value in terms of security if we want the REST API to only be used within our company's network.

We can preprocess the API call input data (such as a header or URL manipulation) just by defining an OnRequest action in the REST API properties.

In the same way as we handle input with `OnRequest`, we can also handle output (we can use this to handle response codes or messages), but this time with `OnResponse`.

There is an interesting item in the **Advanced** parameters of the properties: the **Send Default** values. If **Yes**, send the input parameter value in the response payload (if it is holding its default value).

We can parameterize any of these values at any time during our API development.

But now we need methods! So, let's go!

Right-click the new **REST API** and select the **Add REST API** method.

Set the method name and create logic for it.

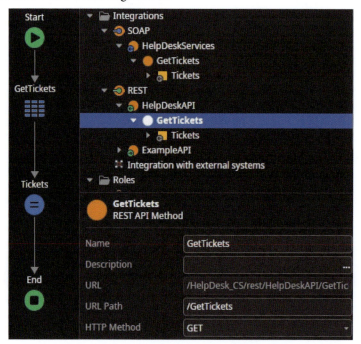

Figure 14.33 – REST API method and its logic

Note that the **HTTP Method** property is set to the HTTP verb corresponding to the action your method will perform:

- `GET` – Read
- `POST` – Create
- `PUT` – Update
- `DELETE` – Delete

> **Tip**
> For manipulation methods where the input parameter is a record (such as
> **POST** or **PUT**), you will have to add the content-type header to the request
> with the application/JSON value.

When it's done, just publish it. The REST API method is available at
`http://<hostname>/<ModuleName>/rest/<RESTAPIName>/swagger.json`.

If you want, and if it is necessary to provide to everyone that will integrate the services
created, we can open the documentation by right-clicking on the **REST API** created and
selecting the **Open Documentation** option first. Check whether the **Documentation**
value in the **Advanced** properties of the REST API is set to **Yes**.

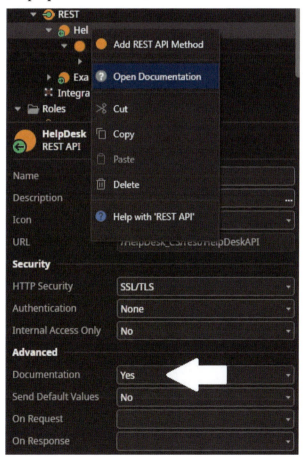

Figure 14.34 – Opening the REST API documentation

Through these two integration protocols (SOAP and REST), OutSystems covers most of the standard scenarios existing in the recent market. We can see that the integration or service exposure procedures are very similar between the two variants and that they are even simple to do.

When exposing services, we must always consider the generality and context of possible consumers in order to assess which protocol to use, be it REST or SOAP (we may have consumers that do not integrate with one of the protocols, thereby creating a technical barrier to the growth of the ecosystem).

A useful piece of advice is that, in the SOAP and REST services consumed, we must always pay attention to reading the documentation provided by their producer so as to understand the correct functioning and details.

Summary

This chapter is very useful when working in companies with an ecosystem composed of multiple systems, as well as when working with multiple third parties. The OutSystems platform becomes a much more attractive proposition with these features.

Thus, in this chapter, we saw how to create our own code in C#/.NET to extend the platform's functionalities, and we realized how we can easily connect to external systems databases and how to consume and expose SOAP and REST services.

Here, we realize that the OutSystems world goes far beyond the code we create, allowing a global expansion in the ecosystem in an extremely fast and practical way.

At the moment, a hot topic is missing regarding the platform's potential. We need to talk about the ability to create process flows and sub-processes to guarantee agility as regards our applications. This capability in OutSystems is called **BPT** (**Business Process Technology**) and is the topic covered in the next chapter.

15
BPT Processes and Timers – Asynchronous Tools in OutSystems

The OutSystems platform has an extremely useful tool to manage the business Processes integrated into our applications. In this tool, called **Business Process Technology** (**BPT**), business Processes are simply referred to as *Processes*.

These Processes are the flow that a given task or event must respect, having a life cycle independent of the rest of the application logic, and may have manual or automatic activities during its execution. Note that a Process occurs **asynchronously**.

Furthermore, a Process can run other Processes, which become sub-Processes of the parent Process. The parent Process can then deal with these sub-Processes in different ways, either waiting for the results or continuing to run.

However, this is not the only asynchronous functionality that OutSystems provides. For processing massive data (also known as batch jobs) and for longer operations, we can use tools called **Timers**. Basically, we configure a Timer to run at a certain time and date with a defined priority, and it runs the logic associated with it at that time (or as close as possible – it always depends on the availability of the server). The logic associated with the Timer is a server action with the logic needed to accomplish what we intend.

In order to fully understand this subject, the chapter is divided into the following topics:

- Process BPT overview
- Timers and how they work
- BPTs versus Timers
- Monitoring Processes and Timers

When we finish the chapter, we will be able to build simple BPT Processes and have knowledge of how we can scale them, such as understanding what kind of artifacts to use and when.

We will also be able to use and configure Timers to Process data, understand the major differences between BPTs and Timers, and how to monitor both in Service Center.

To start, let's take a tour of BPTs, seeing how and where we can implement them.

Process BPT overview

First, what is a Process?

In OutSystems, a Process is seen as a way to carry out all the steps and phases of a task within a company, such as a recruitment Process, handling an order, or a help desk support request.

In order to create the Processes for our application, we have to understand very well the guidelines that they must follow and what kind of activities must take place during them. It is important to define the business rules very well so that the Process runs and guarantees the correct functioning of the application.

To support these business rules, the platform provides a set of visual artifacts, all of them very intuitive and easy to use.

Let's work through the following steps in order to start creating our Process:

1. We open the **Processes** tab, right-click on the **Processes** folder, and choose **Add Process**:

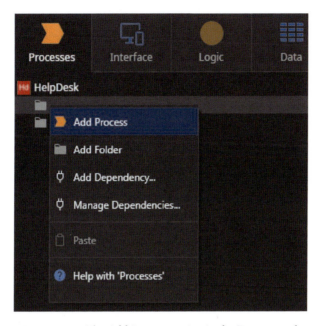

Figure 15.1 – The Add Process option in the Processes tab

2.   Then we name our Process and fill in the details for its properties:

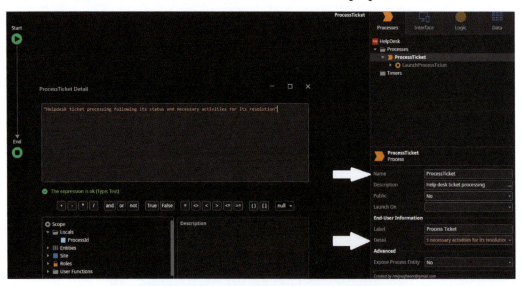

Figure 15.2 – Fill Process name and detail fields

3.   Then we have to choose how to start the Process. We can start it by setting a CRUD operation in the **Launch On** field or we can use the **Callback** Action of the **Launch Process** in our logic:

Figure 15.3 – Process launch options

4. If we want to expose the Process entity so that we can get information about the Process in our code, we can do it simply by going to the **Advanced** properties section of the Process and choosing **Yes** for the **Expose Process Entity** attribute:

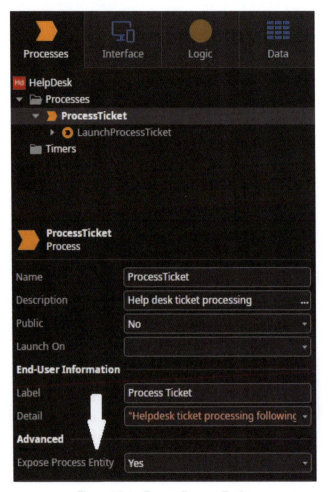

Figure 15.4 – Expose Process Entity

5. From this moment on, the Process entity becomes available in the **Data** tab, which has a read-only property, since the only available method is `Get`:

Figure 15.5 – Exposed Process entity in the Data tab

We can use the data of this entity to control the state of our Processes at runtime, for example, if a Process is suspended or there has been an error.

We can also, in more advanced scenarios, use the Id of a Process returned by this entity to terminate a Process.

Then, in order to create our flow, the following visual artifacts are made available:

1. **Start**: This is where the Process will begin. We can only have (as with actions) one node start per Process.

2. **Conditional start**: This is a special start used to initiate alternative flows. You can check the following documentation link to see in what context you can use them: `https://success.outsystems.com/Documentation/11/Reference/OutSystems_Language/Processes/Process_Tools/Conditional_Start`.

3. **Human activity**: This is an activity that will be performed by a human being on the frontend. It can usually be configured to be performed by a specific user, a group, or all users. You can check in the documentation how this artifact works in general: `https://success.outsystems.com/Documentation/11/Reference/OutSystems_Language/Processes/Process_Tools/Human_Activity`.

4. **Automatic activity**: These activities are performed automatically without user interaction. They are usually used to automate Processes in repetitive tasks. Via this link, you can check its general use: `https://success.outsystems.com/Documentation/11/Reference/OutSystems_Language/Processes/Process_Tools/Automatic_Activity`.

5. **Execute Process**: We can run another Process as an activity, these being called sub-Processes of the parent Process. We can investigate this in a little more detail at the following link: `https://success.outsystems.com/Documentation/11/Reference/OutSystems_Language/Processes/Process_Tools/Execute_Process`.

6. **Wait**: Sometimes we may need to put the Process on hold for a condition to be met. For this, we use the wait artifact. It is parameterized so that it only continues execution when a certain condition is validated. We can find out a little more at the following link: `https://success.outsystems.com/Documentation/11/Reference/OutSystems_Language/Processes/Process_Tools/Wait`.

7. **Decision**: This artifact allows us to follow different paths of our flow based on the conditions we define for it. We can see it as a switch in the flow where, derived from the verified condition, it follows the corresponding path. We can check its general usage at the following link: `https://success.outsystems.com/Documentation/11/Reference/OutSystems_Language/Processes/Process_Tools/Decision`.

8. **Comment**: As with our actions, we may have to record something important and in detail. For this, we can use comments.

9. **Process End**: As it begins, a Process must also end. To finish, we use the End node. There can be more than one End node in our stream, as it can have several branches caused by Decisions. We can configure this End node to terminate the Process or not (we should always pay attention to what context this Process is used for, since it can run as a sub-Process in another parent Process and can cause anomalous behavior). We can find out a little more on this at this link: `https://success.outsystems.com/Documentation/11/Reference/OutSystems_Language/Processes/Process_Tools/Process_End`.

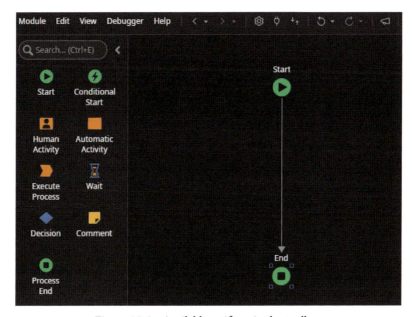

Figure 15.6 – Available artifacts in the toolbox

Each activity generated in the flow of a Process using a Process tool has an independent life cycle.

With the knowledge of these artifacts and how to initialize a Process, we can already begin to understand the implementation part of a procedural flow and make decisions. These tools that we've seen so far allow us to adapt a Process to the applicational need, always keeping everything abstracted and centrally manageable.

Now let's see how to define a Process flow, invoke sub-Processes, and make decisions.

As with almost everything in OutSystems, the visual concept is also applied to Processes.

For that, we have a canvas where we can create our logic, and the way it is done does not differ much between server, service, or client action logic. The big differences are the artifacts that are available, but everything happens in sequence.

Another difference, as already mentioned at the beginning of this chapter (but it is so relevant that it won't hurt to go back to remind yourself), is that Processes occur **asynchronously**.

The canvas is the central area of the Service Studio workspace where you drop tools from the **Process Flow Toolbox** to define your Process logic.

To see the properties of a Process activity, select it in the **Content View** and the properties will be displayed in the **Properties** window.

To define the flow of a Process, connect elements in the **Content Screen** starting from the **Start** element – there can only be one **Start** node in our Process flow. To finalize a flow path, use the **End** element – depending on the elements you use in the Process flow, you can have one or multiple paths.

Within a Process flow, you are allowed to use other initialization tools to define alternative flows to handle specific events:

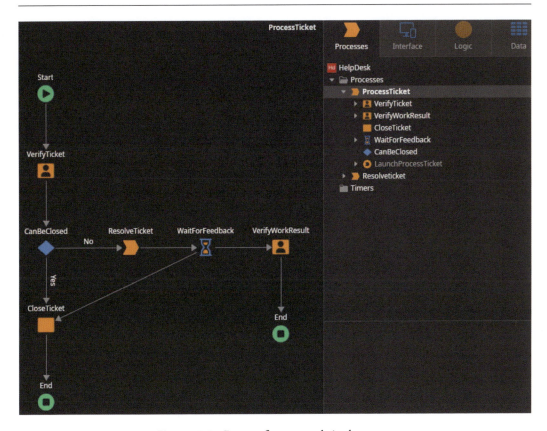

Figure 15.7 – Process flow example in the canvas

While designing the flow of our Processes, we can introduce validation rules for their execution. If for some reason we need to block or give up on the Process, we can do it using the callback actions. How do we do this?

In the module tree, under **Processes**, right-click on the **Process** element, choose **Add Callback Action**, and pick one of the available actions:

Figure 15.8 – Available callback actions in a Process

Some of the callback actions are at the Process level and some are at the activity level, as shown in *Figure 15.9*:

Tool	On Ready	On Open	On Start	On Close	On Skip
Start	-	-	-	-	-
Conditional Start	Yes	-	Yes	-	-
Human Activity	Yes	Yes	-	Yes	Yes
Send Email	-	-	-	-	-
Automatic Activity	-	-	-	-	-
Execute Process	-	-	-	-	-
Wait	Yes	-	-	Yes	Yes
Decision	-	-	-	-	-
End	-	-	-	-	-

Figure 15.9 – Activity (artifact) callback actions

We may come across scenarios where we repeat multiple business rules in multiple callback actions for different activities during our Process flow. In these scenarios, we must then change the common rules to a single callback action, but this is done at the Process level, as we can see in *Figure 15.8*. We must add the callback action to the Process and develop the business rules in it, thus centralizing the code and allowing it to be better maintained, also avoiding repetition.

Otherwise, we can create the callback action at the activity level:

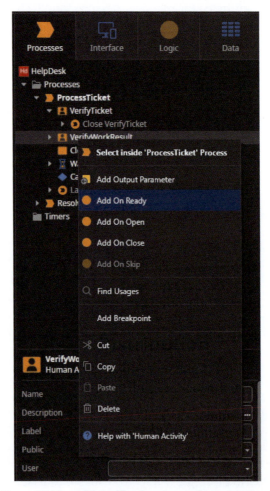

Figure 15.10 – Add a callback action at the activity level

Info

The sub-Processes that are defined in our Process flows do not inherit the Callback Actions. Basically, each Process has its own scope for the callback actions. BPTs have a variant for cases where we need data-driven Process management and have no need for human intervention. This variant is called Light BPT and allows more threads simultaneously than traditional BPT. In this case, while traditional BPT only allows 10 threads, Light BPT allows 20 as shown in Figure 15.11

	BPT	Light BPT
Threads	10	20
Activities	>3500	1 Automatic
Automatic Activity Timeout	5 Minutes	3 Minutes
Callbacks	✓	✗
Output Parameters	✓	✗
Process Logging	✓	✗

Figure 15.11 – BPT and Light BPT differences

How can we create a Light BPT?

First, the Process we created can have one and only one automatic activity and no other activities of any other type. Also, it can only be triggered through a database event and never by the Process **Launch** Action, otherwise it will run like a traditional BPT Process:

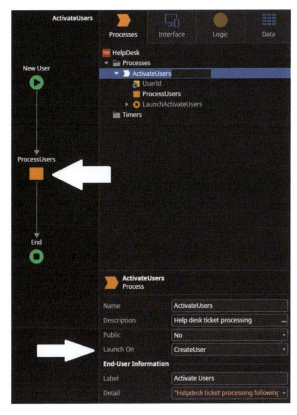

Figure 15.12 – Add only one automatic activity and define the Launch On property
for the Users entity event

The next step is to enable the Light BPT in the module settings in Service Center. In the module definitions inside the **Operation** tab, activate **Light Process execution**:

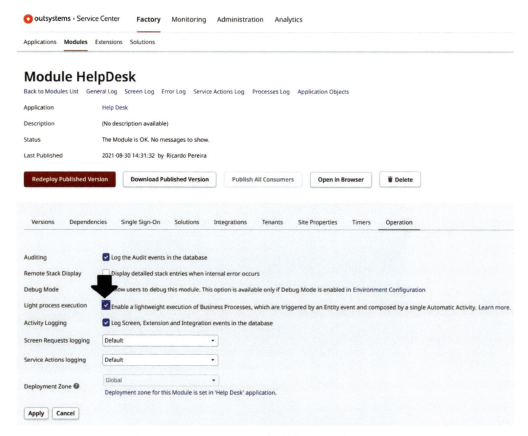

Figure 15.13 – Activate Light BPTs in Service Center

After these steps, we click on **Apply**. Then we must publish the module again, which can be done through Service Center or Service Studio.

Now the Process is enabled to run lightweight Processes.

Remember that just one trigger by a database event runs the Process as a Light BPT. Starting the Process using the **Start Process** action runs the Process as a traditional BPT.

OutSystems has another tool for asynchronous events. In this case, this tool is used to run Processes at a certain date and time, despite allowing its execution through its call in our code. This is the Timer.

Timers and how they work

Timers are tools that allow us to run logic periodically at a scheduled date and time, and this event is usually called a *batch job*. It can also be invoked from application logic, via the **Wake** event.

There are a set of elements on the platform related to Timers that allow us to have a better understanding of their context:

ELEMENT	DESCRIPTION
OutSystems Scheduler service	This service commands and controls the running of the Timers. It is multi-threaded and allows different Timers to run in parallel.
Runtime database	This database contains the system entities related to the Timers, storing the following information: - A record of all existing Timers - The schedule for executing Timers - The current execution of Timers: when they started, their timeout value, and/or next execution
Log database	This database logs when a Timer starts running.
Configuration Tool	In this tool, we configure the number of teams to be run simultaneously on each of the frontends.
OutSystems Log service	This service writes to the Log database information about Timers that we access in the Service Center
Deployed module (application)	The module contains the actions and code that will be executed when the Timer runs. It also has some built-in code that ensures that the system database is always up to date with regard to Timer status.

Figure 15.14 – OutSystems elements related to Timers

With this information, we will be able to understand the following further examination of this topic.

To create a Timer, work through the following steps:

1. Click on Service Studio's **Processes** tab, right-click on the **Timers** folder, and select the **Add Timer** option:

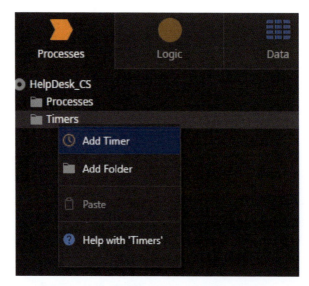

Figure 15.15 – Create a Timer in Service Studio

2. Then we select which server action will be executed when the Timer runs. Alternatively, we can choose the **New Server Action** option, thus creating a new server action where we can create our logic:

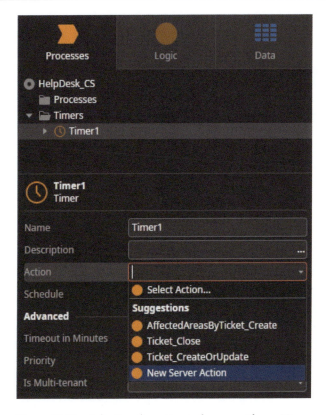

Figure 15.16 – Selecting the action to be run with our Timer

If there are input parameters, their values must be defined when the Timer is created and, if there are output parameters in this same action, their values are not accessible after its execution.

3. The next step is to adjust at what point in time the Timer should be run in the **Schedule** attribute:

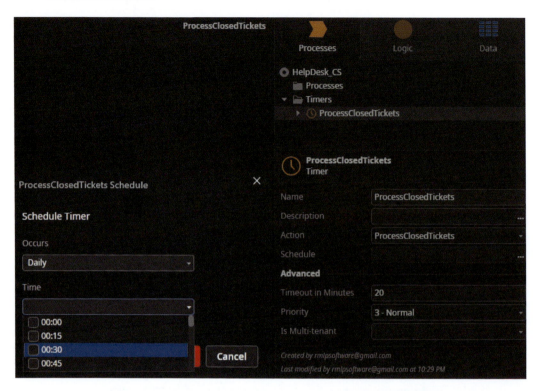

Figure 15.17 – Defining the schedule for the Timer in Service Studio

> **Info**
>
> The effective schedule of the Timer is defined in Service Center. If you set the Timer schedule when designing the app, the first schedule will be ignored. This ensures that you can customize the Timer schedule when deploying an application in another environment, without having to change the application itself.

Another way to run the Timer is to call it directly in our application code, via the built-in **Wake** action:

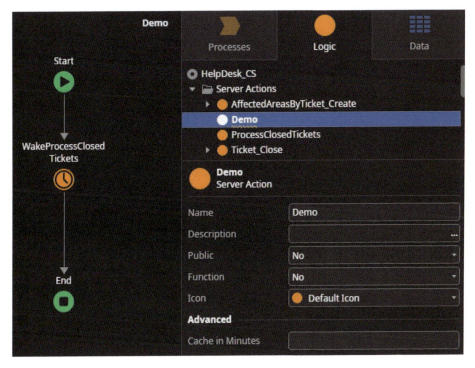

Figure 15.18 – Calling the built-in Wake Timer action in a regular server action

If we explicitly need to run the Timer at any time, we can do it through Service Center by accessing the Timer and clicking on the **Run Now** button:

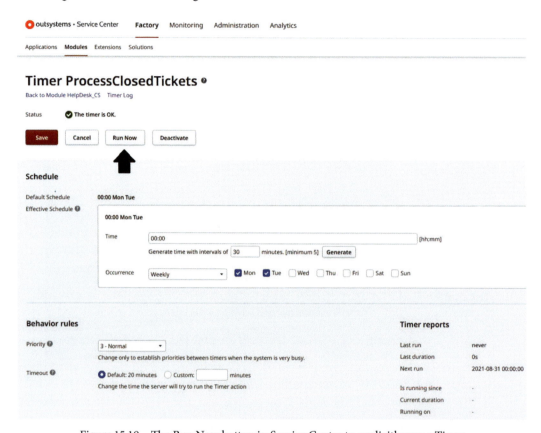

Figure 15.19 – The Run Now button in Service Center to explicitly run a Timer

Another attribute that we must consider is **Timeout** (default 20 minutes). Essentially, the value defined here is the time in minutes that the Timer is given to run. If the operation does not finish within this defined time, the Timer returns an error, and will try again later. Note that Timers only make three execution attempts. If on the third attempt it fails again, it will only run again on the next schedule.

In addition, we also have the **Priority** attribute, which can take one of four possible values: **Low**, **Normal**, **High**, and **Top**.

What is **Priority** for? If there are several Timers set to run at the same time, which one will run first is defined by this attribute: the higher the priority, the sooner it starts running in relation to its competitors.

Figure 15.20 – Timeout and Priority attributes are defined in the Timer properties

> **Tip**
> You can see more details about Timers here: `https://success.outsystems.com/Support/Enterprise_Customers/Maintenance_and_Operations/OutSystems_Platform_Timers_and_Asynchronous_Processes`.

Timers are a useful tool when it comes to longer and/or massive processing of information. Furthermore, there are techniques being developed to Process Timers that run actions with very high processing load Process and heavy access to databases, with these Timers being called heavy Timers.

There are guidelines on how to act to handle these cases, and how to solve each of the possible bottlenecks that can result. We can introduce techniques such as having a "soft timeout" (a control variable that allows the Timer to finish before reaching the predefined timeout and can call itself (the Timer) starting from the point where the previous iteration ended) or using a history file.

> **Tip**
>
> You can see more details about heavy Timers here: `https://www.outsystems.com/training/lesson/1749/odc-2018-heavy-Timers`.

With all this information, you most likely understand the pros and cons of BPT and Timers, and when and why to use each of them. When choosing which to use, it is best to compare them side by side, taking into account the benefits of each to better adjust our choice to the solution we need. In the next section, we'll consider BPTs versus Timers.

BPTs versus Timers

Although both BPTs (both light and traditional) and Timers are asynchronous tools, their purposes are not that similar.

Factors such as parallelism and competition differ between the types of Processes.

By default, there are 20 threads per frontend to run Light BPT Processes, 10 threads for traditional BPT Processes, and 3 threads for Timers.

Furthermore, BPT Processes are driven by database events, while Timers are triggered by a programmed schedule (they can also be triggered in the application code with Wake, but a Timer is not an event focused on a database event).

Also, while the Timer makes three attempts to run successfully, BPTs try until they succeed or until someone cancels them in Service Center.

All these factors have to be considered when deciding on the ideal tool to use; that is, in practical terms:

- Timers are recommended for massive or time-consuming processing of data that is not oriented towards a specific database event but more for scheduling or application background processing such as sending emails.

- Traditional BPTs are recommended for automation of database event-driven Processes with or without human intervention, but with the definition of several procedural steps that lack logging.

- Light BPTs are recommended for database event-driven processing, which needs speed and does not need logging mechanisms (Light BPTs do not use the log mechanism of traditional BPTs). Also, they are the right choice when we need thread-level parallelism.

As already mentioned, Light BPT does not support the logging mechanism of traditional BPTs. However, it is useful to understand what logging is done and how we can use Service Center to check them and monitor our Processes. In addition, we also have the Timer logging component to understand and how it also helps us to monitor the Timers of our applications.

Monitoring Processes and Timers

The monitoring of asynchronous tools, like all other tools, is done in Service Center. All logs are recorded in the database and can be searched in the Service Center window related to the type of tool in question.

To monitor the Timer logs, we open **Service Center**, and in the **Monitoring** tab, click on **Timers**:

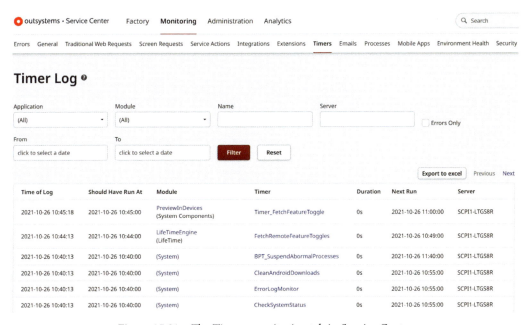

Figure 15.21 – The Timers monitoring tab in Service Center

In this tab, we can find out the following:

- The date and time the log was created

- The expected date and time when the Timer should have executed

- The module the Timer belongs to

- Which Timer was executed

- Timer run duration

- The scheduled date and time for the next run

- Which frontend server the Timer was run on

We can also find useful information regarding Timers in the **Environment Health** tab in the **Monitoring** section:

Timers ❷

Module	Tenant	Timer	Last Run (duration)	Next Run	Running since (duration)	Running By
LifeTimeEngine		FetchRemoteFeatureToggles	2021-10-26 10:49:22 (0s)	2021-10-26 10:54:00		
LifeTimeEngine		InvalidateCache	2021-10-26 10:40:13 (0s)	2021-10-26 10:55:00		
LifeTimeAnalytics		HarvestAndGroupData	2021-10-26 10:40:13 (0s)	2021-10-26 10:55:00		
(System)		ErrorLogMonitor	2021-10-26 10:40:13 (0s)	2021-10-26 10:55:00		
(System)		CleanAndroidDownloads	2021-10-26 10:40:13 (0s)	2021-10-26 10:55:00		
(System)		NativeBuildStarter	2021-10-26 10:40:13 (0s)	2021-10-26 10:55:00		
(System)		CheckSystemStatus	2021-10-26 10:40:13 (0s)	2021-10-26 10:55:00		
lifetimeapi		APIDownloads_CleanExpired	2021-10-26 10:00:26 (0s)	2021-10-26 11:00:00		
PreviewInDevices		Timer_FetchFeatureToggle	2021-10-26 10:45:18 (0s)	2021-10-26 11:00:00		
ECT_Provider		RetrievePageTimer	2021-10-26 10:10:11 (0s)	2021-10-26 11:10:00		

Figure 15.22 – Timer monitoring info in the Environment Health tab

An interesting point in this section is that we can see information about Timers running at the respective moment of the query, both their duration and which server is running them.

Errors that occur in Timers, as with all aspects of the platform's error log, are shown in the **Errors** tab of the **Monitoring** section, and we can access their details by clicking on **Error**.

To monitor our BPT Processes, we access the **Monitoring** section and click on the **Processes** tab:

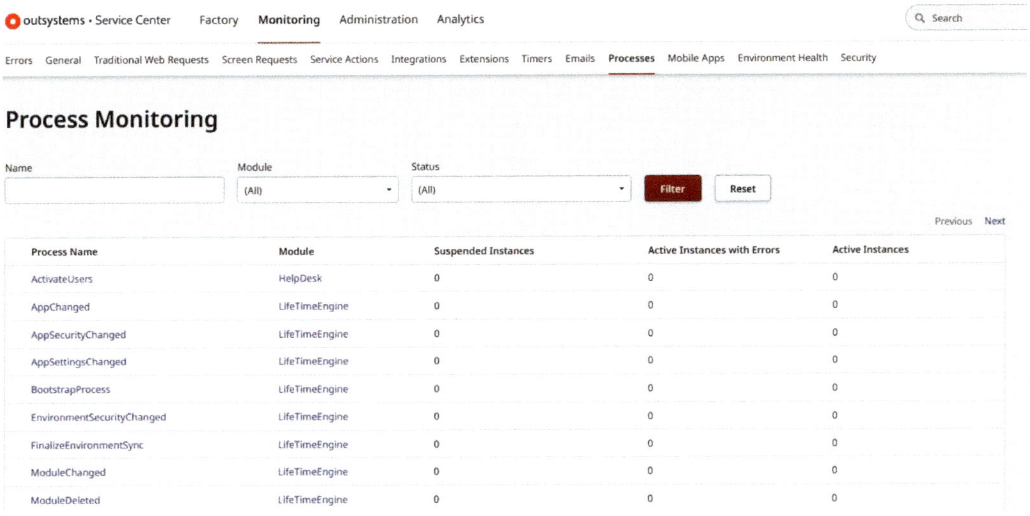

outsystems • Service Center   Factory   **Monitoring**   Administration   Analytics   Search

Errors   General   Traditional Web Requests   Screen Requests   Service Actions   Integrations   Extensions   Timers   Emails   **Processes**   Mobile Apps   Environment Health   Security

Process Monitoring

Name	Module	Status			
	(All)	(All)		Filter	Reset

Previous   Next

Process Name	Module	Suspended Instances	Active Instances with Errors	Active Instances
ActivateUsers	HelpDesk	0	0	0
AppChanged	LifeTimeEngine	0	0	0
AppSecurityChanged	LifeTimeEngine	0	0	0
AppSettingsChanged	LifeTimeEngine	0	0	0
BootstrapProcess	LifeTimeEngine	0	0	0
EnvironmentSecurityChanged	LifeTimeEngine	0	0	0
FinalizeEnvironmentSync	LifeTimeEngine	0	0	0
ModuleChanged	LifeTimeEngine	0	0	0
ModuleDeleted	LifeTimeEngine	0	0	0

Figure 15.23 –Processes monitoring tab in Service Center

On this page, we can check the following fields:

- The name of the Process
- The module to which the Process belongs
- How many instances are suspended
- How many instances are active with errors
- How many instances are active

When we click on the name of the Process, we are directed to a page that shows us the details of that Process, which instances have taken place and are taking place, along with their status.

Also, on this page we can lock the Process, preventing further activities from occurring.

If the Process is already locked, the **Unlock** functionality is available.

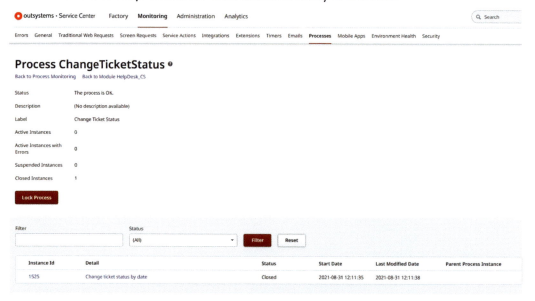

Figure 15.24 – Process detail in Service Center

If we click on an instance of a Process in the table on a Process's detail page, we can follow the entire event history of that instance, including what activities occurred, when they occurred, and what their status was. In addition, here is an example of the information of the Process instance identifier generated in the database:

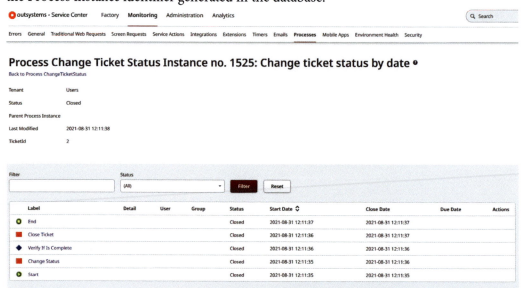

Figure 15.25 – Example of instance details in Service Center

Worthy of note here is that if any Process generates an error, we can visualize in which instance and activity it occurred by consulting the pages we've covered here. Errors generated in the application logic executed by the Processes are logged in the **Errors** tab of the monitoring section.

In order to add more monitoring capability, OutSystems' R&D team created an application called **Business Activity Monitoring**, available for download from OutSystems Forge at `https://www.outsystems.com/forge/component-overview/132/business-activity-monitoring`.

The monitoring capability can go even further in the case of custom logs, since we can always use the LogMessage server action in our code to generate logs adapted to the scenarios we are developing, therefore allowing for more effective monitoring.

We can see that in terms of monitoring, asynchronous Processes follow the same method as the rest of the platform (apart from the specificity of the BPT technology), always following a very transversal path of checking the logs and generated information related to BPTs and Timers.

Summary

In this chapter, we had an overview of how BPTs and Light BPTs work, as well as how to implement each of these models.

We also saw the functioning of Timers and their implementation.

Furthermore, we realized that all of these three models are asynchronous activities, that is, they do not occur at runtime; rather, each of them requires a trigger to run.

We detailed the main differences between them and what their purposes are, and got a brief idea of some scenarios in which each one of them should be used.

In the final part, we saw how we can monitor Processes and Timers in Service Center and what information is available to us.

The purpose of this chapter is to highlight that we do not need to process all the information in real time if this is not necessary, thus improving our control of Timers and Processes life cycles, performance, and data robustness.

The asynchronous capabilities of the platform were left to the end of this book because it is a more complex topic, and also because the tools explained here are the target of continuous improvement and optimization, both by developers and by OutSystems itself.

I hope this book has given each of you the motivation, foundational knowledge, and context to start your career in OutSystems (for those who are starting now), along with the necessary clarification of your doubts about any topic even if you're already working with OutSystems.

I always advise doing some additional reading of the OutSystems documentation (`https://success.outsystems.com/Documentation`), as well taking their online courses (`https://www.outsystems.com/training/paths`), which are full of objective, high-quality information.

May it be the beginning of something good, and I hope I have contributed to your journey of becoming a Jedi!

`Packt.com`

Subscribe to our online digital library for full access to over 7,000 books and videos, as well as industry leading tools to help you plan your personal development and advance your career. For more information, please visit our website.

Why subscribe?

- Spend less time learning and more time coding with practical eBooks and Videos from over 4,000 industry professionals

- Improve your learning with Skill Plans built especially for you

- Get a free eBook or video every month

- Fully searchable for easy access to vital information

- Copy and paste, print, and bookmark content

Did you know that Packt offers eBook versions of every book published, with PDF and ePub files available? You can upgrade to the eBook version at `packt.com` and as a print book customer, you are entitled to a discount on the eBook copy. Get in touch with us at `customercare@packtpub.com` for more details.

At `www.packt.com`, you can also read a collection of free technical articles, sign up for a range of free newsletters, and receive exclusive discounts and offers on Packt books and eBooks.

Other Books You May Enjoy

If you enjoyed this book, you may be interested in these other books by Packt:

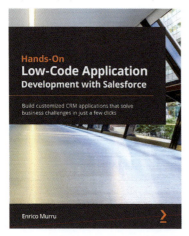

Hands-On Low-Code Application Development with Salesforce

Enrico Murru

ISBN: 978-1-80020-977-0

- Get to grips with the fundamentals of data modeling to enhance data quality.
- Deliver dynamic configuration capabilities using custom settings and metadata types.
- Secure your data by implementing the Salesforce security model.
- Customize Salesforce applications with Lightning App Builder.
- Create impressive pages for your community using Experience Builder.

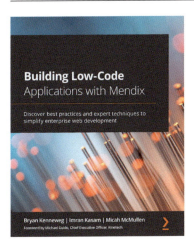

Building Low-Code Applications with Mendix

Bryan Kenneweg

ISBN: 978-1-80020-142-2

- Gain a clear understanding of what low-code development is and the factors driving its adoption.

- Become familiar with the various features of Mendix for rapid application development.

- Discover concrete use cases of Studio Pro.

- Build a fully functioning web application that meets your business requirements.

- Get to grips with Mendix fundamentals to prepare for the Mendix certification exam.

Packt is searching for authors like you

If you're interested in becoming an author for Packt, please visit `authors.packtpub.com` and apply today. We have worked with thousands of developers and tech professionals, just like you, to help them share their insight with the global tech community. You can make a general application, apply for a specific hot topic that we are recruiting an author for, or submit your own idea.

Hi!

Me, Ricardo Pereira author of *Rapid Application Development with OutSystems,* really hope you enjoyed reading this book and found it useful for increasing your productivity and efficiency in software development in OutSystems platform

It would really help us (and other potential readers!) if you could leave a review on Amazon sharing your thoughts on *Rapid Application Development with OutSystems.*

Go to the link below or scan the QR code to leave your review:

`https://packt.link/r/1800208758`

Your review will help us to understand what's worked well in this book, and what could be improved upon for future editions, so it really is appreciated.

Best wishes,

Ricardo Manuel Lopes Pereira

Index

Symbols

3 Layer Canvas 297

A

Android device
  steps, for debugging applications 286
application architecture
  validating rules, reference link 301
applications
  naming conventions 81-83
  creating 185-198
architecture
  significance 296
Architecture Canvas
  about 297
  Core Layer 298
  End User Layer 298
  layers 297
  sub-layers 297, 298
Architecture Dashboard
  about 51, 305
  reference link 305

architecture design process
  about 299
  applications distributed, in
    Architecture Canvas 300
  assemble 299
  disclose 299
  identified logic, moving to
    another module 304
  identified logic, moving to
    new module 304
  logic, referencing through Manage
    Dependencies window 305
  module button, moving in
    Service Studio 303
  module, creating in correct layer 304
  organize 299
  split application ownership 302, 303
  violations, avoiding 300
architecture layers
  modules, applying to 77
architecture violations
  no cycles 301
  no side references, among end
    user modules 301
  no upward references 300

architecture violations, rules
    different owners, splitting 302
    different sponsors, splitting 302
    layer your applications, correctly 301
    layer your modules, correctly 301
attributes 251
attribute values, database Entities
    delete 87
    ignore 87
    protect 87

B

batch job 355
blank modules 72, 81
blank sheets 81
block lifecycle events 181-184
breakpoint
    about 276
    adding 276
    disabling, temporarily 280
    removing 278, 279
Business Activity Monitoring
    about 367
    download link 367
Business Process Technology (BPT) 42

C

cache 15, 16
cascade effect 87
C# code
    reference link 313
characteristics, of database Entities
    attributes 86
    foreign keys 87
    indexes 87
    primary keys 87

Client Actions
    about 37
    creating 241-247
    using, on frontend 241-247
client logic actions
    about 238-240
    properties 239, 240
    reference link 240
C#/.NET code
    about 54
    code, creating 308-313
    code, using inside OutSystems
        platform 308-313
conditional paths
    used, for taking logic decisions 121, 122
Content Distribution Network
    (CDN) 13, 14
content security policy (CSP) 48
Cordova Plugins, using
    reference link 209
core layer
    modules, applying to 79
Create, Retrieve, Update, and
    Delete (CRUD) 33, 89
CSS
    themes and styles 176-179

D

data
    fetching, from local storage 256-260
data actions 235-238
database Entities
    characteristics 86
    exploring 86
data bootstrapping, into Entities
    data, populating into existing Entity 93
    Entity, creating from Excel sheet 94

from Excel spreadsheet 93
reference link, for official
    documentation 95
data model
  AffectedAreas by ticket auxiliary
      Entity, with their foreign keys 105
  AffectedAreas Static Entity,
      with records view 104
  application details, filling in
      Service Studio 98
  application type, selecting in
      Service Studio 97
  attribute, creating on Entity 101
  creating 95
  developments, publishing in
      Service Studio 112
  Entity, adding to database 100
  entity diagram, adding in
      Service Studio 110
  entity diagram view, in
      Service Studio 111
  foreign key properties 106-108
  module, publishing in Service Studio 98
  new application button, in
      Service Studio 96
  new module, creating in application 98
  record, creating on Static Entity 103
  starting from scratch, in
      Service Studio 96
  Static Entity, adding to database 102
  Status Static Entity, with
      records view 104
  ticket entity, with attributes 110
data modeling
  about 91
  many-to-many relationship 92
  one-to-many relationships 91

one-to-one relationship 92, 93
reference link, for official
    documentation 93
data synchronization patterns
  analyzing 260-273
  reference link 273
Data tab, Service Studio
  Client Variables 35
  entities 33
  entity diagrams 33
  Multilingual Locales 35
  processes 43
  Resources 36
  Site Properties 35
  structures 34
  Timers 43
delete rules
  reference link, for official
      documentation 88
Discovery
  about 306
  reference link 306
Dynamic Entity 34

E

Electronic Canvas
  about 305
  reference link 305
end user layer
  modules, applying to 80
end users
  managing, with Users application 53, 54
Entities
  data bootstrapping, from Excel
      spreadsheet 93-95
  reference link, for official
      documentation 88

Entity Identifier 87
error log
   accessing 288
events
   used, for propagating changes
      from block to parent 184
Exceptions
   Abort activity change Exceptions 148
   Database Exceptions 146
   handler flows 149-151
   handling 153-160
   raising 144-148, 153-160
   Security Exceptions 147
   types 145
   User Exceptions 145
Extension and Integration
      Framework (XIF) 56
extension modules
   about 73, 79
   elements 79
extensions, official documentation
   reference link 79
external databases
   connecting with 313-320

F

Flow 40
foreign keys 87, 251
foundation layer
   modules, applying to 77

G

global Exception
   handler 151, 152

H

hardcoded values 91
HTTP Strict Transport
      Security (HSTS) 48

I

If artifact 121
indexes 87
infrastructure
   managing, with LifeTime 51, 52
Integrated Development
      Environment (IDE) 28
Integration Studio
   about 8, 54, 55
   multi-tab editors 56
   multi-tree Navigator 56
   opening 66
   server info 56
   specific editor 56
   starting 66, 67
   status bar 56
   toolbar 56
Interface tab, Service Studio
   Images 41
   Scripts 41, 42
   Themes 41
   UI Flows 40, 41
iOS device
   steps, for debugging applications 286

J

JavaScript
   in OutSystems 179-181

L

libraries, official documentation
  reference link 78
library modules
  about 73, 78
  artifacts types 78
LifeTime
  about 9, 10
  used, for managing infrastructure 51, 52
local storage
  data, fetching from 256-260
  entities, creating 250-255
  entities, using 250-255
logic actions 114-117
logic decisions
  taking, with conditional paths 121, 122
Logic tab, Service Studio
  Client Actions 37
  exceptions 39, 40
  integrations 38
  roles 39
  Server Actions 38
  Service Actions 38
loops
  creating 123, 124

M

Microsoft Visual Studio 54
mobile app screens
  creating 215-230
mobile design, considerations
  about 203
  design 204
  process and concept 203
  security 204
  target audience 204, 205

mobile plugins
  about 205-207
  adding, to applications 208-210
module logging level
  reference link 291
modules
  applying, to architecture layers 77
  applying, to core layer 79
  applying, to end user layer 80
  applying, to foundation layer 77
  blank 72
  distributing, across applications 75-77
  extension 73
  for mobile applications 74
  for web applications 73
  library 73
  naming conventions 81-83
  Reactive web app/phone
    app/tablet app 72
  service 72

N

native app generation 210-215
native mobile applications
  debugging 286, 287

O

OutSystems
  JavaScript 179-181
  pricing and editions 58, 59
OutSystems applications
  reference link 305
OutSystems factory
  options 21
OutSystems IDEs
  installing 62, 63

OutSystems platform
  application, publishing 10-12
  cache 15, 16
  components 24
  Content Distribution Network
      (CDN) 13, 14
  deployment options 21-23
  external tools 24
  Forge and Community 24, 25
  Integration Studio 8
  logging 12, 13
  monitoring 12, 13
  overview 5
  Platform server 5, 6
  Search Engine Optimization
      (SEO) 16-21
  Service Center 8, 9
  Service Studio 7
OutSystems system requirements
  reference link 314
OutSystems UI
  patterns and templates 166-170

P

patterns 202, 203
Personal Environment
  setting up 59-62
Platform server 5, 6
pricing and editions, OutSystems
  reference link 59
primary key 87, 251
Process BPT
  monitoring 363-367
  overview 340-354
  versus Timers 362, 363
producer module 284

producer modules, debugging
  reference link 285
Progressive Web App (PWA) 32
Progressive Web Apps (PWA) 205
PWA distribution
  reference link 210

R

reactive web applications
  debugging 276-285
Reactive web app/phone
      app/tablet app modules 72, 80
REpresentational State Transfer
      (REST) 37, 237
REST API
  exposing 334-338
REST services
  consuming 327-333

S

Screen Client Actions
  about 234, 235
  properties 235
screen events 181-184
screens
  scaffolding 173-176
Search Engine Optimization (SEO) 16-21
Server Actions
  about 38, 114-117
  creating 125-141
  reference link 116
Server Actions, variables
  input variables 118
  local variables 120
  output variables 119

Service Actions 38
Service Center
  about 8, 9, 44
  features 44
Service Center, features
  Administration tab 47-49
  Analytics tab 49-51
  Factory tab 44, 45
  Monitoring tab 45-47
Service Center logs
  using, to support
    troubleshooting 287-291
Service Center, OutSystems platform
  LifeTime 9, 10
service modules
  about 72, 80
  artifacts types 80
services, official documentation
  reference link 80
Service Studio
  about 7, 28-33
  Data tab 33
  Interface tab 40
  Logic tab 37
  opening 64
  Processes tab 42
  starting 64-66
Simple Object Access Protocol (SOAP)
  about 38, 237
  consuming 320-323
  exposing 323-326
Static Entities
  about 89-91
  attributes 90
  Id 90
  Is_Active 90
  Label 90

Order 90
  reference link, for official
    documentation 90
Static Entity 34
Switch artifact 122

T

technical debt
  reference link 297
templates 202, 203
Timers
  about 355-362
  monitoring 363-367
  versus Process BPT 362, 363
  working with 355-362
TrueChange section 7

U

user experience (UX) 148, 238
Users application
  used, for managing end users 53, 54

V

variables
  types, in Server Actions 118-120

W

Web Services Description
  Language (WSDL) 38
widgets 170-172, 202, 203

Printed in Great Britain
by Amazon

20478200R00226